ABOUT THE AUTHOR

Brian Hirst was born in Batley, West Yorkshire, on December 1st 1946. His first book of memoirs, *Rag-Oyle Town Family,* was published in March 2011 and consisted of 14 chapters, each giving mini-biographies of his Mam, Dad, eight brothers and four sisters. In *I Can See You But You Can't See Me* Brian writes about his growing-up years, from his first memories of the early 1950s to his education at Infant, Junior and Secondary schools, ending in 1965. His first two books are written in the third person voice of the adult Brian, which he felt gave him a measure of detachment from the deeply personal content of both books. He has just begun his third and final memoir, written in first person voice, and hopes to publish it early in 2013.

I CAN SEE YOU BUT YOU CAN'T SEE ME

BRIAN HIRST

FOR MY MAM
MARY HIRST
30th APRIL 1915 – 21st MARCH 2011

© Brian Hirst 2012

Published by Brian Hirst

ISBN 978-0-9568363-1-1

All rights reserved. Reproduction of this book by photocopying or electronic means for non-commercial purposes is permitted. Otherwise, no part of this book may be reproduced, adapted, stored in a retrieval system or transmitted by any means, electronic, mechanical, photocopying, or otherwise without the prior written permission of the author.

Book and cover design by Clare Brayshaw
(Cover image Brian at Filey Beach aged 14, 1961)

Prepared and printed by:

York Publishing Services Ltd
64 Hallfield Road
Layerthorpe
York YO31 7ZQ
Tel: 01904 431213

Website: www.yps-publishing.co.uk

CONTENTS

Foreword	vii
The Hirst Family	xiv
Chapter One "Mr King" Dies; Coronation Party	1
Chapter Two: Ice Slide; Club Trips; Christmas	27
Chapter Three: Healey Seniors; Fierce Growing Lad	126
Chapter Four: Ahm Gooin Teh Bi A Teacher	136
Chapter Five: "Social Mobility" and "Difference"	181
Chapter Six: That Word! Butlins; A Death	225

FOREWORD

Sadly, my Mam died just a few days before *Rag-Oyle Town Family* was first published in March 2011 and so she never saw the book she had so looked forward to reading. Mam was admitted to Dewsbury Hospital with heart problems in late December 2010 and she stayed there until mid-March 2011 when she was transferred to a nursing home at Birkenshaw (quite near Batley) where she died a few days later. I visited her at Birkenshaw three days before she died. She was physically very frail by then and was being given "end of life care" which kept her calm and free of pain. Apart from some mild hallucinations, (caused by morphine treatment) she seemed to me as mentally vigorous and full of love and concern for her family and community as she had always been. Mary was a major force of influence in the lives of her thirteen children and in many of her thirty grandchildren's lives. She lives on in the hearts of all of us who loved her and her influence will last for years to come as it is passed down through present and future generations of her family. God Bless, Mary luv!

*

I predicted in the Afterword of my first book that family members would spot errors or distortions of fact. That turned out to be true but to my pleasure the overwhelming family response to my first memoir ranged from positive to enthusiastic. Many small factual errors were pointed out to me, too many to list here, but some of the major ones follow.

1 My brothers John and David have no memory of the tortoise and outhouse wall incident which I included as an example of John's fiery temper as a boy. If the incident described in the book gave readers the impression John was unkind to animals, I want to refute that absolutely. John loved and cared for animals as a boy and he loves and cares for them still.

2 I apologise to my brother Malcolm and his wife Caroline. It was, in fact, Malcolm, not my younger brother Stephen, who broke the family "tradition" of conceiving his first baby less than nine months before marriage. I want also to re-affirm my respect for Malcolm's single-minded determination and ambition. I do not regard these qualities as negative and I think they far outweigh the "coolness and distance" which existed (to my eyes) between Malcolm and other members of the family during his boyhood and growing-up years.

3 An apology to my cousin Ann who told me how much she loved my first book while pointing out that her Dad, Uncle Horace, died of bowel cancer, not cancer of the lung.

4 The bigot-priest who refused to marry Bob and Mary in the Roman Catholic Church in 1934 was not Father Shine. Father Shine was, in fact, a priest at Birstall during the 1960s and was much loved and respected. I am sorry for making that mistake but I suppose such time slips are inevitable in a family story which starts in 1912, when my father was born, and ends almost 100 years later.

5 Michael was not a football hooligan aged 17. The incident with the police man took place after a night out with mates, not after a football match.

6 It was not Paddy Mac but Tommy Morley who went to war with Bob and Tommy Tighe in 1939. Paddy was in the army throughout the war and after but was never posted abroad, let alone to Egypt. It must have been Tommy Morley, or another of Bob's pals, who told us Hirst bairns about life in wartime Egypt.

*

I have used the real names of my family in this book and have provided a family outline for those readers who might otherwise become defeated by all the names. I have given the real names of the teachers who played such a strong positive part in my early educational development and I have either not named, or have not used the real names, of other adults and school friends appearing in this book.

I have not included a glossary. As far as I am aware, there are no major additional colloquialisms or dialect words to add to the glossary in *Rag-Oyle Town Family*. I was disappointed not to find an opportunity of using two intriguing dialect words still sometimes used by the broad Batley speakers in my family:

Minesht – Pronounced as one syllable consisting of "mine/sht." It means: "mind you!" For example: "Minesht! E's alus be-ern a nasty bugger as ower Arry!"

Translation: "Mind you! He's always been a nasty bugger has our Harry!"

Agate – pronounced "a gate" as one syllable. It means something like "saying" or "said" and only tends to be used in reported speech and gossip. For example: "Ah wor agate 'Wotsta me-ern, thee? Callin me a liar.'"

Translation: "I said, 'What do you mean, you? Calling me a liar.'"

And another old word I love, which you never hear now: "Amn't," meaning "I am not." For example: Mam: "Brian! Stop nibbling that cake else there'll be none left feh tea." Brian: "I amn't nibbling it, Mam. Honist!"

*

In the Afterword to *Rag-Oyle Town Family* I said the need to write the book came when I was diagnosed with leukaemia in 2004 and was given three-to-ten years of survival by my haematology doctors. (My survival chance now, in 2011, is two-to-three years. This is an "average" prognosis, meaning my survival could be shorter, or longer.) The CLL diagnosis made me face the prospect of my death and that realisation made me want both to shed, and share, some of my own life "history." I also said that I wanted to "reveal the story of my family." Looking at it now, the word "reveal" is significant. For years and years I hid as much as I could about my family's social status – and at worst told downright lies about it – as I travelled that difficult, troubled road to widening my social standing and began mixing more and more with "aspiring" middle class fowk. Thus, on a crude level, the book was an attempt to shed all those evasions, lies and masks I so carefully constructed throughout my life about my family background and upbringing. But to my great joy and pleasure, while revealing the truth about my family background, and shedding the lies, I found myself sharing – with my prospective readers – the stories of an outstandingly wonderful mother, a deeply damaged father and eleven siblings who have all, in their own ways, inherited my mother's strengths and perhaps some of my father's flaws. While writing the book I often found myself laughing out loud at the humour and dogged vigour of the people portrayed. And I was often tearful, wrapped in intermingled emotions of pride, shame and regret that I had never looked so closely at my family's lives before.

Writing *I Can See You But You Can't See Me* has been in many ways a parallel experience to writing *Rag-Oyle Town Family*. It began with a firm intention in my mind about what I wanted to achieve. On one level, I wanted to reveal the lies I told, which grew more and more pathological as time went on, about myself, my family and my social class. I also wanted, rather late in life, I know, to reveal my homosexuality to all those of my family and friends who are not already privy to it. While writing about my sexuality I more and more began to realise it was a deeper "shame" within me, lurking behind the "shame" of my social class, and together those two "shames" led to telling all those lies. But just as happened with the first book, I found myself becoming less and less concerned with the "confessional" elements as I became more and more engaged in the younger me, and in the time and place – in the history – of the story. I found myself laughing out loud at those wonderful remembered moments, from mixing-up Mr. King with King George V1, to those marvellous communal occasions such as the Annual Club Trip. And needless to say tears came too while recalling sad occasions and events such as my cousin Glynne's death. Alongside the laughter, sadness and regret, I also felt a great sense of love, recalling the places and people of my early world: a love which became a kind of rhapsody, elegy, eulogy, especially when recollecting those early years before puberty hit, described in the first three chapters: a love which I think still makes up a large part of who I am. (*Who Am I?* was my first working title, covering both books.)

I am a former teacher and teaching is rather irremovably etched into my psyche. Over the last two years, while writing and editing the final copy of this book, the subject of "social mobility" was cropping up more and more often in the world outside my computer screen and writing room. It is a topic which is so intrinsic in who I am that it became another theme, another character, in this book.

I worry though that the teacher in me has made me fall into that awful pitfall in creative writing: telling rather than showing. If you the reader find the telling sections irksome then I won't mind. I've no right to be hurt or offended. After all, I have only ever read the "Peace" sections of Tolstoy's *War and Peace,* as the fact-based war sections bore me to tears.

The photographs of places, and those showing myself at various ages, are for me powerful visual aids supporting the written text. The photographs of "Brian" brought back vivid memories, especially those such as the one shown on the front cover passed on to me by my sister Shirley after Mam died, which I had not seen since they were taken forty or more years ago. I spent a sunny warm day in Batley in August 2011 going back to many of the places described in the book, taking snapshots. Some buildings have disappeared entirely, notably Healey Juniors. Other places, such as the "piece" at Bunkers Hill, have been "tidied-up." Some places have barely changed at all, such as the railings and triangle stones at Purlwell Infants School. I was struck by how different present-day Batley is, compared with the pictures in my head of those early years of my life there. Many of the black grim buildings have been cleaned and are now a beautiful sandy gold. The town is so much greener now. You cannot see the Bradford Road from Mount Pleasant because of the trees that have grown there since my early days of living in 1950s Batley and the stark expanse of grass in front of Batley High in its early years is also now full of sturdy trees. The Bradford Road has also changed. At the peak of the textile industry in the Heavy Woollen District there were over sixty working mill chimneys between Batley Carr and Birstall* – a stretch of a mile or two – and right up to the late-1960s many of those chimneys were still in use. The mill chimneys have gone completely now.

Time and space constraints prevented me from including events which interested, intrigued and bothered me during my last four secondary school years: the Cuban Missile Crisis; President Kennedy's assassination; the Viet Nam War; the arrival and inexorable rise of The Beatles. Other matters, too, such as whether to use the old or new system of naming year groups in schools involved some agonising. This attention to detail fits in with another theme of both memoirs: the theme of continuity and the past being always present in our lives now, even though we live in an age which constantly seeks to assert the "end of history." But enough. I need to focus now on finishing the third and last of my memoirs. I expect you just want to get on with the story, if you have not already dismissed it with disgust, that is.

Brian Hirst. Scarborough. December 2011

* See "Historical Snapshots Of Batley And Birstall" written and published by Malcolm H Haigh, 1994.

THE HIRST FAMILY

GRANDPARENTS
Robert Hirst and Winnie Coleman
John Wolstenholme and Elsie Poskett

PARENTS UNCLES AND AUNT
Robert (Bob) Hirst and Mary Wolstenholme
Horace Chadwick and Louie Wolstenholme
James Hirst

COUSINS
Glynne Chadwick (1946-1965)
Ann Sheilds (nee Chadwick)

SIBLINGS, FOLLOWED BY THEIR SPOUSES AND CHILDREN
Barry (1934-1993) and Sheila Hirst – parents of Linda, Christopher
Shirley and Jimmy Colleran – parents of Julie, Linda, Stephen
Moira (1936 – 1979) and Jimmy Colleran – parents of Timothy, Michelle, Paula
Margaret Hirst (1938-1942)
Robert (Young Bob) and Dot Hirst – parents of Jane, Sally, Lisa
John and Pat Hirst – parents of Kate, Moira
Malcolm and Caroline Hirst – parents of Tracey, Debbie, Peter
Brian Hirst

David and Mary Hirst – parents of Donna, Tammy, Wayne
Richard and Lynne Hirst – parents of Nicola, Joanne
Richard and Linda Hirst – parents of Gemma, Liam
Stephen and Maggie Hirst – parents of Richard, Elizabeth
Lynne and Mick Cribb – parents of Hayley, Paul
Michael and Sandra Hirst – parents of Michele
Michael Hirst and Donna Flatley – parents of Scarlett, Otis

"MR. KING" DIES; CORONATION PARTY

Brian became explicitly aware of his shame over the size of his family in the third year at Batley High when his form teacher began the hateful ritual of filling in the class register on the first day back in September after the six-week holiday. It was a whole interminable morning filled with the teacher's droning voice, asking every boy his full name, address, names of parents, siblings – and then the final dreaded question:

"An' do you have free dinners, Hirst lad?"

And a mumbled, "Yessir," followed by surreptitious sneers, from some in the class.

It was three hours of excruciating boredom for everyone, including the teacher, and the boys became more and more restless, having nothing else to do but snigger at the unfortunate lad whose turn it was for questioning. For Brian, it was nerve-wracking and humiliating. He was at that age when just having to talk out loud in class was torture. Being forced to call out all the names of his eleven siblings and then say "yes" to the free dinner question, with the whole class staring and listening, was his idea of nightmare. There were three good things he clung onto that made the ordeal bearable. First, his surname came early in the alphabet and so by the time the ritual ended most of the class had forgotten his huge family and free dinners. Second, the names of his Mam and Dad were normal, unlike the weird old-fashioned names that some parents had. And third, neither he nor any of his siblings had middle names at all, let alone risible or dated ones.

It was around this time that he became expert at putting on a blank expressionless face to the outside world. Inside, he was full of imagination and fantasies, which enabled him to escape from the real and perceived sneers from other boys, and from his inner fears and shames. The fears and shames had been stacking up inside him for years but it was only at this stage that he was becoming consciously aware of them, though he could not articulate them yet. His fantasies were an escape route from the feelings and half-shaped thoughts inside; feelings and thoughts which were increasing in intensity and taking on a shape he was starting reluctantly to half-understand, at the age of fourteen.

Even in Brian's earliest memories the feelings were there in a cloudy shape. He began his formal education at Purlwell Infant School in September 1951, three months before his fifth birthday. His adult recollections of his classmates at infant school are vague but memories of one boy, Jeffry, and one girl, Margaret, remain. Jeffry was busy, loud and confident. He wore glasses and posh clothes and had thick black curly hair, and Brian felt both fascination and attraction toward him. Jeffry was dominating, always at the centre of classroom life, while Brian was on the edges, wanting Jeffry to notice him and be his friend. But he was fearful of pushing himself forward; fearful of rejection. Perhaps it was then that he first developed his habit of playing the spectator: hiding himself, standing on the sidelines, fearing rejection, holding back from participating in play and classroom activities, avoiding the limelight. As he ran home at the end of the school day, Jeffry was sometimes in Brian's head: his lustrous dark hair, glasses, posh clothes; his noise and bravura. And when Brian began exploring the roots of his sexuality at the age of fifty, he recalled a story he made up in his head when he was five, involving himself and Jeffry. In the story, Brian is lying on his back in the school sandpit and Jeffry is lying on top of him. The image excited him but he knew it was "wrong" and it became one of his first guilty secrets, bottled up inside; just like his Dad bottling up the war in his mind for all those years after.

Margaret was tall and bossy and acted like a grown-up. She lived in a high stone Victorian house at the end of a terrace not far from school and had her very own playroom right at the top of the house with a big window overlooking Batley Rugby Club grounds at Mount Pleasant. One day she took Brian and another boy and girl to play at her home after school. Her house seemed enormous; quite unlike Brian's cramped crowded house at Woodsome Council Estate. She had to shout from the front hall to be heard by her "Mum," who was in the kitchen at the back of the house. When Margaret's "Mum" appeared in the hall he thought she did not look like a Mam. She looked more like his big sister, Moira, with her permed hair, lipstick, make-up and tidy clothes. She was the opposite of his Mam, with her pinny, worn-down slippers and un-made-up face.

"Yes, yes. Goo on darlin. You can all play upstairs."

So they climbed endless-seeming steps, past bedrooms on the first landing, until they reached Margaret's vast playroom crammed with toys. Brian wanted to stand at the window and look out at Mount Pleasant grounds, already feeling a dim sort of shame about his own family house at Woodsome. He imagined this was his house and Margaret his sister. Meanwhile, Margaret briskly donned her nurse's clothes and then interrupted his reverie.

"Right. Tek your closes off Brian an cum an lie down on the bed. I'm the nurse an yoor the patience. An you ave teh do what I tell yeh."

He went along half-heartedly with the game, allowing Margaret and the other girl to examine his chest and touch his belly button and willy.

"Right. It's ower tern to be patience and yoor the doctors. Cum on. Yeh've got to zamin *us* now."

The girls undressed and Brian watched the other boy touching them, preferring not to join in, worrying about her Mum suddenly appearing and catching them being naughty. But her Mum soon called Margaret down for tea. And they all went home.

Even at the age of five he knew intuitively that he was "wrong" not to be interested or excited by the undressed girls. He knew the picture-story in his head of Jeffry lying on top of him was "wrong." He knew his large family and the house at Woodsome were in some way "wrong." Shame and guilt feelings about himself, his home and family were already layering-up inside. The worst shame though was what his Dad thought of him. His Dad thought he, Brian himself, was "wrong." Most of the time his Dad ignored him, as if he did not want him to exist. Sometimes he told him off. He did not tell him off often but when he did it hurt.

"What did thar jus seh teh yeh Mam? Yeh'll doo-er as shi bluddy tells yeh – YOW LITTLE MARY-ANN." Or. "Stop that bluddy screeching, thee. YOW LITTLE MARION-ETTE."

And his Dad's face would screw up in contempt and loathing and the words, and the look on his face, *cut* into Brian, making him feel wounded inside, inhibiting him emotionally for years after. Even as an adult, he was reluctant to remember the pain. He could see Bob's face, suffused in withering contempt, and he still felt the effect of those spat-out words. It was like having acid thrown all over his body. The first time it happened, he curled into a tight ball to protect himself from the acid while Bob turned his back, after the look and the words, and walked away.

He stayed ages in that tight ball; shrinking from Bob's look and contemptuous words. He felt a sense of utter diminishment. There was just him; curled in his stinging ball. No Mam. No brothers and sisters. Just Brian: curled up, soaked in stinging mental pain.

After the pain he felt hurt and anger, which deepened and grew into hatred of his Dad and the hatred stayed inside him for years. His hatred of Bob grew so strong by his early teenage years that it made him unable to say the word "Dad" anymore. "Dad" was a loving word which other lads used with respect and affection. The taste of the word on his tongue was sour and bitter and Brian could not utter it without feeling sick and pained. He relegated the word into abeyance, avoiding uttering it throughout his growing years to save himself from inner pain and bitterness. He copied his Dad's example. He made Bob invisible; just as Bob had done to him. He envied other boys, who had no idea how lucky they were, when he heard them talking about their Dads. Even as a young man the word "Dad" still felt false on his tongue and so he used the neutral word "father" instead, when forced in conversations to name Bob.

Another less introverted and introspective child might have defied Bob and asserted his "Mary-Ann and Little Marionette-ness," like Ray Stevens did, Brian's friend during his junior and early secondary school years. Ray's older brother played professionally for a while in the Batley Rugby League team but Ray stuck two fingers up right from the start at the efforts of the world around to force him into being a macho rugby-playing Yorkshire lad, like his big brother. Brian, on the other hand, did not stick two fingers up at anyone, least of all at Bob. Instead, when the pain lessened enough to enable him to think, he stayed curled up inside himself, pondering the meaning of the words and the contempt in them and their relationship to himself: to what and who he was. He pondered over why Bob made him invisible and concluded there was something deeply wrong about himself, Brian. There was something wrong about the high squealing pitch of his voice when he became excited. And there was something wrong about his hand gestures, his walk, his gait, when he was happy and at play. These seemed to be some of the things Bob hated about him. Wrapped up inside his ball, he came to the conclusion that it was wrong for a boy to behave like "a girl." Perhaps it was then when his yearning to be someone he was not began; when guilt and shame and concealment of the things that made him guilty and ashamed started; when he began to create a different Brian, in his imagination, outer actions and words. And as the years progressed, guilt, shame and concealment became intrinsic parts of his nature, as well as yearning, imagination and creating a "right" self in place of the "wrong" self with which he felt he began life.

Bob's contempt, indifference and stinging words were imprinted on him in those early years, wounding and prisoning him, but beyond that he led a happy life, marred only occasionally by an unhappy experience. One of the experiences that made him unhappy was the dreaded moment of being sent to bed in the afternoons during his first year at Purlwell. His teacher – a young lass with a permanently red wet nose, a sniff, a swirling skirt and a cardigan with a frilly damp hanky sticking out from a sleeve – took all the bairns to the sleeping-room after dinner. The sleeping-room was in a long narrow wooden hut out in a corner of the playground behind the main stone school building. It had white painted walls outside and small prison-like windows. Inside, it was lined with narrow iron-framed single children's beds ranged down both long sides of the room and there was a central walkway where the teacher patrolled as the children slept or fretted. The flock mattress on the bed was hard and cold. Just one grey rough blanket, and no pillow, was provided for each bed.

The children each had their own bed, unlike at home, where Brian shared with his brother David.

Every afternoon the sniffy cardy-wearing teacher ordered the class to climb onto the beds and lie down to sleep. Some of the children did exactly as they were told, sleeping as soon as their heads touched the hard mattresses. Brian was fretful. He did not want to sleep and was frightened of wetting the bed if he did – another of his shaming secrets. He lay on the bed, missing David beside him, looking at the high windows above and imagining he was in a prison or a dark tunnel, fearful of being swallowed up by something awful if he slept. He resented the teacher patrolling and watching, knowing she only wanted a rest from all the bairns. It was torture: tossing, turning, not being able to sleep, fretting about peeing, seeing prisons and tunnels inside his head.

Another unhappy memory from that time has no clear beginning or end – in Brian's adult mind. The memory is comprised only of weather, emotions and physical sensations. One minute he was in school, but then he ran out of class, sobbing and crying, without the teacher's permission. It was after he wet himself and saw the pale yellow pee on the light beech chair he was sitting on, and felt his wet warm pants and the fish-smelly pee seeping down his legs. Afterwards he must have reached home. (Appen Mam towd im off feh runnin aht er schoo-il, then calmed an stripped im, an weshed im, afoower tekkin im teh bed?) Later in life, he barely remembered the beginning, before he ran out of school, and after, when he reached home. What happened between the before and after is what he remembered most. After peeing hissen, he ran out of the school building, then ran-walked-stopped-cried all the way to Colemans Grocers. The final leg of his journey, from Colemans to Woodsome, remains blank. His distress and misery were at their most intense in the fragment of time before he blanked-out, when he was able to examine and reflect upon his misery and distress as it was happening, while simultaneously examining minutely the world around him, as he made his way home wrapped in misery.

*

It was pouring with heavy slicing warm summer rain. He looked up, sobbing. The sky above was thick and grey. He ran down the short path from the main entrance door to the gate, still sobbing, licking the salty snot sliding down his lips, catching his breath in searing rasps, trying to pull hissen away from the heavy wet patch on his short trousers, feeling a stinging stickiness where pee dripped down to his knees and onto the tops of his long wool socks. There was an iron barrier railing with flaky rusty white paint, rough to the touch, which he had to negotiate his way around to get outside the school grounds and onto the Purlwell Road causa outside. The rail felt wet and warm as he slid his hand over the flaky bumpy surface. He paused to savour the textures of the iron rail and to examine the peeling shards of white paint clinging to his wet hands before reaching the causa, which was made with old Yorkshire flagstones, from monumental in size and area, to small square slabs. Some slabs were cracked, and small diamond and triangle shaped stones were used to fill-in gaps, while glistening silky moss and tufts of grass filled other gaps. He saw how the rain made puddles on the uneven rippling causa surface and noticed various shades in the stone, from jet black to the palest sand, shimmering alongside each other.

Another rasping sob caught in his throat and he started to wail in earnest, hearing the sound inside filling him. Once outside the gate he turned right and ran the few yards by the low stone wall that fronted the school, before reaching the snicket. The wall was made of black and tan stone which mirrored dully the grey summer rain. Thick privet, cut low to just a few inches above his head, grew behind. Every few yards the wall built up into a pillar with a triangle stone at the top and, when he looked closely, he saw a rusty iron railing showing through the privet growing between the triangle pillars. On happy days he loved pulling a leaf from its stem and squashing it until his fingers were smeared in dark privet green, then sniffing the acrid pulp on his hands. But on that day the pillars looked like prison walls and the privet was soaked with rain dripping down every tiny leaf. Bigger wetter heavier plops of water came down from the trees lining the road. The rain drenched him, making his thin shirt and jersey cling, soaking his trousers.

He did not wear underpants (coss Mam sed thi cudn't affoo-erd em) and his trousers stuck to his bottom and crotch. Not wearing underpants was another wrong thing. Other boys, like Jeffry, *could* afford them. His socks prickled his legs and the holes hidden at the back of his ankles chapped and irritated his skin. He wailed louder, wanting someone to notice him as he neared the snicket, but there was no one around. He cried and ran and at the same time noticed how the cobwebs in the shrubs took the weight of the rain; how clearly the concentric patterns stood out; how the busy small spiders ignored the rain. Then he reached the snicket corner. It was a narrow cobbled snicket. To the right was the high back wall of the school grounds and to the left were the high walls and gates leading into the back yards of the big stone terraced houses on Dark Lane. Those stinky creeping plants, the ones with big white trumpet flowers, like those Down Wheatcroft, covered the school wall. They smelled more pungently of piss than usual in the rain and the thick rhododendron and laurel bushes behind the trumpet flowers seemed to be hissing and spitting, closing the snicket in. The cobbles glistened, stretching a hundred yards ahead between high walls and heavy overhanging creepers, until the snicket ended and opened into the street where Colemans Grocers stood. Crying, wanting someone to notice him, he ran through the snicket while simultaneously noticing how the cobbles sloped down to the centre, making a broad v-shape, and how there was a smooth stone channel with small iron drain grills in the middle. He paused to watch the rainwater gush, froth and bubble, noting small leaves, petals, stamens, a paper sweet wrapper, all swirling in the vortex of rainwater around the drainage grill.

He moved as close as he could to the back walls and gates of the houses on the left, avoiding the stinking creepers and dank hissing vegetation to his right. He looked up, stretching his neck, the rainwater blurring and stinging his eyes. He could just see the high bedroom windows of the big houses. He imagined being dry and warm inside one of those high rooms and looking out at the incessant rain. He knew about "dopting." Moira told him one of the bairns in his class was dopted. He wished a nice lady would come out of one of the back yard gates and take him inside and dopt him. He wailed louder and louder as he ran up the snicket, still hoping the nice lady would rescue him. But no one appeared. He felt as if he were swimming, drowning in water, and all his body was stinging, chapped and red raw. As he neared the other end of the snicket he felt something warm sliding from his trousers. He looked down and saw shit spreading down his leg to his knee socks, mixed in with rain and pee. He started to scream. The lane was a tunnel: entrapping him: closing him in. Then blankness.

He ran out of Infant School without permission twice more. The first escape was because of a hole at the elbow of his green jersey. He was older than when he was poorly and messed hissen. He was becoming more aware, more sensitive and easily hurt, about his wrongness; his difference; his shame and guilt. Sometimes at school he was acutely aware of the poverty of his clothes. He did not notice there were other bairns in the class whose clothes were as poor as his nor how some children, like the H girls who lived near him at Woodsome, wore even poorer clothes. He only saw the nice clothes that bairns like Jeffry wore: red leather sandals, hole-less knee socks with deep maroon stripes at the top, short corduroy trousers, new, smooth, bright checked shirts like those in picture books at school (an in Mam's catterlogs an magga-zeens). And best of all, Jeffry's belt, made of red and black stretch cotton, with an alluring silvery buckle in the shape of a snake.

On the day he ran out of school, Brian was wearing worn plastic sandals bought new but now too small. Old grey socks sagged at his knees and forever flopped down to his ankles where they scrunched up. Underneath the green jersey he wore a thin hand-me-down frayed vest under a thin hand-me-down frayed shirt. He wore no underpants under his baggy flannel short trousers, which were held up with old loose braces in faded red; braces which made his trousers bounce up and down like a clown when he ran. Mam had hand-knitted his green jersey and he was once proud of it but he was outgrowing it now and the hole had that very day appeared at the elbow, causing him agonies of embarrassment. He was restless and inattentive in class, fretting over the other bairns noticing the hole in his jersey. The sniffy teacher called him out to her desk.

"Listen ter me, yung man! Stop lookin round the room all the time. Ah want *yoo* ter pay attention ter *mee,* when ah'm speekin. D'you ear mi?"

He stood in front of the desk, shutting himself off from her words (waitin fer er teh shurrup naggin an tell im teh gu back ter is seat). She sat far back from him in her chair as if he smelled like a toilet while she towd him off. He gazed at her and her clothes, shutting off her words and voice. She was young, bony and thin, like Moira. But her chest did not heave up and down like Moira's did; it sagged floppily instead underneath her white frilly blouse. Her arms were crossed tightly just below her floppy chest. She wore her customary pink knitted cardy and he could see the damp white frilly hanky peeping from one of the sleeves. He saw some damp in the corner of her nostril as well but tried not to stare because it was "rood," Moira said. She had a thin red face and she sniffed as she talked. (An er snivly voice sownded like shi wah talkin throo snot.) She kept darting angry looks at him, her lip curling in a disdainful way, her voice droning on and on. To distance and distract himself from her, he looked under the desk at her long skirt covering most of her legs right down to her dull black shoes with low heels. She was wearing nylons; wrinkled proper ones with a real seam at the back, not like the seams Moira and Shirley drew with mascara on the backs of their legs (when thi went teh Gaiety Dance Hall, Down Bah-li, on Satdi neets).

"You jus look at me, yung man, when ah'm speekin teh you."

So he did and he saw that all the time she spoke she was staring at the hole in his jersey. He could not stand her staring. He stopped scrutinising her and burned with shame and humiliation and he looked down, seeing her legs under the desk.

"Look up, when ah'm talkin teh YOW! Look at MEE!"

He could stand it no longer. He kicked at a bony leg under the desk and ran out of school and back to Mam at Woodsome. That night Mam cuddled him and stroked his hair and later, after he went to bed, she darned the hole in his jersey from the spare green bobbin of wool she kept in her knitting drawer with all the other wools, cottons and needles. And at Christmas that year the best thing in his stocking was a bumble bee yellow and black striped stretch cotton belt, with a silvery clasp shaped like a snake.

The third time he ran home was because of what Miss Blackburn, the headmistress, said in assembly. He knew something was wrong that February day in 1952, a few weeks after he turned five. One minute they were all playing in the sandpits and the next minute Miss was leading them into the big hall with all the other classes and everyone had to sit on the floor. It was not like a usual assembly, with cheerful music coming from the wooden wireless, or Miss playing the piano and singing hymns. *This* morning the wireless was silent and the big wooden record player was placed at the centre of the stage on Miss Blackburn's desk, playing solemn music with muffled drums and muted horns. He could see the thin needle at the end of the play arm bobbing up and down on the circling disc and he smelled the vinyl and heard the hiss of the turntable behind the music.

He was mystified by this disruption to the usual routine. He watched his teacher, in a whirl of cardys and billowing skirts with the other two young teachers, all three of them standing at the front below the stage. They whispered and giggled in their cauldrony huddle, occasionally snapping at a misbehaving bairn. He watched them carefully. They looked full of some important news which only they knew about. Suddenly they stopped talking and stood up straight in a line and smiled sweetly, like bairns showing an adult they were being good. They were looking toward the back of the hall where Miss Blackburn had just come in. All the children smiled and craned their necks to try to catch her attention as she walked slowly from the back of the hall to the stage. She looked at the children and smiled and mouthed "good morning" as she walked to the front. He liked Miss Blackburn. Everybody did – even Miss. She was a very nice lady.

Miss Blackburn talked to the teachers before she went on the stage. Then she stood behind her desk and listened to the music and looked at the children gazing up at her.

She was smiling but serious. She looked at the record player, waiting for the arm to reach the end of the big black disc. The music ended and the record player hissed and crackled and Miss Blackburn carefully lifted the arm and put it back on its resting place before switching it off. She moved to the side of the table near the front of the stage and clasped her hands lightly together and stood with legs slightly apart. He loved watching Miss Blackburn. She had tight curly black hair with steely wisps of grey. (Mam sed shi ad a luvli perm.) Her clean wrinkly face was dusted with white powder, behind rouged cheekbones and red lipstick lips, and her thick glasses had lenses like the bottoms of empty jam jars, just swilled-out for pickling. You could see her brown eyes behind the glass, like white marbles with a floating of brown at the centre. Today she wore a long dark green knitted cardigan with big brown buttons coming down to below her waist. Under her cardy was a crisp white blouse tightly buttoned at the neck with a lace of milky artificial pearls floating over her chest. Her skirt nearly came down to her ankles, almost reaching her gleaming black flat shoes. It was coloured in reds, browns and the same green as her cardigan, all in big checks. (Ower Moi sed it worra "tartan kilt" – frum Sco-lund.) And at one side of the kilt was a huge silver pin. Then Miss Blackburn's bright red lips opened to speak, distracting him from his examination of her clothes. Later, he could not recall the sound, timbre, accent, of her voice. Only the words.

"Children: I have some very sad news to tell you this morning."

She paused a long time.

"The King is dead."

Brian heard no more. A wave of sorrow, distress, excitement, a huge sense of importance, overwhelmed him. He wanted his Mam. He wanted to tell her what had happened; because she did not know. He fled the hall sobbing and panting. It was not long after the move from Woodsome to Staincliffe and he ran all the way past the snicket that led to Colemans, across Dark Lane into Staincliffe Estate, past the two side roads to the left, without even pausing to look at the big posh houses down there, not noticing anything, full of his portentous news. When he reached home Mam was in the scullery baking bread, or wringing nappies through the mangle, or preparing ham shank and peas with carrots and onions for tea, or scrubbing the floor, or changing Richard's nappy. Her mouth went into an "O" of surprise when he ran in – panting, tearful, big-eyed with self-importance.

"Mam, Mam. Mr. King, Mr. King. E's DEAD. Miss Blackbern towd us."

"What the – bluddy ell? Eee, cum on, luv. Calm dahn. Tell mi what's up."

Brian liked Mr. King. He used to be a cobbler Down Batley before he retired and he lived in one of the bungalows which right-angled off Chapel Fold on the other side of the road from them. He was tall and stiff with wavy white hair and he often sat on an old wooden stool outside the bungalow door, puffing on his pipe and greeting anyone passing, including dogs, cats and bairns. It was horrible he was – DEAD. Mary laughed.

"Ey, Brian, owd cock. Yeh daft bugger. It's not Mr. King et's dead. It's King. Yeh naw. Im oo lives i' Buckinum Palice an gus rahnd Lundun in a gowden coach. Not Mr. King, wi is rusty bike an cowncel bungerlow!"

There were intensely happy times in those early years when guilt, shame, wet soiled pants and misery did not fill Brian's soul. Some days at Woodsome he spent hours sitting on the scullery door-step at Mrs. Naylor's next door, stroking her red setter, Rex. Stroking Rex's coat, burying his nose in it, sniffing his doggy smell, murmuring, talking nonsense, watching his ochre-red nose twitch and his ears going alert then restful. They spent hours and hours, him and Rex. Drowsing on the back doorstep, together.

*

The Coronation of Queen Elizabeth II in June 1953 was special. In common with the vast majority of lower working class people in Britain at that time, the Hirst family could not afford to own or rent a television and so they were not able to view the Coronation at home on the day it took place. Brian watched a special Saturday morning children's showing of the event at Collins ("fleapit") Picture House, Down Batley Carr, several days after the Coronation took place. No doubt Moira and Mam, both being avid BBC Home Service fans, listened to some of the Coronation service broadcast on the wireless, while Barry and Shirley probably watched highlights on the Pathe News, at a stylish cinema in Leeds. Bob stood back, sceptical about the flummery of it all, his mind still full of memories of the war and working in the mines before nationalisation and also, no doubt, thinking of the lessons his Uncle Bill taught him as a boy about the rulers and ruled of this world. He did go to the Coronation Party at Mount Pleasant Miners Welfare Club – "Bur ee went feh beer, noo-en feh new Quee-ern."

Brian adored the Coronation Party. It was an outstanding event of his infant years, happier and more enjoyable even than the annual Whitsuntide Walk, with its penny rewards. He was not sure who "The Queen" was and what the word "Coronation" meant. He had seen black and white pictures of Princess Elizabeth in the Daily Herald and Yorkshire Post, at home. He listened to the gossip of the females in the family and heard reports of the forthcoming event on the Home Service, coming from the big rented wireless which had pride of place standing at the middle of the "winder bottom" in the back room of the house at Chapel Fold. He listened to Miss Blackburn and the teachers talking about the Coronation. It made little sense to him but he did not let his ignorance spoil his enjoyment of the party.

Before working men's clubs started to pass into history, it was customary for men to take-up membership of several clubs. There was an unspoken hierarchy in the clubs that working men joined. At the top was the Club of the heart; the Club your Dad had belonged to and his Dad before; the Club which identified who you were and where you belonged. Bob's number one club was the Nash. It was situated at the heart of the area of Batley where he was born and it was Catholic, with Irish Republican sympathies. After his number one club, a man might also join another, with affiliations to a Trade Union and the Labour Party. He might also be a member of a club associated with a particular district, or a club known for good entertainment turns, or for serving good beer at a reasonable price, or one having an especially convivial atmosphere and ethos. At various times, Bob and his oldest three sons – Barry, Young Bob and John – were members of the Nash, Staincliffe Cricket Club, Carlinghow Club, Batley Carr Club and the Miners Welfare Club.

And so it was that Bob and Mary took the family *en masse* to the Miners Welfare Club Coronation Party at Mount Pleasant, where Bob and Uncle Horace were members. The Welfare was a glorious place to hold a big community party, situated neatly as it was on the edge of the Batley Rugby League and Cricket Club grounds. There was great excitement at Chapel Fold on Coronation Party morning. Apart from towder-ends' weddings, which came a few years later, it was the only time the whole family went out together on a social occasion: from Bob and Mary, to Barry, who was twenty, down to Richard, who was just a few months old. It was chaotic with eleven people breakfasting, washing and dressing in the house – all at the same time, instead of the more normal staggered mornings. The older three females and the three youngest children took over the bathroom, while Barry and the two Bobs washed and shaved downstairs at the big pot scullery sink, with Malcolm and John being snapped and swatted at by the adults, like nuisance bluebottle flies, as they ran and played between the two main camps. Eventually everyone was washed and dressed in best clothes, and shopping bags and brown paper carriers were packed with blankets to spread on the grass on the Mount Pleasant pitch, along with myriad sundry items to sustain a family of eleven for a day-long open-air summer party.

When Mam and Dad and the nine Hirst bairns processed down the front path on their way to Mount Pleasant they were amazed to see the rest of the world also processing to numerous parties being held across town. Brian gazed at all the smiling happy fowk and noticed even Bob was smiling. Everyone, in an understated way, seemed determined to have a good day. No one mentioned "The Queen" or "The Coronation" like Miss Blackburn at school and the posh fowk on the wireless did. The talk was all about, "Which dow ivvribody wah goo-in teh." Brian loved the tangible sense of bonhomie in the air; the graspable sense of happy anticipation everyone was feeling. He wanted to jump as high as he could and shout at the top of his voice with joy and he would have, were it not for Mary's, Shirley's and Moira's restraining hands, facial signals and indulgent but firm commands "Teh be'ave is-sen."

"Nah then, Bob, owd lad! Weer's thar lot bahn teh tehdee then?"

"Weer off teh Miners. Weer's thar bahn?"

"Cricket Club dow, us. Thiv gor a reight good tern feh tehneet an yon stooward theer pulls a reight good pint."

"Ey up, Barry Summerfield. Thar's looking smart tehdee. Weer's thar gooin then?"

Mrs. Summerfield, their next-door neighbour – who Brian and David called "Mrs WhatsterdewCOCK?" on account of her funny Manchester accent, with its questioning lilt at the end of everything she said – did not give their Barry the chance to speak.

"Weer gewin dewn Sent PatrICKS. The Father's givin a blessin befewer the dew gets gewin in the pres-bi-teery gardINS."

Brian wanted to giggle: at her high pitched voice and funny way of speaking: at the way she seemed to push spit into the big gap between her middle top front teeth when she spoke. But he could feel Moira's, Shirley's, or Mary's hand, squeezing his, warning him not to. It was busy all the way down, past his school at Purlwell, to the Welfare. The whole world was out. Everyone was going to a party, and Mount Pleasant did not disappoint when they arrived. Glynne, Auntie Louie and Uncle Horace were already there. Louie was a natural party person in normal times and her exclamations "ovver ow luvli younguns" looked, and her teasing jokes "wi towduns," only added to the joyful atmosphere. Brian loved the way Mam and Auntie Louie commandeered a nice spot in the centre of the grounds while Bob, Uncle Horace and Barry spread big blankets over the grass for them all to sit on, making sure there was no dog muck first. The big Welfare Club hut was festooned in long strings of red, white and blue bunting shaped in triangular pieces, which fluttered and shook in the breeze. Brian wanted to *be* one of those triangles and flutter and shake with them. The bunting did not end there. It was strung all around the edges of the vast pitches, too. To Brian's eye, there were thousands of people gathered at Mount Pleasant – grown-ups and bairns: milling, talking, playing, running. There were huge marquees smelling of tea, beer, food, sweat, grass, earth, pee and poop, all mingled in, and the tents were anchored into the ground by thick white ropes. He loved the white of the canvas and rope, even the toilet one that stank worse and worse as the day went on. He loved the contrast of white against deep summer green grass.

There was more fluttering white from crisp starched cloths spread over long trestle tables. Big tin tea pots and urns stood on the table covers, preventing them from fluttering onto the grass, like Mam's washing sometimes did in the back garden at home, making her curse or cry with frustration. Some areas of the pitches had been roped-off: for Maypole and Morris dancing, for a brass band, for games where grown men and women tugged on ropes, or where you could hurl wet sponges and water at fowk locked into things called "socks." Children played running, jumping, skipping, hopping and throwing games. And there were prizes and competitions everywhere. Singing voices came from big loudspeakers and sometimes a man on a loud hailer shouted things out. Even the mayor came for a few minutes, arriving in his big black car, wearing his gold chain and speaking a few words on the megaphone before leaving for another party. (It was well before the Thatcher Era, when miners were belittled and diminished by her. The mayor dared not neglect paying the Welfare members a respectful visit.)

Brian, Glynne and David spent the whole morning running round and round the amazing spectacle that Mount Pleasant grounds had miraculously been transformed into – just for that day. If you had asked the infant Brian what heaven was like he would have said "Mount Pleasant on Coronation Party Day." The grounds were indeed on a pleasant mount and from the far edge you could see all of Batley Carr and the Bradford Road spread out in the valley below. Just there, was the mill where Granma an Grandad once worked. And further down was Burrows Mill, where Auntie Louie worked. And right below was Smiths Mill, where Shirley would eventually work. From Mount Pleasant edge, he could see more high stone mills imitating classic Greek and Roman architecture, towering along the sides of the snaking Bradford Road. Perhaps it was on that day that his love of high places with expansive skies above, and human detail and landscaping below, began. He loved the space and detail; the sense of feeling simultaneously exalted, yet grounded to earth. Perhaps Mount Pleasant that day gave him his first sense of the heavenliness of earth.

The best bit though was dinner time. Everybody had to come and sit down on the big blankets and Brian, David and Glynne were warned, even by Auntie Louie, "Teh bi good." Then Mam, Auntie Louie, Shirley and Moira went over to the tables with all the other women and after a few minutes they came back, loaded with big white pot plates and mountains of food. They put the plates in the middle of the blankets. (Mam sed ivvribody ad teh wait till food wah passed round. An shi slapped David's arm when e tried teh snee-erk a sanwich, an towd im teh watch is bluddy manners. E nearly cried bur Auntie Louie squeezed is cheek an winked at im when Mam want lookin an e laughed instead.) Then everybody had to say what they wanted to drink. There was tea and hundreds of different pops, including Brian's favourite – cherryade. Then the women went to the tables again and brought back drinks. The tea was in proper white cups with saucers and the pop was served in tall thick glass tumblers. There were potted meat sandwiches, salmon paste ones, salad and tomato ones, and cheese with onion ones. And sausage rolls, pork pies, pickles, fairy cakes, coconut slice, covered in tiny coloured sugar seeds, and jelly and custard. And if you wanted more – and Brian did – all you had to do was go back to the big table and wait for someone to notice you and then tell them what you wanted. He went back again and again, asking in his high clear voice for more, for himself and all the family. He loved standing at the table until a grown up noticed him and gave him whatever he asked for. He loved looking up at the grown-ups and the high tin tea urn hissing out vapour. He loved looking down at the sticky mud puddle the hot water leaking from the urn was making on the ground and standing on tiptoe, trying to see what was left of the food on the long trestle table.

Everyone was lazy after eating. Brian scraped the last of the red jelly and custard from his plate and put it in his mouth. He held it there, glutinous on his tongue. He sucked at his pop, which had lost its fizz, mixing it in with the food, savouring the flavours and textures. (Till Mam towd im teh swaller is food an called im a greedy littel sod.) Bob was lying on the blanket "like a bluddy owd lord" according to Mam.

"Mary, lass. Pass mi thah bit er poo-werk pie fru yonder."

He pointed languidly toward a plate. Mam gave him a funny look as if she was mad at him but she laughed.

"Oo d'yeh think I am? Yeh bluddy maid? Reach fer it yehsen."

Everyone laughed, including Bob. And all the women started telling the men it was their turn to do some work and they all argued and laughed and then Bob, Uncle Horace, Barry and Young Bob collected all the plates and took them back to the tables, and they all had to stand up while Mam and Auntie Louie shook crumbs off the blankets. After the food: more games, more music, more shouting from the man on the loud hailer, while Brian ran and ran around the Welfare Club hut. He saw Barry with George Harwood, Bernard Lee, and some of his other pals from grammar school days, all holding pints of beer. They were shoving and play-punching each other and laughing. Bob was nearby with Uncle Horace and some older men and they had pints, too, and Bob was laughing. He looked really happy, in a way he rarely did at home.

Some other women came and joined Mary and Louie on the spread-out blankets and Brian went to lie down next to Mam. He listened to the soothing sound of the women's voices and rested his head on Mam's lap, and she ran her fingers through his hair again and again while she talked. He squeezed his eyes together until sights and sounds became blurred. A while later, he opened his eyes and the women were still talking. One of them looked over toward the men standing nearby, laughing and talking, pint beer glasses held in their hands.

"Ah see thar Bob's enjoying is beer ovver yonder."

Mam did not get mad. She smiled ruefully.

"Aye. An the'll be moo-er pints gooin weer that wun's gooin afoo-er tehneet's aht, an all. Cum on then, Brian. It's bed time feh yow. Yeh tired aht. Weer's Ower David? Ower Malcolm? Ower John? Moira luv. Gu an fetch em. It's time wi worr off."

And all he remembered after was someone carrying him back to Chapel Fold. And being put to bed. And sleeping.

Railings at Purlwell

Path from main door at Purlwell

Thick privet and triangle stones at Purlwell

White trumpet flowers

*The snicket
behind the school*

Brian aged five

ICE SLIDE; CLUB TRIPS; CHRISTMAS

Staincliffe Junior School was nearer to Chapel Fold than Healey Juniors but, for reasons Brian only dimly apprehended at the time, all the Hirst children, from Young Bob down to Michael, attended Healey rather than Staincliffe. (Barry, Shirley and Moira grew up in Batley Carr and went to Warwick Road Juniors.) Staincliffe Juniors was a ten minute walk from Chapel Fold. The walk to Healey Juniors, on the other hand, took thirty minutes. The Hirst children passed Staincliffe Juniors every day to reach their school at Healey. Brian had a vague notion that Staincliffe was for "posh" bairns and Healey was for "poor" ones. He knew most of the children at Staincliffe went on to grammar school whereas most of the Healey bairns went on to secondary modern schools.

"Mam, Mam. It's not fey-er. Why can't ah gu ter Steyncliffe insted'n Eeli Jewnyers? Derek Bryden gus ter Steyncliffe, an e ony lives two doo-ers away."

"If ah've towd yer once, ah've towd yeh twenty times, Brian. It's cos wi not Church'n'England. Steyncliffe's ony feh Church'n'England fowk."

Fifty years later, when Brian knew a little more about the way education works in England, he realised the junior school to which he was allocated had as much to do with social class, and whether or not you had aspiring pushy parents, as it did with your Church. Before the war, Bob took a keen part in the education of towder-end but by 1954 he had lost interest in his younger bairns. He was still traumatised and wrapped up in his own bitter life experiences: memories of fighting in the war; the injustices of the mines; the dogmatism of the Catholic Church. Mary remained an aspiring mother. She wanted all her bairns to do their very best but above all else she valued their happiness at school. She praised her children's successes, and sympathised and comforted them when they felt they had failed, pointing out other skills and talents they had outside of school. She chided them when they were lazy or badly behaved at school and she invariably unquestioningly supported whatever the teachers said about her children, and whatever punishments were meted out on them. She did not push her children over schooling, or bribe them, or give them extra tuition, as middle class and aspiring working class parents often do. Pushing her children educationally was something she did not do instinctively and she did not bribe them because she had nothing material she could bribe them with. Instead, she looked askance, with a touch of envious whimsy, when she heard from one or other of her bairns how someone's Dad had promised his son a bike if he passed the eleven-plus exam. As for tuition, there was little she could offer, beyond helping with the basics of numeracy and literacy. Mary herself and those most close to her – her parents, friends, sister, husband – all left school at fourteen and anything beyond a basic education was a mystery which posh fowk knew about and "ower soo-ert" did not. She and Bob accepted the "religious" reason given for their children's exclusion from Staincliffe Juniors. Bob was still estranged from the Roman Catholic Church and so the option of the children attending the local RC Junior schools was ruled out. And besides, Mary reasoned, both St. Mary's Juniors, Down Cross Bank, and St. Joseph's, Down Batley Carr, were even further away from Chapel Fold than Healey.

Brian's adult memories of his move to Junior School are at best hazy. Mary was too busy to find time to take him to his new school on his first day. Possibly Young Bob, who was mature, dependable and nearing fifteen, took him instead. After the first few days Malcolm, who was two years above Brian at school, might well have been put in charge of making sure he arrived at Healey Juniors safely. But if this *was* the case, it is a certain bet Malcolm would quickly have lost patience with his slow and dreamy younger sibling and left Brian to find his own way to school. In 1954 it was normal for a child of seven to walk unattended to and from school no matter how far and during the four years Brian spent at Healey Juniors most days he walked to and from school alone, or with David, and no one thought anything of it.

Brian was happy at Healey Juniors. Most of the children there were not expected to pass the eleven-plus and the teachers and parents (with rare exceptions) did not push them to do so. The school was not a "sink" school in the way some schools are branded in England nowadays. Nor did Healey Juniors have the huge challenges which junior schools in cities and socially deprived areas face today. The vast majority of Brian's contemporaries at Healey were from a similar background to him. They were lower working class and lived either in the Victorian terraces around Healey (many still back-to-back and lacking bathrooms, indoor toilets and gardens) or in nearby council estates. The council estates were then new symbols of a bright post-war future for the British working class. They were nothing like the devastated areas many have become in Britain at the onset of the twenty first century.

Two children in Brian's junior school class – Jennifer and David – were different from the rest. Their difference fascinated him and he observed them closely, making up stories about himself and them, hoping they might notice him, just as he had done at Purlwell with Jeffry and

Margaret. Jennifer was short and plump with small bumps on her chest. She had smooth olive skin and black hair which looked as if it might be permed and she was the only child in his class who always wore the non-compulsory school uniform: a crisp blue check dress, a navy cardigan, clean new sandals and white ankle socks with a blue stripe, neatly folded at the top. Jennifer was the only girl in his class who later went on to Batley Girls Grammar, rather than Foxcroft or Princess Royal, the two girls' secondary modern schools in Batley. Jennifer did not like boys and made no secret of her dislike. If she could, she turned her back on boys and went into huddles with girls, pretending the boys did not exist. Because she so clearly wanted to deny their existence, the boys crowded around her, teasing her and trying to force her to notice them. When they did this she had a dignified way of drawing her short plump self up and she would rapidly blink her eyes, refusing to respond to the taunts, blotting the existence of boys away with the blinking of her eyes and somehow managing to look down on her tormentors from her short height.

But it was not her clothes, her perm, the small protrusions on her chest, or her dignified refusal to be taunted, that fascinated Brian: it was her voice. Or rather, it was her accent, which did not have a trace of Yorkshire in it. To Brian's ear, Jennifer's accent was exactly the same as the voices of the females in *Mrs. Dale's Diary* on the wireless, or what he imagined Elizabeth Violet Bott spoke like in the *Just William* books he so much enjoyed reading at that time. Jennifer spoke like the Jennifer in the stories he made up in bed at night; stories which excited his imagination but sent David to sleep. Brian could not get enough of Jennifer's accent. He listened to her speaking in rapt fascination and then imitated her sounds until he reproduced them to perfection.

"Ew, Brai-en Haarst. Wai dewn't yew gew ahway end leave ass gels alewn? Horrid bw-oy!"

It might have been then, imitating Jennifer, when he started to change his own accent from the broad industrial Yorkshire of his family, to "posh."

David was shy and introverted and although he always seemed happy he rarely spoke to anyone. He wore nice clothes like Jennifer, and Margaret and Jeffry at Purlwell Infants. He had pale golden skin and thick blond hair. The teachers talked differently to David than they did to other children. They were quieter and gentler. David lived in a big stone house surrounded by high hedges and long gardens on Staincliffe Hall Road. Mam said David's Dad owned one of the woollen mills on the Bradford Road, the one with David's family name painted in big letters in faded white all across the stone mill front.

"Oo aye, luv. That mill's been in is famly feh years. Is Grandad owned it; is Dad owns it nah, an one day David'll own it an all, when e's grown up."

But the mill closed down in the 1970s along with dozens of others spread along the Bradford Road and is now occupied by a bedding company. David was given extra special attention the day he left Healey Juniors and Mr. Knott, the headmaster, made a rare appearance from his smoky office.

"Now then, boys an girls. I'm sure you all want teh join with me in wishin ower young friend David here good luck at his boardin school. What's a boardin school, did you say? Well, it's a school where you go to live with all the other children and you only come home in the holidays."

Brian was intrigued by Mr. Knott's description but he was also appalled by the idea of sleeping in a school and not seeing your family for weeks and weeks. It reminded him of those horrible iron beds in the prison-like hut at Purlwell Infants. Brian saw that going to boarding school also clearly worried David, who cried all through his last day at Healey Juniors. Brian was not especially interested in David himself. It was his differences from most children at Healey that interested him: the big house on Staincliffe Hall Road and the mysterious, sinister boarding school. For some time after David's departure from Healey Juniors, whenever he passed by the big house on his afternoon walks back from school, Brian wriggled inside the bushes at the bottom of the long front garden and spied, afraid to go any further. Hiding in the bushes, he hoped David or his "Mum" might see him and ask him to come inside and play. Maybe David's Mum might let him stay overnight and give him his own room? Maybe she might adopt him? But there was no sign of life in the garden or house and Brian never saw David again after he left Healey Juniors.

There was one unhappy period during Brian's four years at Healey. His class teacher during the first two years was in the same powdery face, pink cardy and long drab skirt brigade as his infant teacher, although she was older and less fluttery and girlish. She wore fearsome winged spectacles as grotesque and rebarbative as "Dame Edna's" are now, though not nearly so comic. There was a bitter spell of cold Arctic weather in the early years at Healey, when Brian's class was taught in a room situated in the school's main Victorian building. The classroom had high ceilings and windows which you could not see out of except by committing the unthinkably bad crime of climbing onto a desk. There was a coke pile in a corner of the schoolyard; a forbidden area for playing. The coke was used to heat the radiators and there was additionally a stove in the classroom into which the teacher piled coke from a small shovel, when the weather turned cold. Big iron radiators, layered with thick cream paint, stood under the windows. The paint stank when the radiators were at their hottest and the iron was marked with patches of grey undercoat, shaped like land masses on a world map, where the paint had flaked or had been scratched off by restless bairns.

During the cold snap the children were allowed to go out into the snow and ice at playtimes. When they came back inside they spread hand-knitted mittens, scarves, hats, balaclavas and oversocks to dry on the big iron radiators, and lined wet shiny black wellies across the floor nearby. The knitwear and rubber wellies steamed as they thawed and clumps of ice still clung to the wool and rubber before slowly and smellily melting; dripping down the radiators until wet puddles formed on the wooden floorboards. The milk bottles in the crate the caretaker dumped in the classroom each morning were frozen solid during the cold snap and the "free milk" was by no means completely unfrozen when the children drank it during morning playtime.

There was one enchanting playtime when Brian and several other children grabbed a corner of the playground and made a slide on the thick crisp snow, gradually transforming it into a pure sheet of ice. Brian loved the sliding game and wanted it never to stop. The children did not fight or squabble or argue over the game. Instead they systematically worked on making the ice slide better and better. They stood in an eager line and each took his turn to run to the start and launch himself down the slide, making it smoother and glassier with each turn. Brian stood tensely in the line, watching the slide constantly transform. He felt the shock and thrill of being on the slide and the delirious anxiety and joy of keeping his balance for the few seconds he floated over it. He loved it. But more than the sliding, he loved the ice slide itself. He loved the magic of the schoolyard, transformed by snow that playtime. He loved watching the slide change shape, colour and texture – and being a part of that transforming process. What started as a narrow track of flattened white snow gradually changed into a steely grey shimmer of pure ice, with small indentations, scratches, marks and bubbles, just like a marble, or old shards of glass dug from the back garden at Chapel Fold. He loved the coke pile in the corner, now a small white mountain with just a few grey coke shapes showing through the smooth white snow. He loved the high stone walls with their thick lacing of snow and ice – like topping on a cake. Winter surrounded the children, closing them inside the enchanted space of the schoolyard. And a blue-grey sky above promised even more snow soon.

The joy of the ice slide had to come to a close. Brian and his group did not hear the hand bell signaling the end of playtime, nor did they at first hear the teacher angrily calling them inside. When he eventually heard the teacher's calls, Brian ran with the others to the classroom. But in his head he was still outside. He was full of the enchantment and joy of the playground slide and was smiling, his head buzzing with the zest, physicality and beauty of the outer wintry world. The end was sudden. The teacher was furious with the latecomers and she reached out to Brian, the nearest child to her, stopping him from reaching his seat. She grabbed a clump of his thick dark hair and swung him round, almost lifting him off the ground, and shrieked in a high voice, like a cat or a vixen crying in the night:

"YOU – BRIGHT – SPARK. What do you think you're doing? Not coming straight inside when the bell goes? GO – AND – SIT – DOWN – QUIETLY!"

And she shoved him away, pointing him to his seat, pulling him out of his joy, forcing him into her visceral angry world. The pain he felt from being grabbed by his hair was awful. He was mystified by the expression "bright spark" and even in his fear of the teacher and the sudden shock of pain she inflicted on him, he mused over what she meant by the strange words. Years later Mary told him he was badly affected by the incident.

"Y'ad terrible nightmares ovver it. Wekkin up in neet, screamin – an wettin yeh bed. Cryin not ter gu teh school in mornins. Yeh used teh luv gooin teh school afoor then."

He must have been reluctant to tell Mary about the incident with his teacher. Perhaps he was afraid she might be angry with him. But it is more likely he expected her to dismiss him if he told her about what the teacher had done, being the sort of parent who invariably supported the authority of the teacher over the child:

"Serves yeh right yeh daft bugger. Yeh shud do what yeh teacher tells yeh!"

But when Mary finally coaxed out of him what the teacher had done she was full of cold anger. Uncharacteristically, she marched to school and demanded to speak to the headmaster. Mr. Knott was a kindly man and Healey Juniors was not a harsh regime. The headmaster liked his children and staff to be happy; he liked a smooth running school where he could bunker down in his office and smoke cigarettes, drink tea and enjoy cosy chats with the school secretary. He must have spoken to the teacher after Mary's visit and devised a plan to settle Brian back into school. After speaking to Mr. Knott, Mary reassured Brian.

"It's or-reight, Brian luv. Ah promise yeh. That teacher'll not dow that teh yer agen."

Next day Mam took him to school and delivered him to the headmaster. Mr. Knott was an affable man nearing the end of a long career. He was quite unlike Miss Blackburn at Purlwell who loved children and exuded an air of professional dignity and charisma which children and staff respected and admired. He had a loud braying laugh and joshed and teased children but Brian was never convinced about the sincerity of his interest in his charges. Mr. Knott was waiting outside his office when Mary and Brian arrived. He was an elderly man with the same salty-peppery hair as Grandad Wolstenholme and, like Grandad, he smelled of cigarettes. He brayed and rumpled Brian's hair and put a reassuring arm around his shoulder.

"Thank you feh bringin Brian back teh school, Mrs. Hirst. I'll just tek him back to class now shall I? Say bye-bye to your Mum, Brian. Come on. Chin up, owd chap.

Here we are. Good morning Mrs. X. Good morning class. Would you like to go and sit in your seat now Brian?"

Mr. Knott and the class teacher smiled gently at Brian as he made his way to his seat. He was not fooled by the smiles and the lighthearted words; some kind of code was going on between Mr. Knott, his teacher and Mam. And it involved him. But he could not fully fathom their secret code. The teacher was sweetness and light toward him from that day on. He was even chosen for the honour of carrying her schoolbag down to the bus stop on the Halifax Road at the end of the school day, where he chatted with her until the Dewsbury bus arrived, when she dismissed him, and waved goodbye. He liked talking to her out of school. She asked questions about his family, his home life, his interests and activities. He rarely had the undivided attention of an adult and he answered her questions eagerly, sometimes making things up to impress her. He could see a disbelieving look on her face when he made things up but he did not care. Talking to her, making things up, was a way of stretching himself beyond the confines of his life. It was an escape, like peeping through the bushes and imagining he lived in David's big house, or talking in his Jennifer voice. He was not especially flattered, being given the role of bag-carrier. In fact the diversion to the bus stop meant a longer walk home. But he was curious about why she was being so nice to him. It had something to do with the secret code between the grown-ups. When he told Mary about his new honorary role he noticed she smiled secretly and smugly to herself.

"Nah then! Yer er bag-carrier, are yeh? Well, int *that* grand?"

In his third year at Juniors Brian changed teacher and classroom. The new teacher was young and burly. She had a deep voice and short cropped hair and simian facial features. If Brian had known what a Sumo wrestler looked like, he would have said she looked just like one of them. In class, she growled when anyone annoyed her and not even the cheeky boys and girls tried to cross her, due to her size. The classroom was in an overspill hut situated at the bottom end of the playing fields of Healey Boys Secondary, just across the road from the main Junior School building. The junior school shared the playing fields, having no outside space of its own, apart from the playground behind the main building with the coke pile in the corner near the outside toilets.

Miss loved being next to the playing fields. While the children were working at their desks she gazed out of the window with an expert critical eye, watching the senior boys playing football, cricket or rugby. More than anything, she absolutely loved sports lessons. It was the only time she really came alive. She changed her clothes eagerly in the privacy of her stock room before the games lesson began, taking off her dark long skirt and floppy jumper and donning a short netball skirt, under which you could sometimes see her knickers, and a tight sporty blouse with a number on the back, before finally putting on her clean white ankle socks and whitewashed pumps. She kicked footballs around, showing her class how to dribble and tackle, or she showed them how to bowl overarm in cricket, or she put hurdles up for them to jump over. She loved teaching hockey above all other sports and hockey lessons were a nerve-wracking time, even for the bravest players. Wildly wielding her big stick on a mad charge, she mowed anyone down who stood in her way. She loved wearing her sports kit so much she often did not bother to change at the end of games lessons. Mavis, who worked in Moira's office Down Batley Carr, knew Miss. And Mavis said Miss played for Dewsbury Women's Hockey Team, where she had a fearsome reputation for rough and ruthless tactics. Mam and Moira used to tut over Miss.

"T'sh. Onist. It shun't be allowed. Fancy weerin them short skets all day int classroom. It's fair blay-tent."

For the life of him Brian could not understand why they disapproved.

In later life Brian remembered virtually nothing of lessons, or how he was taught, from infants right up to his last year at junior school. He must have been taught reading, writing and arithmetic, but only the faintest memories remain. He recalled droning through the words in reading primers, his only concern being to get through them quickly and do something else. He must have been taught a little history, geography and religion but remembered nothing of this. He enjoyed singing hymns in the mornings, and listening to posh fowk talking and singing on the big wooden school wireless during music and story times. But he was more interested in *how* the posh fowk spoke, rather than in what they said: all of that just went over his head. He enjoyed art, with paint powders spread out on a tin tray, and mixing-in water from a little glass jam jar and then watching the miracle of loud primary colours appearing on the paper as he stroked the brush across the surface. He loved mixing primary colours to make secondary colours and was full of wonder at the transformation. But even art could be dreary and grim during those austerity days, with frequent warnings not to use too much paint powder. After just a few minutes, the paint faded into the mushy cheap art paper and instead of the vibrant colours he eagerly anticipated, dour shades of mud appeared on the sheet when the powder dried. The difference between the colours he imagined and the actual dreary non-colours on the art paper disappointed and dispirited him.

Mr. Walsh taught Brian during his final junior school year, back in the main Victorian school building. Until then Brian's female teachers had all been remote figures but when he moved to top class at Juniors, to his surprise and interest, Mam knew all about Mr. Walsh and his family.

"Oo, aye. Yeh Dad knaws Mr. Walsh's Dad reight well. E drinks reg'lar in Nash wi yeh Dad, an Paddy, an Tommy Tighe. Theer a reight big Cathlic famly is Walshes. Theer clever an all. Two on ems on town council – Labour, er course. An theer Gerald's a priest. An, em, wots is name? Bernard! That's it. Bernard Walsh. E's a *doctor*. In *Leeds*."

Brian eagerly absorbed this information. It was one of the first hints in his life that people like him could end up being posh: a priest, a doctor, a teacher.

Mr. Walsh's class only ever saw him from the chest upward, or so it seemed. He kept iron control but rarely moved from his seat. He never came to you: you had to go to him. He was fair skinned with hair coloured between blond and grey. He had a long thin face and a sardonic expression. He was the same physical and facial type as Alastair Campbell in today's world and he treated his pupils rather as Campbell treated the press lobby in his days of power at Number Ten: with iron control and sharp lashing humour. As Campbell did with the media, Mr. Walsh played power games with his class. One of his tactics involved creating an unsubstantiated rumour which gradually transformed into an absolute fact of existence, such as the "fact" that if you achieved less than the mark he decreed you should reach in a test then you would be slippered. Brian never saw Mr. Walsh slipper anyone, nor did he ever see the rumoured slipper but throughout the final year he was convinced he would both see the slipper and feel its effects if he scored less than eight out of ten in any of the many spelling and arithmetic tests set by Mr. Walsh. The slipper threat notwithstanding, Brian was fairly confident about his ability to score his target marks in the tests: targets set by Mr. Walsh that is, not by armies of government education enforcers, as happens in schools today. But there was always that small shadow of fear over the elusive slipper as he was called to the desk to have his test scores checked by "Sir." Miraculously, or perhaps with some doctoring of the score by Mr. Walsh, he never fell below the eight out of ten ticks that Sir decreed he should achieve.

In the final year at Healey, Brian sometimes played with children who went to Staincliffe Juniors, in his free time outside school. They told him how the teaching at Staincliffe was geared toward passing the eleven-plus and how their parents were also relentlessly pushing them to pass. There was no such atmosphere at Healey, or at home, regarding the eleven-plus. His Mam just said: "Yeh can ony try yeh best, owd cock," and his Dad said nowt. Mr. Walsh barely mentioned the exam but Mr. Knott himself every so often took out three or four children from class, including Jennifer, for "special" lessons in his office. Brian knew no one expected him to pass the eleven plus, not even Mam, though it was never said out loud, and so he himself did not expect to pass. The exam was not an issue in his life. Scoring the right marks in Mr. Walsh's tests however was a major issue. He was intrigued when his Staincliffe Junior friends talked so much about the eleven-plus and whose Dad was going to buy who what if they passed. He was intrigued as an outsider to all this exam fever and Dads who were interested in your schooling and could afford to bribe you with bikes and other rewards. It was something the Staincliffe Juniors tribe could afford to be passionate about. In contrast, the Healey Juniors tribe had Mr. Walsh and the elusive slipper to worry over. And the only treat their Dads could afford was an occasional penny or two as a reward for running an errand or cleaning shoes.

There was no build-up to the eleven-plus for Brian's class. Mr. Walsh took a casual approach, telling the class to try hard but urging them not to worry over the tests. The sub-text of his approach seemed to be that he did not expect them to pass. There was a test involving reading and writing and another involving sums, all of which Brian took in his stride. But there was one test that bothered him. It involved putting shapes together to make them fit. He had never done a test like it before. He was mystified and had no idea what he was expected to do and so he sat staring dully into space, waiting for the strange test to end. One morning in assembly Mr. Knott announced gleefully that Jennifer and the other children he took for special lessons were the only children in the final year to have passed the eleven-plus tests. Brian was not disappointed he had failed; it was what he and the majority of his class expected. He was surprised though when Mr. Walsh singled him out after assembly.

"Now then, young man. You did very well in the arithmetic and English tests. It was the IQ test you failed. Never mind. Well done, son."

*

School was peripheral in Brian's world during those junior years; it happened on the edge of other more important things. It was a dull interlude, passively and obediently endured, between the things that *really* mattered in his life. The walk to and from school, for example, was much more interesting and absorbing than school itself. On his morning walk to Healey Juniors he had first to turn right at the bottom of the garden path. On a hot summer's day the earth in the bedding border of Mr. Dewhurst's garden next door was dry and crumbly to the touch and as he walked by the garden wall he loved to reach out and take a handful of grey earth, and crumble it to a fine grey dust in his palm until it reached the same consistency as the paint powder at school. Then he would blow the dust back onto the garden border, watching it sift between his fingers until there was only fine grit left on his hand: tiny glistenings of coal, brick, minerals. He loved seeing things change from one thing to another. He loved the power he had in his hands to change a dry clump of earth into fine powder, full of miniscule glistening jewels.

Mr. Danes's garden, next door to Mr. Dewhurst's, was boxed in tightly by a thick privet hedge, meticulously clipped every few days during the growing season by Mr. Danes and so dense and impenetrable that only tiny insects found a way through. He wanted to pluck the privet leaves and pulp them into green acrid mush in his hands but his desire not to spoil Mr. Danes's immaculate hedge was stronger and he refrained. On a good day the Danes's golden Labrador, Rusty, ambled down the path to greet him. Rusty was a burly muscular dog, fearless and aggressive toward other dogs who tried to invade his territory. Brian loved watching him from a safe distance, warning another dog off. His normally cheerful waggy tail rose up still and stiff, looping into a tight curl at the tip and he swayed it from side to side, dangerous and menacing. He growled low, circling the intruder, daring him to answer back. Brian closely observed Rusty's macho mood, noticing the way he displayed his bulk and powerful frame, as he growled, circled and threatened the intruder. When there were no enemies to ward off, Rusty happily submitted to Brian stroking him, feeling his floppy ears, blowing into his beige wet nose and talking nonsense. But time was strictly rationed. After a minute, Rusty shook Brian off and trotted up the path to the side kitchen door, hoping for breakfast from the ever-busy Mrs. Danes.

After Rusty Danes's house came the bungalow half-moon crescent which Brian loved to roar around on a shopping errand for Mam, driving the maroon Tansad with his youngest brother Michael, gleeful and grinning, strapped tightly inside. On either side of the crescent were two blocks of semi-detached bungalows. The only person he knew in the old people's bungalows was Mrs. Boothroyd, who lived alone next-door-but-one from the Danes's. If he was in the mood and had time, on a school morning he would stand on the pavement just a yard or two from her living room window, staring cheekily, trying to discern if she were sitting on her high chair by the fireplace inside. Sometimes, staring in, he caught her eye and she raised a slow arm and waved her wrinkly fingers, and he smiled and waved before walking on. Mam used to fret and natter over "Poor Mrs. Boothroyd."

"Malcolm, gu an ask poor Mrs. Boothroyd if shi needs an errand runnin. Gu on! Don't argue -

John, luv. Slip on ter poor Mrs. Boothroyd's an fill er bucket up ter top wi coil. An mek sure yer bank er fire reight up. Shi can't lift that bucket on er own. Shi'll freeze ter death one day, poo-er sowl. All on er own -

Brian, owd cock. Tek this Sundi dinner ter poor Mrs Boothroyd, else towd lass'll be avin nowt. Mek sure tea towel dunt soak up gravy. That's it. An stop an ave a talk wi er, wee-ernt yer, luv?"

Mrs. Boothroyd was no doubt poor in the financial sense as well as being in frail health and alone, which was what Mary meant by "poor." In another bungalow lived Mrs. Terwiterwoo Owl. She was a large robust insatiably nosy lady who spent all her time standing at her living room window, watching the world outside through her round pebble glasses. During one school holiday, when Brian's friend Ray Stevens came up from Purlwell Estate to play at Chapel Fold, a favourite game with the two boys was to stand outside her bungalow staring back at her, flapping their arms and calling: "Mrs. Owl. Mrs. Owl. Terwit-terwoo," in owly voices. Then they rolled around on the grass, laughing fit to burst at their brilliant wit. That game rapidly came to an end when the owl lady complained and Mary gave Brian a tongue-lashing lecture which left him deeply ashamed of his behaviour and made him more wary in future of sharing Ray's penchant for cheekiness toward adults.

"Ah'm reight ashamed on you, Brian Irst. Fancy! Upsetting that poor owd lass like that. You just mek sure yeh don't do it agen. An yer cummin wi me now the tell er yeh sorry. An another thing! Yeh can stop playin wi that Ray lad. E's a cheeky little bugger, an nor arf!"

After the bungalows there was a row of three or four soot-grimed stone Victorian houses. Frank Wilson, Malcolm's best mate, lived in one of the houses, with his older brothers and widower Dad. Mr. Wilson owned a garage near Staincliffe Library and was rich, so Malcolm said. He drove an old Jaguar, which partly confirmed the claim. Mr. Wilson seemed to Brian more ancient than his car and he looked older even than Grandad Wolstenholme, and wore shabby clothes and down-at-heel shoes. Beyond Frank's house was a long winding avenue which took Brian to the "top-end" of Staincliffe Estate, to a field with a cinder footpath to one side. The cinder path led to Staincliffe Juniors and Staincliffe Hall Road. He liked the cinder path part of the walk; it was still familiar territory and sometimes there were horses tethered in the field. He liked the horses, imagining feeding or stroking them but too timid to do more than watch from his safe distance. The cinder path ended with a high sooty drystone wall to the right, behind which were spooky high trees and Staincliffe Vicarage garden, and to the left was the stone gable end of the Victorian part of Staincliffe Juniors. Bairns at Staincliffe Juniors started and finished the school day earlier than Healey bairns. Brian wondered if the difference in school times was due to Staincliffe parents and teachers not wanting their bairns to mix with bairns like him, who walked past Staincliffe School every day on their way to Healey Juniors, not to mention the tough older boys reluctantly trudging to Healey Seniors. Sometimes as he walked by Staincliffe School he could hear teachers talking or shouting from inside the building; on other days he heard the singing of morning assembly hymns.

Mary never complained about her children having to walk all the way to Healey, when Staincliffe Juniors was so much nearer to Chapel Fold, but she nattered about them having to cross the busy and narrow Staincliffe Hall Road, where a child was once killed by a lorry. She nagged her boys every morning.

"An listen teh what ah'm sayin, yow tow. Are yow lisnin, David? Mek sure yer look both ways afoor yer cross that main road. Ah doo-ernt want yeh gerrin run ovver. Ah mean it: LOOK BOWTH WAYS!"

She must have tutted too over the fact that the lollipop lady went straight home after the Staincliffe children were safely inside, leaving the Healey bairns to risk crossing the road unaided. Staincliffe Hall Road was the half-way point between Chapel Fold and Healey Juniors and it was where Brian changed from ambling, dreaming, talking to dogs and watching horses, to a more serious and nervous state of mind. The road frightened him when he suddenly came to it from the cinder path and a big rag-oyle lorry roared by. He became nervous as well about time and being late. Everywhere beyond Staincliffe Hall Road was alien territory and, apart from the other Staincliffe Estate children who attended Healey, he knew no one around there. This part of the walk to school scared him and he tried to shut the world out. He put his head down and rushed the remainder of the journey, telling himself a story for comfort, anxious to get the walk over and be inside the familiarity of school.

On the other side of Staincliffe Hall Road at the brow of Bunkers Hill was a "piece." Batley seemed full of "pieces" in those days. "Pieces" were small plots of land, sometimes rubble-strewn, sometimes grassy, usually surrounded by buildings, and open to anyone to walk across. They were not exactly common land; they were just pieces of land which had been forgotten, or land where formerly there were buildings before they were hit by stray bombs in the war, like the one at Batley Carr where Granma fell, not long before she died. There was a dirt pathway across the grassy Bunkers Hill piece. It saved Brian having to walk the longer way round and so most mornings he walked across the piece, careful of the piles of dog muck when he remembered. Reaching the other side of the piece, he put his head down, blotted out the alien world and ran down Bunkers Hill before turning right at the bottom into Bunkers Lane. Just a few yards along Bunkers Lane was the junction with Healey Lane, where the friendly Healey Juniors lollipop lady was waiting to guide him across the busy road.

During the winter of heavy snow and the schoolyard slide, there was one special morning walk to school which Brian never forgot. Thick crunchy snow was falling silently and heavily from the sky when he and David reached Bunkers Hill that morning. A real blizzard was blowing and the hill was covered in massive snowdrifts way above their heads, where the snow had banked-up against walls and fronts of buildings. It was bitterly cold and scary but utterly wonderful, too. The two boys dived into the high drifts, squealing with fear and excitement, scared they might be buried in snow and then struggling, panic-stricken, to extricate themselves.

"Ey up, Bri. Wi cud bi ESKIMOS an bild an igloo ter live in, cun't wi?"

"Yeh. An wi cud ave a fire inside – an roast RAYN-DEE-ER meat on it."

"Yeh, yeh! An we cud ..."

Even the normally distant and taciturn adults on Bunkers Hill were excited and jocular that morning. One man stopped and joshed them and then walked off laughing.

"Nah then, yow tow lads. Istah bahn ter Eley Jewniers? It's dahn theer under-nee-erth yond mountin er snow. Tha'll av ter *dig* thissens i theer this mornin."

Another remembered morning walk to school, in the summer. Brian is on his own, rushing down Bunkers telling himself a story, shutting the world out. Suddenly he is aware of a man approaching him, walking his dog. The man is staring and laughing at him.

"Ey up, owd cock. Thars tellin thissen a reet owd tale this mornin, ant tha?"

He realised he must have been telling his story out loud. It made him feel stupid and he was annoyed with the man for making him feel daft. So he stuck his nose up in the air and walked on, determined if the man said anything more to him he would turn right round and tell him teh get lost: because he lived in a big posh ouse on Staincliffe All Road: an he would tell him in his poshest Jennifer voice, an all.

Brian became a little more adventurous in his last summer at Healey. Goaded and entreated by David, he agreed to vary the route home. Near to Bunkers Hill Piece was an alternative footpath which took you to a little known, secretive, part of Staincliffe. On one side of the footpath was a high stone wall marking the boundary of a filled-in mill dam. Lying on the tufty grass, where the dam had formerly been, were several huge concrete sewer pipes which some unknown adults had left lying around forever. The pipes were wonderful for walking on; the curve constantly threatened your balance if you were careless or went too fast. A favourite game with David and Brian was to see who could walk-run over the pipes fastest without losing his balance and toppling off. Brian tended to forget it was a speed competition and instead turned it into a story where he was a circus tightrope walker inching his way slowly across the rope, hundreds of feet above a breathless audience with mouths agape far below. David soon became bored with Brian's internal game.

"Or, cum on Bri. Ah'm fed up wi yeh. Yeh serpooersed teh bi runnin, aren't yeh? Let's gu through inside et pipes. Wi cud be sowdyers er else prisners escapin frum gards."

"Now. Ah'm not gooin in theer. Ah might get stuck inside an starve teh death. An big lads mite cum an block us in an *kill* us!"

David only once persuaded Brian to crawl through the pipes but it was a real ordeal. He hated enclosed spaces, and clambering out of the pipe at the end of the slow crawl felt like a huge liberation. Beyond the old dam and drainpipes the footpath opened out into a mossy green cobbled courtyard. The dam wall had collapsed in the top corner where an ancient tree stood. Some of the senior lads had rigged up a "Tarzan" rope swing onto one of the branches of the old tree and, provided the senior lads were not playing on the swing themselves, it was understood that juniors could play on it too, especially if you had credentials such as Brian's and David's, with respected older brothers at Healey Seniors. The swing was dangerous. It was high and involved climbing over broken masonry to reach it. The idea was to grasp the rope in your hands and hurl yourself several yards from the broken wall and then land on the grassy old mill dam mound. Brian tried it once but ended up dangling ineffectually, before letting go of the rope halfway across and landing in an ignominious heap among the rubble.

While David played the lethal swing game, Brian preferred to sit on the old dam wall nearby, from where he could observe the "secret courtyard." Beyond the main entrance to the yard was Staincliffe Hall Road and he sometimes watched the busy traffic flowing past, the drivers unaware of this secret place. He could see the swaying trees of Staincliffe Parish Church graveyard on the other side of the road and when he peered closely he could just discern headstones. On one side of the yard was a small terrace of three-storey stone mill cottages dating back to the earliest times of the industrialisation of wool production in West Yorkshire, where the top floor of the cottages might once have housed looms. On the other side was a small wool mill built later than the cottages. The mill was still in operation and a rusty iron hoist and a dangling heavy chain for lifting wool bales protruded from the side of the building. The people in the cottages and the mill workers must have been aware of the unofficial adventure playground at the top of the yard but they never attempted to put an end to it. An occasional passing elderly dog-walker might sometimes take fright, observing the dangerous swing game, and threaten "ter tell a copper." Mam would have been furious and banned the boys for perpetuity from going near there again had she known about the rope game or seen some of David's wilder gyrations on it. But she never found out.

*

The mill and cottages have long since disappeared although the trees in front of the mill dam can still be seen. The courtyard is now taken over by a car valeting company and what used to be a steady traffic flow on Staincliffe Hall Road is transformed into gridlock at Junior School turning-out time, with today's children sitting inside cars, being "safely" ferried home while playing "dangerous" games on their hand-held electronic gadgets, unaware of, out of touch with, secret courtyards, drainpipes, crumbling walls and rope swings, which once were there. Personal computers and electronic games played no part in Brian's junior school years in the middle 1950s and cars were remote objects of desire. The family doctor, Alan Hinchcliffe, had two cars: an ordinary nondescript Ford and a beautiful sleek yellow and black vintage Lagonda, which he drove around Staincliffe Estate on his visiting round. There was Frank Wilson's Dad's ancient Jaguar and Mr. Booth, who lived in a private semi-detached house further along the other side of Chapel Fold, and who Mam said was "a manager," had a purring bull-nosed tank-like Rover 90. One or two council house neighbours down Chapel Fold were just beginning to hope of one day owning a car, and the only car-owning person in the Hirst family was Barry.

Most children nowadays seem to spend their time indoors, enclosed in the world of computers, while outdoors they are ferried around in cars. Indoors, Brian spent his free time playing with two or three toy cars, or reading, or listening to the wireless. Outside the house he travelled mainly on foot, with the occasional luxury of a bus ride. His solitary walks to and from school, the errands he was regularly expected to run, or just playing and wandering outdoors with David and Glynne, would strike most of today's parents as dangerous. Nowadays parents in comfortable areas worry about the real danger for their children from traffic, or the largely perceived danger from strangers. Those in less comfortable areas worry about muggers, bullies, stabbings, guns, attack from roaming gangs of teenagers. Traffic, strange adults, bullies and aggressive youths all existed in Brian's childhood but his biggest concerns when he was outdoors alone were sudden horrible hailstorms falling from the sky, or an occasional threatening dog.

*

Brian grumbled or sometimes complained bitterly when he was dragged from his toy cars, or his book or comic, to run an errand. But more often than not he was happy to run to the shops, especially if it included a bribe of a penny, or "threppence." (Three old pennies – pronounced "thruppence" in most places outside West Yorkshire.) Presents, treats and rewards of any sort were in short supply, so he grabbed them when he could. He was a curious child, a people-watcher already, and running errands satisfied his people-curiosity. By the time he reached his eleventh birthday he ran a regular round of errands each week. On a Friday evening there was the walk down to Granma's at Batley Carr with the clothes money Mary had scrimped and saved up during the week. Sometimes on a Sunday dinner time, if Bob was not imbibing at the Nash, he gave Brian an order.

"Sithee, Brian. Thes a shillin ere. Geh thissen dahn teh Cowlmans an fetch a quart er dandilion an burdock. Goo on! An doo-ernt dordl."

Colemans was the only nearby shop which opened on a Sunday. Brian resented Bob's curt orders. Unlike Mary, who gave him a penny when she was flush, Bob never considered the idea of rewarding him. When he returned with the pop, however, he was allowed a potful to drink with Sunday dinner. He loved the sweet frothy fizz in his mouth and mingling the pop with the Yorkshire pudding, gravy, peppery mashed carrots, fatty roast beef and milky mashed potatoes. Colemans was a gloomy miserable dump of a general corner shop, and its owners perfectly matched the ambience, with their suspicious stern demeanour toward all customers, but more especially toward those vile creatures – bairns! It could be a brilliant blazing Sunday morning outside but it was always cold, damp and clammy inside Colemans, like a tomb or a long forgotten sepulchre. Brian ran as fast as he could through the estate down to Colemans, sweating and itching all over when he reached the shop. There were two shop windows on either side of a corner where two streets met, with the shop doorway between. One window was covered in an ancient faded advertisement – Cherry Blossom Shoe Polish, or was it Persil washing powder, or Capstan Full Strength cigarettes? In the other window was a sad display of dusty cans of Heinz soups, faded HP sauce bottles and jars of onions, pickled well past edibility. In the top half of the door was a grimy pane of glass with a tattered "open" sign dangling below a mucky dark blue blind, always drawn at half-mast, as if to say: "Go away. We don't want you here. We're closing now." No matter how elated he was by the run from Chapel Fold, Brian cooled on arrival at Colemans. He thought about running back home and swearing on his Mam's life that the shop was closed. But instead he gingerly, reluctantly, pushed the door open and entered directly from the stone flagged causa, to the sound of the battered wooden door scraping on the stone step and a rusty mean bell pinging faintly, like a tolling somewhere far away as the hangman puts the noose round the condemned man's neck.

The shop was even more dismal inside than out. It consisted of just one room, originally the front parlour of the Victorian corner-terraced house before it became a shop. To the right of the door, underneath the side window with its grudging display, was a sad collection of cardboard boxes. Decaying soft onions lay in one box, withered slack carrots in another, worm-riddled potatoes in another, and black-skinned bananas in another, like devilish half- moons. Eviscerated oranges and shrivelled apples decomposed in other boxes. To the left were shelves, blocking out the advertisement window and holding sundry household cleaners: Fairy Household Soap, Persil, Brillo, Vim. They were like a litany, reminding poor housewives that life was all about drudgery and work: endless lifetimes of drudgery and work, work, work.

Opposite the door was a narrow counter with a dim glass top and more shelves along the walls behind, sparsely filled with bottles, cans and packets of everyday household products. Pop bottles were ranged along the floor behind the counter. Underneath the smeary glass counter top the "penny-farthings" for children were grudgingly displayed. They consisted of various sweets but only posh fowk called them sweets. Brian knew them as "spice," which was accepted usage, or "spogs" – a word frowned on by better-class fowk such as Moira and teachers. The spogs ranged in price from a penny at the luxury end to a farthing at the economy end. On one of the shelves behind the counter was a range of big spice jars but you had to have at least threppence to buy a two ounce bag. Brian adored spogs of any kind and voraciously devoured them whenever he could. At the farthing end – a farthing being a coin the value of a quarter of an old penny – he loved to buy a dark Black Jack toffee, which lasted ages if you sucked and chewed it slowly. Another farthing item was "spanish," a small twig of real liquorice root which could vary in flavour from just the taste of wood to an intense tang which lingered ages in the mouth and on the tongue. For a penny you could buy a black stick of what Brian called "proper" spanish, such as liquorice allsorts and Pontefract cakes are made of. If he was really flush and had threppence to spend he bought a two ounce bag of his favourite spogs: sherbert lemons, sucking them slowly, relishing the fizz of sherbert at the end.

In a dim corner behind the counter was a doorway which led into the private quarters of Mr. and Mrs. Coleman. The door had been taken out and a grey blanket, like the one at Granma's house at the stairs bottom, was threaded onto a rusty squeaky iron rail. The shop was always empty when he went in on a Sunday and the blanket was drawn, protecting the privacy of the owners lurking in the back room. The shop *appeared* empty but it was in fact full of the ghastly essence of the Colemans. Brian knew if he so much as dared touch one thing, even a manky onion, wrath would descend upon him. A powerful skeletal hand would wrap itself round his neck, choking him, before throwing him into some unknown hellish pit, a punishment for his sin. He pushed open the scraping door to the chill ping of the bell and waited in the ghostly gloom, hating the lavatory stink of cabbage filling the shop. The stink was caused by Mrs. Coleman's over-boiling of the Sunday lunch vegetables in her scullery behind the grey blanket. He stood in the shop and waited, feigning an intense look of interest in a black banana or a tube of Vim, steeling himself for the entrance from the back of Mr. – or more rarely – Mrs. Coleman.

Mrs. Coleman's entrances were sudden and swift. She was a tiny slim woman, not much taller than Brian, who was himself quite small. She had dark swarthy skin and grey shadows below her eyes and jet black hair pulled back with vicious tightness into a bun. She wore dark blouses and long dark skirts over which was wrapped a tight grimy pinny. She never pulled back the blanket. Instead she slithered into the shop from behind the blanket and stood at the counter rubbing her wet cabbage hands on her pinny and glaring at child customers as if they were the worst adversaries in the world she could think of. In a snappy bored voice she would ask:

"Nah then, lad. What's tah want?"

"A-quart-bottle-er-dandilion-an-burdock-pleeze-Missis-Cowlmn."

She would then bend quickly, surprisingly lithely, down behind the counter and then re-appear, placing the pop bottle on the glass counter, both hands wrapped tightly round the neck. And then: snap-snap:

"Is tharit, then? Or dustah want owt else?"

On a lucky Sunday, Brian might have an "ayfpence teh spend." He knew what he wanted – two Black Jacks or a stick of spanish. But in spite of the loathing emanating from the small dark dragon behind the counter, he could not prevent himself from dithering over the pathetic display of penny-farthing offerings, delaying the delicious moment of choosing. Mrs. Coleman waited a second or so, seething and tutting. And then: snap-snap.

"Cum on, lad. Aye ant gorall day. Dinner's ont stove. What's tah want?"

Mr. Coleman was a variation on the same theme as his wife. He was small, thin and wore thick pebble glasses, with skin even paler, ghostlier than his wife's. When he came from the back room to serve, his body was preceded by a white skeletal hand, full of a complex network of bulging blue veins and knots of sinews, and sparse black hairs stuck out from the lower parts of his fingers. The hand appeared at the top of the blanket and pulled it back, to the accompaniment of a teeth-gritting squeak from the rusty iron rail, and Mr. Coleman appeared from behind, clad in a brown paper coloured coat, like the long white coats hospital doctors then used to wear. His demeanour and tone were the same as his wife's: grudging, sour, bitter, utterly taciturn. Everything about his voice, his face, his body language, told Brian he was just a horrible nuisance, like a buzzing bluebottle getting in your way when you are trying to read. Mr. Coleman, he knew, could not wait to be rid of him. Behind that sour grim façade and minimal pretence of service, all he really wanted was to swat Brian out of his shop. After daring to hesitate over the penny-farthing display, Brian quickly made his choice and money was exchanged. And then whichever Coleman it was who had served him would stand behind the counter glaring, willing him to go and never darken their domain again. And he would fumble with the door catch, the big pop bottle and the spanish stick clutched in his hands, slowing him down until at last he was free: and out in the sunlit world.

The walk back home, even on the sunniest day, was wreathed in gloom. The shop infected him with its mood. The Black Jack tasted bitter in his mouth and the big quart pop bottle weighed a ton. A headache started and by the time he reached home he was deep in gloom. And all because of Colemans. He wished he were Shirley, his oldest sister, the possessor of powerful words like those she used to lash that Gestapo bus conductor. He imagined lashing, lashing, lashing those nasty Colemans out of his life: with words.

Brian's regular Saturday morning errand to Nelson Hirst's butchers involved a long walk from Chapel Fold, passing through Purlwell, Mount Pleasant and Wheatcroft Snicket, before crossing a main road to Nelsons, near the town centre. Nelson's butchery shop had also once been a stone terraced house but the resemblance to Colemans ended there. At Nelson's the old sash window had been taken out and replaced with shining plate glass. From the street you could see everything inside, unlike the secretive murk of Colemans. A freshly painted sign shone above the window in a primary colour of shimmering gloss paint: "Nelson Hirst Butchers. Established Since -" And the door was wide open whatever the weather as if to say: "Come in, you're very welcome." Immediately inside the shop was a stone flagged area where customers gathered and fresh clean-smelling sawdust was scattered over the flagstones. The sawdust was spread and swept clean, and spread again, throughout the day. A large wooden chopping table and a small high counter faced the customers and behind these were more chopping tables and a whirring steel slicing machine. There were knives and choppers of all shapes and sizes; a different tool for different meats and different jobs. Gleaming metal chains with hooks at the end hung from the ceiling. Carcasses of pigs, lambs and cows hung heavy from some of the chains. As well as raw meats, there were whole cooked tongues, hams, pork pies, strings of bright red or pale pink beef and pork sausages. There was a back room you could see into, where more meats hung, and behind the shop was the cobbled yard where Nelson kept his new Baby Austin van with his name and business brightly painted on the side.

Nelson's was always busy on a Saturday morning. Behind the counter were Nelson himself, a full-time assistant and a shadowy Saturday-boy who made tea and swept the old bloodied sawdust out before scattering a fresh sprinkling across the floor. Nelson was a small thin man, delicate and refined. His long hair was jet black, combed back and heavily larded in Brylcream. He had dark swarthy skin with distinct black eyebrows and black hairs coming from his nose and two brilliant black jet eyes which sparkled and twinkled with kindness and quiet humour. Nelson's assistant was the opposite. He was a large florid man with a rolling belly and swollen pink arms, hands and fingers. He was loud and garrulous, raucous and rude, and told dirty jokes to the men customers and flirted licentiously with women. Nelson and his assistant were opposites but they worked in unison, like a double act on stage: quiet dignity on the one hand; loud vulgarity on the other; gelling in perfect symbiosis. But Nelson was in charge. Just a flicker of dislike on his face instantly subdued his assistant – when he went too far with a dirty joke, or a suggestive comment to a lady.

Brian loved the camaraderie and jollity of Nelson's on a Saturday morning. He loved the smells of sawdust, raw meat and sausages, mingled-in with warmer odours of pork pies still hot from the ovens. He loved watching the white pots being passed around behind the counter, the sweet milky tea swirling and steaming. He loved the cheerful banter between the grownups, most of which he did not understand. In winter he loved to watch steam coming out of everyone's mouths as they laughed and teased. But most of all, as Brian waited in the queue gradually moving forward, he loved watching Nelson, master butcher in every pore of his being. Nelson watched everybody and everything as he served, or chopped meat, or sliced bacon, or made jokes, or exchanged money, or gave instructions. His shop ran smoothly, efficiently, effectively, just like the perfect steel bacon slicer on the table behind the counter. Nelson was the motor behind it all.

Being the middle one in a big family, Brian was already adept at disappearing, at making himself invisible when he was uncomfortable or insecure in a crowd and did not want to be noticed. And sometimes, being the "middle child" made him feel *forced* into invisibility, into nothingness, under the weight and pressure of all the personalities and egos swirling around him. Sometimes, he used to imagine, he could kill himself with a knife or a gun, right in the middle of the family – and no one would notice. Sometimes he thought of himself as the very embodiment of a game he played when entertaining Michael: "Peek-a-boo. Peek-a-boo. I can see you. But you can't see me."

Standing in the queue, he secretly watched Nelson. He was different from nearly every adult Brian knew. Nelson noticed Brian, instantly welcoming him with just a flicker of a smile as soon as he entered the shop. Nelson's recognition was different from the other adults he knew. It was not like the sniffly teacher noticing the hole in his jersey elbow, or Mam or Moira telling him off for eating his food too greedily, or Bob's dismissive glance blotting him out completely, or Auntie Louie's quick hugs and noisy laughter, or the older Beever girls down Chapel Fold exclaiming over what a grand looking lad he was. Nelson seemed to recognise him for what he was: himself: Brian. As he edged further toward the front of the queue his fascination with Nelson's brilliant orchestration of the shop diminished and a rising anxiety took its place. He worried that Nelson had stopped noticing him. Was he forgotten? Had Nelson wiped him from his mind? Would the worst thing of all happen? Would Nelson attend to another customer and leave Brian in the hands of the loud assistant? He became anxious about having to make his order; about having to say the words out loud in front of everybody, when it was his turn to be served. But when his turn came, all was well. Nelson had not forgotten him and he served Brian personally. He had not wiped him out. He smiled warmly, full of attention for Brian, and no one else.

"Nah then, yung man, what can ah dow feh yow this mornin?"

It was a rhetorical question. It was a ritual that had to be observed between him and Nelson, or the world might fall apart. Brian stood up straight, cleared his throat. Nelson had filled him with a confident smile and in a clear high voice he said the words Mary had drilled into him:

"Ten shillins er beef (or pork, or lamb) feh Mrs. Erst, please – wi a bit er bastin fat on top."

Nelson nodded and smiled, approving Brian's perfectly worded order. Then he cut the meat, laying marble white fat on top, and wrapped it in greaseproof white paper and an outer wrapping of brown before placing it in a brown paper carrier bag decorated with his name and occupation, his business address and telephone number, and a cow's head. And at the very last second, just before he took the ten bob note from Brian, he reached under the counter and dropped into the carrier bag a whole four stick Kit Kat chocolate bar and handed the bag over, uttering those blissful words:

"And that's sumthin feh yow, yung man. Can yer manage that?"

Brian nodded and smiled and held the heavy bag and Nelson smiled him out. The bliss continued all the way up Wheatcroft, as Brian crunched his way through the four sticks until nothing was left of the sweet biscuity chocolate. And he was glowing inside from Nelson's attention and kindness, until the bag became heavy, the string handles biting into his hand. And chocolate and kindness were gone – until next week. And he dragged himself home to Chapel Fold, the bag seeping blood from the meat inside.

One terrible Saturday he felt in his pocket for the ten bob note to hand to Nelson and found it was empty. Tears sprang to his eyes when he realised he had lost the ten shilling note on the way down to Nelson's. He was old enough by then to know the value of money. Ten shillings (fifty pence today) was a big part of Mary's weekly household budget. The "ten bob" joint provided the family with meat for Sunday dinner and the leftover was used for Bob's "snap-tin" sandwiches, or it was shredded and added to a mid-week hash, or to a meat-an-taytie plate pie. Not to mention the drained fat, the best of which was used for fat'n'bread teas and the rest for the chip pan. Tears came too because he knew how Mary would react to the money loss. Initially she would be furious and lash him with her tongue. But this would not last. It was the sure knowledge of her devastation and worry about how to make up for the loss of ten bob that distressed him most. He knew she would be reduced to bitter tears after recovering from anger and shock. It was the thought of her tears and sorrow, and the added burden his careless loss would put on Mary's already overburdened life, that made him cry.

Nelson took it all calmly. He handed over the joint and the Kit Kat as usual.

"Cum on, owd lad. Doo-ernt werry. Tell yeh Mam ah s'll see er on Wensdi teh sort money out."

As always in those days, in such a crisis situation, the adult queue of customers in Nelson's instantly transformed themselves into an eager Greek Chorus, commenting on the situation and its multifarious implications for Brian, and the moral state of the world.

"By ell, yung Esty. Thi Mam's barna gi thee a reight tannin when she ey-ers abaht this."

"Duz thar realise ow much ten bob's weth, owd lad? It's a load a bluddy munny is ten bob. Tha'd avter wek thi bluddy socks off for anole bluddy mornin ter earn that bluddy much."

"Ee, ah doo-ernt noo-er. Bairns, these days. Thiv no bluddy sense."

"Ah nor, owd lass. My lot's same: norther use ner bluddy orn-iment."

"Eee: bairns!"

"Bluddy bairns!"

"Bairns!"

The chorus went on until Nelson intervened and urged Brian to run home bearing the bad news for Mary. Everything anticipated happened on his return. Mary was furious, shocked and finally overwhelmed by the loss of the ten bob note. Towder-end questioned him minutely. Exactly which route had he taken to Nelson's? Then a search party, from Shirley down to Malcolm, set off to hunt down the lost ten shilling note. They combed the route with the precision of a police forensic unit. But to no avail. The ten bob note was gone. And Bob pronounced:

"Sum greedy sod's fund it, an pockited it. Yer nivver knaws. It might er bee-ern wun er them lot in Nelson's queue. Sneakin aht er shop, an rushin up Whee-at-croft, an finndin ten bob noo-ert, an spendin lot, on a bet at Mount Pleasant bookies! Bastard!"

Brian was not at home the following Wednesday when Nelson called at Chapel Fold to deliver the mid-week sausages, liver and stewing meat. But when he returned from school, Mary was wreathed in mysterious smiles and later he heard her and Moira whispering in the scullery over what a "luvly man" Nelson Hirst was.

When it could be afforded, Mary splashed out on a Friday teatime treat. A bairn was dispatched to whichever of the three nearby chip-oyles (fish and chip shops) was currently in favour with the cognoscenti. Sometimes it was the chip-oyle situated in the middle of Staincliffe Estate, which meant nipping through the back gardens of neighbours to Hawthorne Avenue, from where it was a quick dash to the estate centre shops. At other times it meant a run past the private houses on nearby Grange Road to a chip-oyle on the edge of the Halifax Road. Or sometimes the small chip-oyle was in favour, right at the far end of Chapel Fold. The estate chip-oyle was the biggest, busiest, most modern and innovative of the three, branching out from just serving fish, chips and fishcake. (A "fish cake" in that part of Yorkshire meant, and still means, two slices of potato with a layer of fish between, dipped in batter and fried.) The shop was run by a young "entrepreneur" – since Thatcher's days in power, a sacred word in every true Tory's ear, although the word was not then in vogue. At the estate chip-oyle you could buy wet fish, pop, ketchup, pickles and dark brown malt vinegar and a few years later the shop was one of the first in Batley to branch out beyond fish and chips, when sausage and chicken were added to its menu. The estate chip-oyle was always packed with customers and Brian disliked it. He disliked having to run through other fowk's back gardens, using them as a short-cut. You never quite knew when the neighbours might object but he risked it, as it was quicker than trudging the roads. He disliked the long queues, the bright lights and the supercilious look the young owner cast over his queues of customers from his position behind the counter. And already Staincliffe Estate was beginning to be tainted with the "problems" that some of the property owning middle classes have always attributed to council estates: feckless people; loud types; people on the criminal fringes. And sometimes people of that ilk were indeed to be found in the queues of the estate chip-oyle.

Brian preferred being sent to the chip-oyle on the edge of Halifax Road, where he could gaze – and dream – at the private houses, some with cars parked in the drives, on his way there and back. The queues were smaller and the customers less loud than the fowk at the estate shop. On a cold winter's evening he liked going to the little place at the end of Chapel Fold. He could see its dim lights as he approached and smell fish and chip steam emerging from the tin chimney and see more steam billowing from the doorway into the dark street. It was cramped and cosy and Brian liked its black exterior and the greasy wooden panels inside. Stepping inside from the dark cold street, in his imagination, was like stepping from the vast forests of Canada or Siberia into a snug logger's den, escaping howling wolves and freezing winds outside.

Whichever outlet was used, Mary applied her rigorous critical standards on the product as it was unfurled from the greasy outer newspaper wrapping and spread out on the kitchen table. She had a small appetite and a vigilant eye for the cost of things and, for herself, she never stretched to fish and chips. If she was feeling really flush, she ate a fish piece but usually she made do with a fish cake. The workers in the family had fish and chips. The younger-end had a portion of chips or a fish cake, both being the same price.

"Remember ter ask feh bits, Brian," Mary would call as he left and invariably, unless Brian forgot to ask, the portions were covered in golden bits of batter. Spread out on the table when Brian returned was a big pot of tea, a mountain of bread and margarine, the salt bowl and malt vinegar bottle.

"Ee, yeh can't beat is fish. It fair melts in yeh marth."

"Ooo, e's a stingy bugger wi is bits. There's none on mine. Look!"

"Ey up, this taytie in this fish cakes ard. It's last time ah s'll ave wun on *is* fish cakes."

"Look at that luvly batter. It fair fluffs up frum that piece er fish, dunt it?"

Over fifty years later, on his visits from Scarborough to Centenary Way, Mary treats Brian to a fish and chip "dinner" from another little chip shop at the bottom of Carlinghow Lane, just round the corner from her flat. There are "chip shops" in Batley now which serve a medley of foods far removed from fish and chips but the traditional chip-oyle, serving a limited but high quality menu, still survives and prospers. The chip-oyle at Carlinghow now, and the food it serves, are not much different from the shop at the end of Chapel Fold in 1956. And Mary in 2010 retains her critical faculties.

"Er fish is allus good. Look at it, it fair flakes off yeh fork...Them chips look nice, Brian. Nice an well dun, an not greasy."

*

During Brian's early years there were three Conservative Prime Ministers in Britain: Churchill, Eden and Macmillan. "Conservative" and "Prime Minister" meant nothing to him at the time but he was dimly aware of these distant things, somewhere in the background of his everyday life. He knew they were important in Bob's and Mary's and towduns' lives. Churchill's Premiership passed him by but he knew about Eden and Suez. He knew the Suez Canal was in Egypt and that Bob had been there in the war. He listened to Bob, Mary, Auntie Louie, Barry, Shirley, Moira and other grown-ups talking about Eden and Suez and he sensed the worry in their talk and voices. During the Suez Crisis, the younger-end were angrily shushed by the grown-ups whenever the solemn newsreader's voice came from the big rented wireless on the back room window bottom. Bob read the dense columns of print in The Daily Herald with more concentration than usual and Brian heard him "nattering" Mary over "Suez, Bluddy Eden, Bluddy Nasser, Bluddy Eisenhower, an that bastard De Gaul." Brian looked at the photographs and maps of Suez in the Daily Herald, when Bob left it on the chair and headed to the Nash to mull the crisis over with Tommy and Paddy. And he understood one thing. It was all about fear. Fear of "Anuther Bluddy War."

*

News and information about Suez was thin on the ground when compared with news about the wars in Afghanistan and Libya in today's world. In Brian's house the news largely came from three sources: The Home Service, The Daily Herald and the opinions and gossip of the local Labour Party members with whom towder-end worked and socialised. There were few other news outlets available to most people apart from the Pathe News shown at "the pictures." Today there are hundreds of outlets churning out masses of news information yet the adults in Brian's 1950s lower working class family and community seemed to know, and understand, just as much about the political world then as people do now. Very often nowadays the sheer mass of news information tends just to confuse the "person-in-the street" – a problem that did not exist for people in the 1950s.

The "choice culture" barely existed in the 1950s in the way it does today. This culture became dominant from the beginning of the 1980s when everything seemed to be embraced into it: choice of schooling, housing, utilities and consumables. "Privatisation" was the buzz word of the eighties and its zealots were convinced it would give more choice to everyone, workers and bosses alike. The promoters of the choice culture tended to turn a blind eye to the poor, focusing instead on the middle and aspirational working classes, who have the material resources to make choices or who want to be able to choose.

Even though the choice mentality was less prominent than it is today there was still *actual* choice for the consumer in Brian's childhood years. People in 1950s England did not live in a drab uniform Soviet-like society that the promoters of today's choice culture sometimes like to claim they did. Attlee's reconstruction Labour government after the Second World War provided Brian's lower working class parents with the "choice" of a Woodsome Estate council house at an affordable rent, in place of the slum dwelling at Wainwright Buildings in Batley Carr which they had rented from a private landlord since their marriage in 1934. And not long after they moved to Woodsome, when the family grew even larger, they were able to choose to move to a brand new council house at Staincliffe Estate. The house at 77 Chapel Fold, Staincliffe, had a front hall, kitchen, dining room and sitting room downstairs. Upstairs were four bedrooms and a bathroom and outside were front and rear gardens and a solid brick building comprising a second toilet, a coal store and an outhouse. It was a huge improvement on the terraced one-down-and-two-up house at Wainwright's Buildings. There was no possibility of Bob and Mary having the "choice" of raising a deposit for a mortgage to buy their own house – ever. After the rent payment, the little money that remained was needed to feed and clothe the family. The question of being able to "choose" to own a house rather than rent did not arise. Bob and Mary were pleased enough to have the "choice" of a council rented house rather than the privately rented houses they had known until then. The "choice" of where they lived was limited for Bob and Mary and their growing family in the 1950s. They could either rent a council house or rent a private landlord-owned house. The choice was obvious and was based on need. There were no hidden background perils in "choosing" to rent a council house in the 1950s, as there are today for many people who "choose" to take on an unaffordable mortgage and other debts.

In the 1950s Mary could choose from three nearby chip shops. She chose on the basis of which of the three was offering the best quality fish and chips at the time and if chips at one shop were cheaper, then that fact would also influence her choice. There was a newsagent, (Harry Hirst's) a chemist, a baker and a general Co-op store (as well as the chip-oyle) at Staincliffe Estate. At the Halifax Road end of Chapel Fold were Shepleys greengrocers, Oldroyds general grocers, a small general grocers shop and a Co-op store – the nearest thing then to a supermarket. At Mount Pleasant was another chemist, another Co-op store, a greengrocers and of course Colemans, where you could shop on a desperate Sunday lunchtime. There was also an off-licence at Mount Pleasant which stayed open till the late time of 8pm, well beyond the then universal shop closing time of 5.30. In addition to the local shops, Bob the Co-op baker delivered to the door from his small electric van, as did the Co-op milk man with his horse and cart, as did the fruit and veg man, Benjamin Hick. "Down Batley" offered a whole range of shops. The Thursday and Saturday Batley Markets were extensive, spreading well beyond the market place past the Memorial Park and down to the Technical School and Batley Public Baths. Mary could buy anything she needed there, from clothes pegs, meat, fresh fish, pork dripping, to "tripe and elder" (the stomach linings from cows) from a stall where customers had the cows' innards wrapped to take home, or where they took the option of eating at the stall. The tripe was served on a white china plate and sprinkled with salt, pepper and malt vinegar to give the tripe "flavour." It was a popular spot to eat a nutritious snack while catching up on gossip with friends, neighbours and fellow tripe-aficionados. The town centre shops ranged from Woolworths and the Thrift Grocery Store at the cheapest end, to high quality, expensive tailor shops and shops selling upmarket household wares and ornaments. If this was not enough, Leeds Market and shops were a half-hour's bus ride away and Dewsbury Market ran twice a week on Wednesdays and Saturdays. Fifty years later, "Down Batley" is dominated by a vast Tesco Superstore. A few shops not taken over by charity shops still survive and the market is a pathetic shadow of its 1950s self.

*

Aged eleven, Brian was beginning to learn a great deal about people and society; about how complex and multifarious they are, not to mention his growing understanding of money and how far or how little you could make it stretch. He knew, for example, that the Estate shops were not as "high class" as those on the Halifax Road. They overcharged for poor quality products, or were inconvenient. They demanded ready cash whereas home-delivery bills could be paid at weekends when Bob's and the old-uns' "keep" was safely lodged in Mary's purse. Long before the loyalty cards of current superstores and chains, the Co-op had the "divi" system. Brian knew he had to tell the Co-op counter staff the family divi-number (10-11-2) at the end of every purchase and he was mindful there would be trouble from Mary if he lost the divi-slip on the way home, or forgot to give the number.

Occasionally if Mary was feeling flush, Brian was dispatched to the posh fowks' shops: to Shepleys greenrocers for some "nice" apples or oranges, or to Oldroyds grocers. ("Feh two ounces er best boiled am, feh yeh Dad ter ave wi salad feh tea.") He liked going to Shepleys and Oldroyds because he did not have to say out loud in front of everyone the embarrassing fact that the purchase was for Mrs. Hirst, which Mary insisted he said in the shops where she was known. Shepleys and Oldroyds had no idea who Mrs. Hirst was as Mary could rarely afford to patronise them. He also liked going to these two shops because they provided him with real models of "posh fowk," a concept and a reality he was beginning to understand and become fascinated by.

At Oldroyds, the owner and his two daughters served behind the counters while other staff did heavy lifting, cleaning, deliveries and behind-the-shop work. The non-serving staff wore immaculate brown paper coloured coats, stretching to well below the knees, while the Oldroyds themselves wore stiff starched long white coats. The staff at Oldroyds all seemed, to Brian, to have shiny polished clean faces and hands. They treated all customers politely and respectfully but toward better-off fowk they added an extra layer of deference which did not quite reach servility. The shop was spacious and pathologically clean, due to Mr. Oldroyd's deep loathing of "dirt." Delicate odours of fine cooked meats, fresh ground coffee and creamy cheeses greeted you when you stepped inside. Brian sometimes hovered at the back of the shop in a quiet corner, making himself invisible, so he could watch posh ladies sweeping in from cars parked outside and from where he could listen to the hushed, almost reverential exchanges that went on between assistants and posh fowk. Not everyone who shopped at Oldroyds was posh. People like Mrs. Danes used Oldroyds on her way to and from her auxiliary nursing job at the nearby Staincliffe Hospital. Sometimes a foreman or a workman came in from Percy Walker's rag-oyle, which was just further up the Halifax Road in the Heckmondwike direction, to have a sandwich made-up for his "snap" and to flirt with the girls, who tittered decorously or sometimes erupted into loud shrieks, until Mr. Oldroyd calmed them down with a sharp look or a loud clearing of his throat. Brian did not know what "shabby-genteel" meant but sometimes he observed elderly ladies in crumpled headscarves and down-at-heel shoes coming in for "Just a slice en 'am," or "Two ounce er cheddar, please," or "Two eggs, luv," or "Ah'll just ave two bacon slices tehday, please." These women dug into their purses for exactly the right change, whereas the posh ladies with cars casually took out whole pound notes – or sometimes even a five pound note – and blithely handed the notes over the counter, not bothering to count the change.

Shepleys Greengrocers was a little like Benjamin Hick's but everything was in a shop rather than set out on a cart. There were piles of fruit and salad on shelves lined with green plastic mock grass and the floor was covered in sacks from which cabbages and other greens and root vegetables spilled out. Whole rabbit, duck, pheasant and other game, still with fur and feathers, hung on rows of iron hooks just outside the shop. Shepleys was not a place of refined luxury as Oldroyds was. It was a living display of profusion and abundance – of fruit, vegetables and game. There were two Mr. Shepley brothers, both pink-faced and clad in uniforms of straw hats and navy-blue-and-white striped pinnies. One day Mam ran out of potatoes for the mid-week meat-an-taytie pie. She sent Brian off to Shepleys to fetch more tayties, warning him to get the cheapest because as always the money in her mid-week purse was scant. Ever the optimist, Brian nagged for more money to maybe buy an orange or some nuts, until Mary snapped:

"Aw, feh God's sake, Brian. Will yow bluddy stop it. Yeh knaw ah've nowt teh gi yeh. Nah tek that munny and gerroff an fetch them tayties else ah s'll nivver get this pie dun."

He stood in the busy shop, invisible, listening to the way the posh fowk spoke and rehearsing asking for the tayties in his Jennifer voice, saying in his head over and over again:

"Three pewnd ev per-tay-tews, pleeze, Mistah Shep-leh."

As he was waiting a big car pulled up outside: a Humber, Rover, or a Bentley. A tall slim woman stepped from the car and then reached inside for her handbag and wicker basket which she held over her arm as she strode across the wide pavement to the shop. Brian was fascinated by her and he could see all the grown-ups were, an all, even though they were trying not to show it. She was dead posh. She wore an elaborate hat, a tight fitting suit, a necklace, glittering bracelets and rings. Her real nylons gleamed on her legs, the seam down the back immaculately straight. Her shoes were made of shimmering black leather and had long slender heels. She wore lipstick (in the middle of the afternoon!) and makeup which made her face lustrous and smooth, not blotchy and powdery like Miss at school. He smelled her perfume cutting through the fruit odours inside Shepleys. One of the Mr. Shepleys hurriedly gave change to the customer he was serving and wiped his potato-dusted hands on his striped pinafore before greeting the woman. An obsequious smile-cum-leer filled his face.

"An what can ah doo four *yoo* this afternoon, mad-arm?"

"Ai'd laike a la-arge peyn-epple. End, ahm, sam brezil nats, please. End, em, you've got thet plackt dack ai orrdered, hev-ent yew?"

Brian stood by the potato sacks in the corner, mesmerized and enchanted, listening to the woman ordering the exotic items. She had a perfect Jennifer accent. He watched Mr. Shepley carefully placing things in her basket. Then he watched her long slim fingers and bright painted nails reaching into her purse for a huge crisp five pound note to give to Mr. Shepley, who insisted on carrying her basket out to the car and placing it on the car floor at the rear. The woman "thenked" him, sank into the car seat, turned on the engine and smiled at Mr. Shepley, drooling on the pavement. She gave him a little wave before driving toward the big private houses between Halifax Road and Chapel Fold. Even quite posh fowk in the shop seemed entranced by this woman sweeping in and out of their lives for a few brief minutes, and it took a few seconds before everyone went back to normal.

"Nah then, owd lad. Wot can ah dow feh yow then?"

"Three pewnd ev them cheap per-tay-tews, pleeze, Mistah Shep-lah."

Dawdling home with the mucky old tayties in the Shepleys brown bag, Brian thought one day *he* would like to have a life like that lady's.

Mary hated the Thrift Stores, Down Batley. She only shopped there when money was really tight: the times when she could not even afford to buy the weekly bread from rosy-cheeked Bob the co-op baker and instead resorted to baking bread herself with ingredients bought in bulk from the Thrift. Only really poor people went to the Thrift and Brian hated it as much as Mary. Sometimes Mary coerced him into going with her to help carry the heavy bags all the way back to Chapel Fold when she had no spare money for bus fares. The Thrift Store was a precursor to the cheaper end of today's supermarkets specialising in its own-brand bulk buy products sold with minimal packaging and presentation, concentrating on basic selling with low overheads. But it was harsher, much more minimalist, than today's Aldi, Netto or Lidl stores. The customers were poorer and entirely from the bottom social class, in contrast to the more socially varied clientele of comparable stores today.

Facing you as you went inside the Thrift was a long counter and shelves behind piled high with plain unmarked bags of basic products such as flour, margarine, sugar, tea. A number of unsmiling assistants in grubby white coats stood behind the counter taking orders. Mary wrote a list which she read out loud to the assistant when she and Brian reached the counter. The produce was then taken from bulk bags and wrapped in either plain white greaseproof paper or measured into smaller coloured bags. As well as bulk items, there were just a few cheap brand labels, such as Stork margarine. After the items were registered on the till, Brian took them from the assistant and passed them to Mary, who packed them into the big brown unbranded carrier bags provided by the Thrift. It was a family of eleven Mary was buying for.

"Four pounds er Stork marg, luv … A pound er that Red Label tea … Nine pownds er strong white flour, luv … An four pownds er sugar … That's it, thankin yow."

And then a pound in money was handed over and a few coppers in change handed back. It was like being in *Oliver Twist*, Brian thought, asking for more. But the Thrift was more impersonal and brisk than Dickens's story and utterly lacking drama, pathos or humour. And finally Brian and Mary escaped the Thrift, carrying the heavy bags between them and trudging slowly home. And as a reward for helping carry the bags, Mary sometimes gave him a penny.

*

Junior school, Colemans, Nelson's and the Thrift Store were just some of the main parts of Brian's life as an eleven year old. But at the heart of his life were his Mam, David, Shirley and Moira – and the rest of the family. His bonds with Mary and David were deep, visceral, instinctive. There was affection and bossiness between him and his older brothers and sisters and he was fond of his younger siblings with only occasional bouts of jealousy. There was no bond between Brian and Bob; just an uneasy acceptance of each other's existence in the same house.

Chapel Fold and the neighbours were another major part of his life. He rarely travelled in cars and buses and so came into much closer contact with neighbours than today's children generally do. Chapel Fold was a long street stretching from the middle of Staincliffe Estate to the Halifax Road. At the Estate end, walking up from Purlwell, it began with ten council houses on the right; a block of two and then two blocks of four, whose gardens were nothing like the devastated rubbish dumps or unsightly parking lots to be seen on some of today's estate gardens. The worst front garden consisted entirely of wild grass mixed with lawn grown to heights as high as Brian. The grass was hacked down with an inadequate hand mower once a year. The best front garden, Mr. Fitzpatrick's, was an immaculate affair in the English cottage garden tradition. It was crammed with seasonal flowers and shrubs and a lovingly clipped mixed hedge surrounded a beautifully manicured small central lawn. Some back gardens were crammed with seasonal and "organic" vegetables (in those days just called "home grown"). Some had a small greenhouse full of tomato plants in the season, some a chicken or bantam run: a cheap means of supplying the household with regular fresh eggs.

Sometimes during the long spring and summer holidays, when Mary urged him and David to get out from under her feet and "layke ahtside," (play outside) Brian became a solitary dreamy wanderer. David and Glynne, along with most of the bairns in the street around their age, layked semi-organised football and cricket games at the nearby Staincliffe Recreation Ground ("rec"). Brian was an outsider when it came to games. He was ashamed of his poor throwing, kicking and batting skills and avoided laykin games at the rec. Occasionally he agreed to play cricket with David in the passage between his house and the next-door Dewhurst's, safe from the mockery he feared might come from other children laughing at his sporting incompetence. "Passage cricket" was as far as he stretched when it came to voluntarily playing traditional boys games. He was driven to his own company instead

On such days he wandered alone up and down his bit of Chapel Fold, from the Danes's house at one end of the ten houses to the house of the elderly couple at the other end. Some days he played with a favourite toy car, a dark green Packard saloon, running it with his hand along the front garden walls, spraying it with dust to add to its authenticity and commentating aloud on its progress along the mountain drive he was imagining. Sometimes he was a doctor driving at top speed to a hospital emergency. Sometimes, bored with the toy car, he performed an inspection of the ten front gardens, ranking them from best to worst and to his shame the Hirst front garden always came near the bottom. Perhaps it was at this time that his lifelong yearning began: to be someone else, to not be who he was; to transform himself and the world around him into something and somewhere else. He imagined the seedier scruffier gardens (including his own) miraculously matamorphosised to the glories of Mr. Fitzpatrick's garden. Then he imagined the houses changing. The Beevers' house became a big stone villa set in its own grounds like David's house on Staincliffe Hall Road. The Brydon's house had a bull-nosed purple and dark grey Rover 90 parked in the imagined drive, like the Booth's private semi further down Chapel Fold. And his own house was transformed into a massive mansion just like Dr. Hinchcliffe's at the end of Track Road. On the left side of the road opposite the ten houses were six council bungalows including Mr. King's, who Brian once confused with King George VI. The bungalows were situated around a small green and they backed onto the rear gardens of a posh private estate behind. After the bungalows, opposite his own house, was a small green with a high hedge and behind the hedge were the long gardens of a terrace of three stone cottages standing at a right angle off Chapel Fold. The cottages had been there long before the council houses. This was the stretch of Chapel Fold that Brian knew best and the street, the houses, bungalows and people who lived there formed a big part of his world.

Beyond the ten council houses on Chapel Fold Brian knew just a handful of other houses and their occupants, including Mrs. Boothroyd and Mrs. Terwiterwoo in the bungalows. In the older posher houses he knew the Wilsons and the Booths and he knew the grown up brother and sister, both in their forties, who lived in the end cottage opposite. He knew the family at the other end of the row of cottages, consisting of a mother and two sons, both a little older than him. The sons went to Batley Grammar and the family kept themselves to themselves and Moira suspected they looked down their noses at council house fowk. There was also a family living in one of the private semi-detached houses further along Chapel Fold with whom Brian was friendly for a short time. The father ran his own chimney sweep business and Moira knew the oldest daughter, Monica, while Brian made friends briefly with the son, Rodney, and the youngest child, Dorcas, whose name he loved.

Out of the other nine council houses, Brian never discovered the names of the frail elderly couple living at the far end from his house. But next to them were the Robinsons and their grandowter who lived with her granparents on a permanent basis, only occasionally seeing her mother and rarely seeing her father. Then came the Fitzpatricks with a son and daughter some years older than Brian. Next came the Beevers with six or seven girls, from Molly who was as old as Moira, down to Jennifer who was David's age, and the solitary Beever boy, Jack, who was a year older than Brian and went to Batley Grammar. Next to the Beevers came the Mortons with a son and daughter who were both nearly grown-ups. Next came the Brydons with Barbara, a grammar school girl three years older than Brian, and Derek, who was David's age and went to Staincliffe Juniors. Next came the next-door Summerfields with the appalling Barry, the same age as Brian, and his younger sister, Sheila, always overshadowed by her brother. And then came the other next-door neighbours, the Dewhursts, with their mad white bull terrier, Brus, and Robert and his younger sister, Lorraine; Richard's and Stephen's contemporaries. Lastly came the Danes's, and Rusty, and Peter (a little older than Young Bob) who attended college in Bradford and became a reight well-off civil engineer, and his sister Barbara, John's age, who trained as a nurse and then emigrated to Canada.

Some families kept themselves to themselves such as the Fitzpatricks and the Mortons and not even the Stasi-like combined intelligence force of Mary and Moira could penetrate their privacy defences. But even with the most private and reserved of neighbours much more was known about them than people living in a comparable street today know about each other. Brian knew, for example, that both Mr. Fitzpatrick and Mr. Morton were builders and that one of them hardly socialised at all whereas the other had a reputation for downing prodigious quantities of beer in various local pubs and clubs – but always remaining standing and coherent, no matter how much beer he supped. He knew which schools the Fitzpatrick and Morton children went to and how their paths crossed in various ways with towduns' lives. He knew which neighbours were friendly and approachable and which were not.

He knew about the darker, secretive side of some of his neighbours' lives. There was one man who regularly persecuted and beat his wife. The wife sometimes appeared at the back scullery door at number 77 with a blackened eye and bruises and swellings on her face. Mary would listen sympathetically to her sobbing account of her husband's latest act of brutality but eventually she became exasperated when the woman failed to take her advice and walk out on the brute, or confront him squarely with his wrongs. Instead, to Mary's disgust, the neighbour consistently forgave the brute husband as soon as he offered flowers or chocolates to compensate for the beating he had given her the night before.

A worse thing than a wife-beating happened further down Staincliffe Estate once: a young man murdered his wife one night. The young couple and their two small children lived in a flat, further down from Chapel Fold going toward Purlwell. As usual, Mam and Moira and the women neighbours knew all about the man and his "poor wife" but Brian was not able to penetrate their whispers and when he asked questions about the awful incident he was fiercely told to mind his own business. A police car was parked outside the flats the day after the murder was committed and people saw the young man, in handcuffs, being put in the car and taken away. Just that. No flashing lights, TV crews, wailing sirens, or crowds of people barricaded behind security lines. No flowers or notes left outside the flat, as happens today since Princess Diana's death. The day after the murder, Brian was too afraid to go near the flat so he sat on a nearby wall, furtively staring across. But nothing unusual happened. For the life of him he could not imagine this scary thing – a murder – occurring inside the mundane familiar flat, just a few hours before.

One night he was woken from sleep by a strange noise in the bedroom. It was Mary and Moira standing at the window. They were peeping through a crack they had made in the curtains so they could get a good view of something going on out in the street. They were giggling and oo-ing and ah-ing in a hushed stifled way. Once he was fully awake he adopted his invisible act and, listening carefully to Mary's and Moira's disjointed muffled commentary about what was happening outside, he gradually put two-and-two together.

"Ooo, look! Shi's kissin im. Bluddy ell. Shi's bahner swaller him, if shi carries on like that!"

"Ooo, stop it, Mam! Yeh'll mek mi laff out loud."

"Nay but fancy! Thiv parked reight under street lamp, weer ivri-body can see."

"Ooo! Bluddy ell fire. Jus look at em nar! Shi's tekkin er blouse off."

"Ooo!"

It was a neighbour, inside a car parked outside her house. She was with a man who was not her husband. It became a regular occurrence until the husband put his foot down. But the Jezebel neighbour always found another man soon after.

Brian often sought attention from adult neighbours when he felt obliterated as a person in his own right under the weight of all the dramas and tensions of his own large family. The adult Hirsts often had neither the time nor patience to give him the attention he sometimes craved. He was a good looking, polite child; skilled at ingratiating himself and gaining the attention of some of the adult neighbours. Occasionally he wandered down to the Beevers, pretending he was looking for Jennifer and Marjorie, who were around his age, to play with. The Beever house was male-starved and, if he was lucky, the older Beever girls were there. He could be sure of ample attention from them.

"Ooo! Ant e got luvli big brown eyes? An look at them dimples in is cheeks. Oo, an is air. It's a luvli dark brown, int it?"

He lapped up the attention inside, pretending on the outside not to know who they were admiring. One day Brian tried casting his charm on another neighbour. He was inside her scullery where she was busy baking cakes as he chatted and smiled his dimpled smile. Suddenly she stopped baking and forcefully rumpled her floury fingers through his hair. (The Beever girls only ever exclaimed over his looks and hair; never touching him.)

"Eee, yer a gran lookin lad, an nor arf, ant yeh?"

Then she did a strange unpleasant thing. He was wearing short trousers, as most boys under the age of fourteen did then. She held him firmly round the shoulder with one arm and ran her other hand up his bare leg from the knee, pretending to be a spider. She ran her fingers right up beneath his underpantless trousers toward his willy. He felt deeply uncomfortable about what she was doing and, before she could touch him there, he wriggled out of her grasp and stood a few feet from her, troubled and unsure. The neighbour laughed as if nothing had happened and gave him one of her angel buns with coloured icing on top and cream running through the middle. She was an excellent cook and Brian could not resist her treats. So he visited her scullery many more times where she sometimes attempted to grab him again. But once bitten twice shy. He became adept at wriggling away from her approaches.

Many years later, he realised the woman's actions would now be called "child abuse." He was a sensitive and to some extent a damaged child. The damage was centred in the emotional void between him and Bob and the insecurity which Bob's emotional distance created inside him. A more trusting unguarded child might not have resisted the woman's approaches but Brian did resist and so her efforts never became more than partial, attempted abuse, rather than full-blown molestation. The neighbour troubled him when she made these approaches but he liked her cakes more than he was troubled and he became adept, like a wily cartoon mouse, at snatching the treats before the cat pounced. What we call "child abuse" in society today can be a dark and often ill-considered thing. It is naturally enough a subject which raises unthinking reactions from "normal" people. Brian knew if he told any of the adults at home about the neighbour's gropes then he would be banned for ever from visiting her, thus depriving him of tasting her delicious buns, and so he kept it to himself. It was one of his own dark silences. It was something at which he was becoming skilled: watching; keeping secrets; staying silent.

When in the company of the older women in the family, or when he was with David and Glynne, Brian could be as noisy and boisterous as all boys are supposed to be. But he loved silence and the inner sense of solitariness and contemplation that silence brings. A good place to go to get away from the noise and tension of the household was the bathroom, especially on cold evenings. During such evenings he would sit on the toilet for long periods, his short trousers pulled down to the ankles, shivering in the chill but cut-off from John having a temper tantrum downstairs, or the younger-end playing or wailing. He drifted into his own world, telling himself Jennifer stories, or stories about the doctor driving the green Packard over splendid mountainous scenery, or stories in which he lived in a house ten times bigger and grander than 77 Chapel Fold. Often there was only one coal fire burning in the house, in the back room. The only other source of heat came from the hot water tank in the bathroom, heated by a back burner from the fire downstairs, or from a standby electric immersion heater. Before puberty kicked-in, the younger-end never had a fresh bath run just for them. Instead they bathed in the lukewarm water left in the bath by one of the older-end. The water was cool and scummy and Brian loathed having to bathe in someone else's leftover bathwater – especially Bob's – but he knew complaining would just fall on deaf ears from Mary. The family washed themselves using rough old face cloths made out of torn-up fragments of former towels, or hard gritty loofahs, rubbing Fairy Household soap into the cloth or grain and using the soap as a hair shampoo as well. All of the children had clear healthy looking skin and glossily shiny hair after their weekly "second-hand" bath. After puberty set in, Brian and his siblings had the privilege of the bath all to themselves but bath time was restricted to just once each week.

The rooms upstairs were icily cold in winter. During those bitter winter nights, towder-end were out socialising or staying downstairs near the fire. Mary economised on light bulbs, fitting one on the landing and two more in towder-ends' bedrooms, leaving the bathroom and two smaller bedrooms unlit. The lock on the bathroom door was broken but even so it was a private room. Brian enjoyed sitting there dreaming, sometimes reading a comic in the semi-light coming from the landing through a glass panel above the bathroom door. The family never barged in on anyone in the bathroom. The "No Entry" rule was unspoken but absolute. If someone lingered there too long and another wanted to use the room then they yelled or banged on the door and occasionally, out of sheer devilment and to get Brian shouting for Mam, John sometimes pretended to push the door open, ruining Brian's reverie.

In the evenings, after tea and chores were finished and the younger-end were in bed, the house, even with five or six people still awake downstairs, became totally silent during the time remaining before the grown-ups' bedtimes. The big wireless on the back room window bottom was switched off and mass silent reading commenced, with

Mary curled up on a chair reading a women's magazine or a love book, picking at her toenails and mouthing out the words in the racier bits, totally absorbed in the story. Moira was similarly occupied with a fashion magazines or a serious novel and Bob raced through a cheap cowboy paperback story while David and Brian lay curled on the floor sharing a Dandy, Beano, or Eagle comic. When the comics were done with, Brian moved on to the younger-ends' Noddy and Rupert Bear Annuals. Mary told him off for reading "baby books" but he loved the pictures and never tired of looking at them. Although he preferred books with plenty of pictures, and texts that were simple and easy to read, he sometimes read Dickens, delighting in the Boz illustrations interspersed in the complex text, illustrations which truly brought the story alive for him. The silence was broken only when some deep alarm rang inside Mary.

"Ooo, ell. Look at time! Cum on, yow tow. Cum on Brian, David. Gerrup them stairs – NOW. It's well past yoor bedtime."

Another silent place was Staincliffe Library which Brian haunted at least once each week from the age of eight to fourteen. The Library was housed in a fine stone Victorian building near the crossroads of the Halifax Road and Staincliffe Hall Road, just behind Staincliffe Rec. Before entering the building he would stop to admire the decorative stonework outside. Inside, there was a large entrance hall with mysterious rooms leading off. A strong smell of wood, floor polish and musty books hit you as you entered and a wide staircase led up to the first floor where the Library was situated. The staircase had a polished wooden rail full of rippling dents from years of use and Brian loved to run his hand over the rail as he climbed the stairs, which creaked under the cracked, scuffed, dull beige lino floor covering. Swing doors, with dim glass panels in the upper halves, led into the Library from the landing at the top of the stairs and immediately to the right inside was the Librarian's counter.

The Librarian looked like Miss Blackburn at Purlwell but had none of her charisma or presence. She wore pebble-lens spectacles and hand-knitted cardigans in dark strong colours and tartan skirts. But her body was fatter, more blobby, than Miss Blackburn's and her make-up and lipstick looked blobby too. She was an unfriendly distant woman, utterly impervious to Brian's dimpled cheeks and winning smiles. Shirley and Moira would have reduced her to nothing with a scathing remark or a haughty look but although Brian disliked her it was unthinkable to show his feelings by look or word and so he handed books in and took books out, not making eye contact, just saying his name quietly and often Mam's, Bob's and John's names as well, as they all relied on him to choose the sort of books they liked, being "too busy" to go to the library themselves. The adult reading section was situated on the right with the big front high windows overlooking the Halifax Road and to the left was the children's section with smaller windows overlooking Staincliffe Junior School and the Rec. It was an imposing room with high ornate cornicing, huge skirting boards and floor-to-ceiling shelves crammed with dog-eared books.

The Librarian had just enough character to impose silence in the room. When she felt compelled, she shushed a noisy user, be it child or adult. Brian loved to prowl around the room, savouring the creaky silence, broken by his squeaky footsteps on the lino floor and by coughs, wheezes and sneezes from other users. He stopped prowling when he became aware of the Librarian's eyes watching his every move; as if he were a dangerous wild leopard about to ravage her books. Fifty years later the building is still there. It is now a chaotic carpet store; a victim of library cuts in the 1980s. The world's traffic seems to roar by every second of the day and no one seems to walk there. Inside, the creaky book-filled silence is just a memory.

It always seemed to be summer when something out of the ordinary happened or when Brian's horizons stretched to trips further afield. During a hot weather spell, or on a Summer Bank Holiday, Mary took her bairns on a day trip to Wilton Park, more commonly known as Batley Park. Even rebellious contrary John and streetwise Malcolm eagerly joined these trips. Seven children, from teenage John to baby Lynne, would troop with Mary on the long march to the park, where they met Auntie Louie and cousins Glynne and Ann. It was a beautiful park, situated on the Bradford Road between Batley and Birstall, with a large artificial lake and rowing boats for hire, a paddling pool, a café, ice cream vans, swings, slides and a climbing play area. An extensive wood stretched from the valley bottom right up a hillside full of twisting pathways with benches, shelters, a trickling stream, ravines and hidden areas for the adventurous. In the middle of the wood stood the Bagshaw Museum, once a grand house, with insects in glass cabinets, endless stuffed animals and pictures of Batley from when time began.

Mary's picnic was funded from her meagre budget. It did not stretch to the glories and sheer mass of food at the Coronation Party. But the Hirst bairns were happy enough with fat'n'bread, egg and jam sandwiches, buns and tarts baked by Mary and a quart bottle of pop to share between them, all topped by a real treat from Auntie Louie: an ice lolly from Yellands yellow ice cream van stationed just inside the main park entrance gate. On Summer Bank Holidays a brass band played under the bandstand. A Punch and Judy Show performed and there were jugglers and men dressed as clowns walking on high wooden stilts. Many families in Batley could not afford to take a day trip to the seaside, let alone take a whole week or more away from home. A day trip to the park was a welcome outing and every ounce of pleasure was squeezed out of every minute spent there.

As well as trips to the park, there were trips from Healey Juniors to places such as Temple Newsam, Bolton Abbey and Castle Howard; places which seemed to Brian like the other side of the world. But the pinnacles were the Mission and Nash Trips held every August. The "Mission Trip" was a mixed pleasure. Although it was something out of the ordinary, something to look forward to, the problem was: you had to attend the Mission Sunday School to qualify for the trip. The Batley Town Mission had its origins in the Industrial Revolution when West Yorkshire towns and cities were filling with new rag-oyles and woollen mills. Alongside these burgeoning industries came burgeoning poverty and deprivation. Some of the mill owners exploited the workers, threatening the sack, destitution and the workhouse to those who protested against long working hours, filthy conditions and miserly wages. (No one writes better of these times and circumstances than Dickens – especially in "Hard Times.") Not all of the ruling class participated in the callous indifference and exploitation of the growing multitudes of industrial workers. Some were shocked by the housing and mill conditions endured by the workers and wanted to help. Some were Quakers, or churchmen and churchwomen from non-conformist sects. One way these people helped was in the establishment of "Town Missions." The town missions were simple chapels such as the one Brian knew in Batley. The "mission" of these simple plain chapels was to meet the needs, both spiritual and material, of people in the community suffering hardship and poverty. Missions still exist today in some English towns and their aims remain the same.

Brian knew nothing of the history behind Batley Town Mission as a child. He suspected he and his brothers were packed off to Sunday School at the Mission every week because it existed for poor fowk like them. He never spoke of this but he felt it. It was one of the worthy Christian spinsters in the solicitors' offices down Batley Carr where Moira worked who put Mam onto the existence and purpose of the Town Mission. Mary undoubtedly felt Sunday School would do her middle four boys some "good" and this was partly why she sent them there each Sunday. But also Sunday mornings were a busy time for her, preparing and cooking lunch (called "dinner") for as many as eleven, involving a large (ten bob) joint of meat, roast and mashed potatoes, three or four vegetables grown in the back garden, gravy, Yorkshire pudding, a fresh made sauce with mint, also from the garden, or apple sauce made with Bramley apples, and always a thick white sauce if cauliflower was on the menu. For afters, she might make a custard pie, or jam and lemon cheese tarts, or coconut slice. As well as improving her boys' souls and providing them with a free summer trip and a free Christmas Party, Sunday School took them from under Mary's feet during her busiest morning. Sunday mornings were grumbly bad tempered affairs beginning with a hurried breakfast of porridge or toast spread with Stork margarine and Tate and Lyle Golden Treacle. After breakfast, the lads were washed and dressed in Sunday best clothes and combs were dragged through tussled hair by Mary, Moira, or Shirley, before they were bundled off to the Mission.

"Gu on, gerroff wi yeh. An think on: no dordlin; no bein cheeky teh fowk; mek sure yeh keep yeh cloyes clee-ern; no stampin in puddles. An be'ave thissens inside Mission."

The four brothers dawdled down Chapel Fold, through Purlwell, to Wheatcroft snicket, quarrelling, bickering, pushing, shoving, with an occasional sneaky thump or a painful arm-squeezing by an older one on a younger one, until it dawned on them they might be late. All four boys were shy and hated being noticed when they were outside home and not protected by family and familiar surroundings. Standing out, being noticed, was utter anathema to John in particular and so they ran the last few yards down Wheatcroft with Brian, the slowest and least energetic of the four, in the rear. The mission stood on the side of a steep little hill leading to the town centre. The main door was situated right next to the causa and was always wide open. Several steep stone steps led to the inner door which in turn led into the chapel. If the boys were late, the inner door was closed and they could hear the booming voice of Mr. Stone, the preacher, inside. John would rather have died than be first in. Malcolm saw it as losing street cred and David would have collapsed into impossible giggles in the role of leader. So Brian was pushed to the front to lead them inside, stumbling to their seats, John's face burning redder than his hair. Mr. Stone would stop his sermon briefly.

"Come on lads. Get yehselves settled down. Now, to continue..."

The main mission room was square and minimalist with few decorations or icons. Hard wooden chairs were set out in rows facing a lectern and a dusty window high on the wall behind. A narrow strip of carpet lay at the ends of the rows of chairs, covering a narrow aisle. The main floor consisted of cold flagstones. A lady with a hat sat at a wheezy little organ to the right of Mr. Stone standing at his lectern. The only decoration in the whole building consisted of coloured panes of glass in the high windows to the left which, on sunny Sunday mornings, shed coloured light across the room and the people within, alleviating the boredom and providing a diversion from Mr. Stone's droning hectoring voice. The congregation consisted of a dozen or so children from infant to early secondary age. There were more adults than children, most of them ladies with hats, handbags and buttoned up coats; ladies like those who patronised Oldroyds Grocers for a slice of ham, or three eggs; not posh ladies like the one at Shepleys with the big car. There were two or three pale wan girls in their later teens and early twenties who took turns to teach Sunday School. The service was a dull affair. David in particular was restive, shuffling about, kicking the chair in front, turning round and giggling, causing his brothers both amusement and agonies of embarrassment when the ladies in hats tutted and stared. Mr. Stone stood at the front and talked forever. It was a great relief when there was a break in his monologue for singing a hymn or when everyone joined in the Lord's Prayer at the end of his sermon:

"All-things-bright-an-byoo-ti-ful...On-ward Chris-tyen so-o-o-old-yers...Prayse-my-sowl-the-king-ov-e-ven .... Olee-olee-olee ... Ower-far-tha-oo-art-in-ev-en..."

Mr. Stone had a shiny scrubbed face and hands, unlike the rough hands of Bob and other Dads at Chapel Fold. Moira said he worked in an office during the week. He wore a shiny black suit and shoes, and a shirt as white as an iceberg, and a bright, tightly knotted red tie. Brian noted these details as he listened to the loud earnest voice going louder then softer, louder then softer, paying minimal attention to his words and meanings. He knew what it was all about anyway. It was about God, an Jesus, an bein good, an be'avin yehsen, an not showin fowk up. At the end of the service there were an-nownce-ments which were only of interest to the Hirst lads when the Sunday School Trip was mentioned. After announcements the ladies in hats stood around Mr. Oates, nattering and simpering, before they went home. The children meanwhile were ushered inside the small Sunday School room at the rear, where the young teacher handed out Bibles before the children took their seats, already arranged in a circle. Brian hated Sunday School before it even started. It was just like nursery: being *forced* to go to bed when you did not want to sleep. The girl-teacher was nervous and unassertive and the bairns were bored. None of them behaved badly as children do now in classrooms where discipline is weak or where teaching standards are poor: shouting out, swearing, running around, thumping, running out and banging classroom doors behind them. Nothing like that. It was just serial, persistent, surreptitious disruption, preventing the teacher from even starting her moral theme of the week, let alone developing it with readings from scripture. Brian was a spectator in situations like this. He quietly watched what was happening, tending only to giggle nervously out of fear if he felt something bad was about to happen. Bibles were dropped noisily on the stone floor just as the teacher was about to read. There were loud yawns, sneezes and coughs and, one after the other, the bairns raised hands:

"Miss. Can ah gu teh toy-let?"

It caused constant amusement, as the mention of lavatories invariably does with young bairns. Eventually Mr. Stone appeared in the doorway rattling keys, anxious to catch the bus home to distant Mirfield and Sunday lunch. Sunday School ended and the lads were released into the world outside.

Except when the August date of the Annual Seaside Trip was announced, Brian only ever found the Mission interesting one other time. It was a cold winter Sunday and a new boy and girl appeared with their Mam and Dad. Mr. Stone in-trow-dewced them to everybody. They had come to live in Batley all the way from a faraway place in Africa called Row-dee-sha. Brian was intrigued by the new family. He was beginning to understand that the Mission only took "poor" bairns like him. Did poor people live in places like Africa? He looked at the family closely. They were not "dressed poor," like some of the children he knew on Staincliffe Estate and at school; like himself and his brothers. But they were not posh either, like the ladies at Oldroyds and Shepleys. They were inbetween, like the ladies in hats and shabby buttoned-up coats.

Brian barely noticed the girl but he stared at the boy who was about the same age as him but shorter and thinner. He wore a new camel duffle coat, gloves and a check scarf. Even wearing all this he was suffering in the cold winter chill of the Mission. His face looked red and chapped, his nose was runny and every so often he shivered convulsively. Brian was determined to sit next to the boy and be his friend. He wanted to know everything about him; about his life in Africa; why he was here, and where he was living now? He wanted to hear him speak. What would a white African boy sound like? It fascinated and intrigued him. He wanted to escape from himself and enter into the world of this boy from faraway and be carried away by him into another world. But the boy was miserably unhappy and cold and did not want to be friends with anyone. He refused to respond to Brian's overtures and shrank deep inside his duffle coat. Someone coaxed a few monosyllabic words out of him and there was a twang to his accent: "tin" when someone asked his age and "yis" and "neeyo" for "yes" and "no."

Brian was hurt by the boy's unfriendliness and a familiar sense of rejection ensued. But he did not curl up into a protective ball. Instead, walking home from Sunday School, he thought about the boy's coldness toward him. He understood that the boy was physically cold, scared and nervous, finding himself thrown into a new country among children he did not know. But he also decided he himself had behaved wrongly. He had acted in a way which the boy rejected. He was too friendly, too eager, too ingratiating; blatantly showing his need to be carried away. He had exposed an inner side of himself – his need for someone to carry him off – which the boy simply could not do. In future, he decided, he would keep his needs to himself: exposing them only brought pain and rejection. He would be carried off through his imagination; he would make a boy up inside his head who would take him over: an imaginary boy: better, bigger, stronger than himself.

Brian enjoyed some aspects of the Sunday School Trip. Most of all it fulfilled a deep need inside to move away from his usual world-boundaries: to see and feel what lay beyond. It was one of the rare occasions in his life when the opportunity arose to move out of Batley and see something of the wider world. The Sunday School Trip location was always Filey; a sedate little seaside town on the Yorkshire Coast blessed with a huge beach, a prim Edwardian front, a small fishing fleet and a tiny amusements arcade, less brash and garish than the arcades at Scarborough and Bridlington. Filey's sedate primness suited the Sunday School Trip organisers.

During the eighty mile journey from Batley to Filey, Brian loved gazing through the coach window, watching the blackened stone towns of the West Riding change beyond Leeds to green meadows and brassy fields ripe with crops. And then the more golden stone of Tadcaster after West Yorkshire's grim black, and pungent smells from the huge Smiths breweries as the coach passed by. There was a slow crawl around the ancient gold tan walls of York at a time before the bypass and outer ring road were built. Despite a growing hunger in his stomach and a need to pee, and Mr. Stone's incessant droning voice lecturing on the history of York, he loved gazing at the Roman walls, solid and immovable, high above banks of summer green grass. He loved watching the crowds of visitors outside, picking out posh fowk, intrigued at seeing "foreigners" (Americans mainly) with tanned skins, all of them wearing different clothing from the clothes English fowk wore. After York, the coach stopped at a small café where there was a lavatory and pre-booked tea and biscuits for all. The Hirst lads would have preferred pop, crisps an spogs but Mary warned them not to complain, telling them, in a voice quite lacking her usual conviction, how lucky they were to be having a "free trip." The landscape and buildings changed again after York. The fields of the East

Riding Wolds looked massive; the sky above enormous and endless, and the houses in the small villages were called "cottages," their outsides painted in gentle pastel colours. Brian was convinced he could already smell the coast, still twenty miles distant, until they reached Filey at last and were allowed to open the coach windows and smell it: the sea!

The coach pulled up by the fishing landing. The amusements area was semi-hidden under the cliffs and odours of candy floss, fried onion and sausage vied with the more natural smells of fish, seaweed and sea. The boys wanted to charge madly down the landing, run along the beach, jump into rock pools and experience bliss itself: a paddle in the sea. But this was the Sunday School Trip and they were under strict instructions from Mam "teh be'ave emsens." Besides, they were constantly watched; the number of adult supervisors being almost the same as the number of children. The ladies, looking sniffy and disdainful, hastily ushered the children past the amusements and led them down to a "nice" part of the beach. Even Brian, the most timid of the four brothers, wanted to run and shout but instead he submitted to being fussed over by the ladies. The day continued in the same mould; the children being constantly watched and supervised, chaperoned and entertained with silly games. The brothers just wanted to run along the beach, explore rock pools, adventure out to Filey Brigg – and please, please: paddle in the sea! But the ladies and Mr. Stone were reluctant to allow the children to wander too far from their "nice" base on the beach. The Hirst boys were used to being left to entertain themselves although they were always conscious of dire threats from Mam of what would happen if they "did owt daft" when she was not around to watch them. When they were with Mam, Moira, Shirley, or Auntie Louie, the boys played a constant wheedling game where pleadings and winning looks were utilized to squeeze treats from the adults: an ice lolly, a bag of crisps, a ride on the dodgem cars. On the Sunday School Trip everything was set out, rigidly organised, with no room for negotiation. Even the paddle in the sea when it eventually came was a ritualistic affair with Mr. Stone ceremoniously rolling up his trousers and leading everyone to the sea's edge, to paddle sedately. And the middle of the afternoon treat, an ice cream cornet, ("Much better for the teeth than one of them nasty lollies") was given to the bairns more as a duty than a pleasure.

An hour before the return journey the adults finally relaxed and allowed the children to roam. Intrepid Malcolm and madcap John headed for the outer reaches of Filey Brigg where they climbed the rocks and defended England from Viking invaders. Brian and David explored the rock pools nearby and marvelled at a mini-world of sand, sea, mud and rock. They found treasures: little delicate shells, pieces of bone, polished wood, shelled creatures clinging to rocks, small crabs scuttling the sand and wriggly creatures beneath, whose movements made zig-zag patterns on the surface. It made the day worthwhile: the miracle of a small area, full of diversity and life, and the delight of watching constant change and transformation taking place in this small space stayed with Brian for many years after.

There was one year when Filey was shrouded in a heavy cold sea fret all day long. Left to themselves, the boys would have ignored the weather and played on the beach and Brigg. But for some inexplicable reason the adults insisted on treating the day as a disaster. (How could a day at the seaside be a disaster? The idea mystified Brian.) The children were made to huddle under blankets and coats just under the sea wall, being "protected" and kept "warm and safe." The nearest Brian came to exploring was plunging his hand into a small area of sand not covered by coats; running the sand through his fingers, watching it descend like a cloudy waterfall to the ground – and picking up more, and starting all over again.

The journey back was always a blur. He was tired and sleepy. It was the mixture of being kept on a tight rein by kind distant adults and the intense excitement and stimulation on his senses of seeing, smelling, touching, hearing, *being* in different places. Mr. Stone and the ladies, in the safe confines of the coach, livened up and urged the children to sing silly inane songs:

"Nic-Nac-Paddiwack...This Old Man...There Was A Man Called Michael Finnegan...Begin Agen..."

Brian's eyelids drooped, closed; opened, drooped, closed. The return journey was a blur of songs and forced cheeriness in the background. The vast diverse land, and towns and villages, sped by outside in the darkening day until, at last, the coach rumbled over the Market cobbles and pulled up outside the Mission and goodnights and thankyous were said. And the brothers climbed Wheatcroft, crawled through Purlwell and trudged up Chapel Fold to home. Mam asked them if they had a good day and they all said "yes" – because you never know – say "no" and the treat might be witheld next year. Then John and Malcolm grumbled over Mr. Stone and the ladies singing baby songs and telling baby jokes and Mam and Shirley carried the two exhausted younger ones to bed

Did Brian enjoy the trip? Yes, partly. His feelings were mixed. He loved the changing sights and scenery provided by the journey and he loved the fundamental elements of sea, sand, rocks and sky, at Filey. But if he could have articulated it he would have said there was an emotional coldness, a lack of real fraternity, community, togetherness, between the children and the adults. It was the coldness of a certain kind of patronising charity that chilled him. It was being the recipient of charity from those who – he strongly suspected – thought they were "better" than him, like those people in the B+B he would see at New Brighton a couple of years later. But it was worthy, sincerely given charity and he knew without it a trip to Filey was out of the question. It was not the warm spontaneous charity that Mam showed on a cold day when she sent her sons with a Sunday dinner for poor Mrs Boothroyd to warm her up. It was cold charity.

The Nash Trip was a complete contrast. It was a huge feat of organisation by the all-male Club Committee Members involving the hiring of fifteen coaches to transport hundreds of grown-ups and bairns from Batley to Blackpool, or to another northern seaside town. There must have been some trippers who were nervous, difficult, bad-tempered; but if there were, Brian never noticed. From the moment he arrived Down Batley at the departure point outside the Nash, the atmosphere was cheerful, confident and full of camaraderie. There was a determination, as there was on Coronation Party Day, that absolutely everyone was "bahner ave a reight good time." There was a sense that everyone *deserved* this treat. The Hirsts were one family among many who could afford only this one trip a year: one day away from the confines and hardships of life in Batley. The day was organised with superb military detail and precision but in place of barking sergeant-majors and troops there were cheerful committee men and happy club members and their families. The coaches were numbered and each family was allocated to a particular coach. The first hurdle was to find your coach along with hundreds of others doing the same thing. It was an adventure and a great excuse for jokes, banter and deadpan irony.

"Ey up, Mary lass. Ah'm buggered alreddy. An we ant even goh gooin yit."

"Ah knaw, Nellie. At this rate wi s'll oney bi i bluddy Bestell bi midneet."

"Ee. It's worse ner Dowsbri Markit on a Satdi mornin, int it?"

Once the coach was found, a committee man was there to give the parents identity tags to pin on the children's clothes. A faded photograph survives from the early 1950s showing Glynne, John, Malcom, Brian and David smiling at the camera, inside a photographer's tent in Blackpool, all of them wearing prominent Club identity tags. Brian wears a buttoned up suit jacket and David a double-breasted jacket with velvet collar and pocket flaps, similar to the sort of clothes which can be seen on films of the infant Prince Charles: a nice "catch" made by Aunt Louie from Burrows rag-oyle, quite likely.

It was inevitable that some children went astray on the crowded beaches at Blackpool, Bridlington or Scarborough. Mams and committee men together impressed upon bairns how important it was not to lose the identity tag. On his first Club Trip, Brian lost his bearings on the beach at Blackpool. He wandered among the dense crowds of people, whimpering for attention until a concerned adult noticed and took him to a Lost Children Office run by the Blackpool police. He enjoyed his time in the office, watching the comings and goings and being given pop and a Kit-Kat – but only a two-finger one – by a young WPC, until a flustered Mary arrived and took him back to their place on the beach.

After the tagging came the most exciting moment when a committee man gave every child a white envelope containing something quite heavy inside: a whole half-crown coin: the "spend" for the day. It was an enormous amount of money to Brian. He would not earn that amount of spend himself until he received his first paper round payment aged fourteen. Half-a-crown (worth about £4.00 today) could buy seven bags of crisps, five four-finger Kit-Kats, *pounds* of sherbert lemons. But "the spend" soon disappeared on donkey rides, the big wheel, dodgem cars and amusement arcades.

While some committee men were handing out spend packets, others were loading huge boxes of Smiths crisps, biscuits, crates of pop and beer into the storage compartments of the coaches. A whole jar of spogs – the kind you suck slowly – was taken onto each coach "teh shuv inteh gobs" of any bairns who became fretful or sickly on the journey. The banter and jokes continued until the coaches were loaded with their full quota of passengers and fifteen engines burst into roaring rattling life and the cavalcade rumbled down Bradford Road to the Huddersfield Road at Birstall, turning left for the West Coast, or right for the Yorkshire Coast. The coach convoy was like a vast festive army or an enormous circus filling the local roads. People on the causas outside stopped and stared. Some waved, smiled and called out greetings. Someone on the coach knew someone out there and you could almost hear the words on the lips of the fowk outside.

"Ey up. Theer gus Nash Trip."

"Ooo, is it Nash trip tehdee? Ower Marge is gooin, wi er bairns. Theer off ter Brid this year, tha knaws."

"Ah thi? Eee, it's a gran place, is Brid."

Brian felt important, someone of consequence, knowing everyone outside was talking about The Nash Trip, which he was part of. He shied away from interacting with the other lads on the coach, already discussing a favourite Batley RL player, or Dan Dare's latest exploits in The Dandy comic. He was shy and insecure meeting new lads and fearful of being mocked or rejected, so he observed the interactions and listened to the conversations instead. But he felt he belonged. There was none of the chill distance of the Sunday School Trip. And besides, free spogs were on tap, there was a whole half crown in his pocket, and more treats to come. Who in his right mind was *not* going to enjoy the Nash Trip?

Gradually the excitement and noise of the grand departure lessened and settled. The coach crawled along roads less familiar, passing places where the fowk outside had never heard of the Nash. The bairns on the coach were sucking spogs and reading comics, of which there was an abundance, as every Mam had dozens stashed inside big carrier bags. Mams gossiped and so did Dads. The Dads sat together at the rear of the coach except those with a dominant missis demanding her man sit with her and the bairns. Soon they were in York and Mams and Dads were as excited as bairns:

"By eck. Them's bluddy big walls, an nor arf."

"Theer Roman, them is, tha knaws. Thiv been theer fer thousands er years, them as."

"Ah knaw, owd lad. Them's towdist walls in England."

"Tha's reet theer."

"An York's capital er Yorkshire, tha knaws."

"It is that. An Ba'li's i Yorkshire, an all. An Yorkshire's got towdist bluddy walls int world."

"It as. Thas reet theer, an all, owd lad. "

And then there was quiet as everyone contemplated York and being fowk from Yorkshire and Brian felt warm and proud inside, not cold and distant, like he did when listening to Mr. Stone lecturing about York with the ladies twittering over how clever he was. And soon the bus rumbled on to Malton, where they stopped for toilets an re-fresh-mints. Every child was given a packet of Smiths crisps with a pinch of salt inside, wrapped in blue greaseproof paper with a twist to keep it from spilling out. And each bairn had a *whole* gill bottle of fizzy pop, just to issen. The mams had cups of tea and biscuits. Most of the Dads did too but some drank a sneaky gill bottle of beer. All day there was treat after treat. After the half crowns, came sandy, gritty sandwiches and cakes, eaten on the beach. And for "tea," the whole Nash Outing took over the biggest fish and chip café in town and everyone, bairns an all, got a whole plate of *fish* and chips (not just chips) and tea, or pop, an bread spread wi *real* butter, not lardy margarine.

Then it was time to go home to Batley and they were on the coach again. They returned much later than the Sunday School Trip and there was merriment on the coach going back and some arguing and shouting. There was nearly a fight among the men – *and* some of the women – at the back of Brian's coach and there were frequent stops so the grown-ups could "aye a piss." The bairns slept through most of it but Brian awoke intermittently and listened to the raucous voices singing, arguing, shouting and laughing behind. And he heard the comforting quiet murmers of Mam's and Auntie Louie's voices reminiscing with some of the other Mams about previous Nash Trips and their younger days as mill lasses in the Batley rag-oyles.

In spite of the shouts and the drunkenness from some, everyone seemed happy and contented. There must have been some who weren't but Brian never noticed. Everyone seemed to know their place and where they were in the order of things. To use a phrase which was not then in vogue, everyone seemed "at home in their skins." To Brian, his coach was familiar. It felt warm. It felt like home. It was not cold and unsure and anxious to be "right" and "proper," like on the Sunday School Trip, where everyone always seemed to aspire to be someone other than who they were: to be somewhere else than where they were. He would become one of those "aspiring" people eventually. But at this time he was puzzled by such fowk. He was "at home" on the Nash Trip, where fowk just *knew* who they were and knowing that often meant they could not be put down by those who thought they were better. Many of the Nash trippers were at the bottom of the socio-economic scale. Their lives were harsh. They scrimped and scraped all year to pay their "Nash dues" so that for one day in August every summer they could rise above the meanness and harshness of their daily lives and live like kings and queens, knowing full well that tomorrow they would be back to toiling "int rag oyle, downt pit, int mill or at oo-em, wi t'scrubbin booerd en cloyes mangle." But tomorrow was another day. Today, now, was what mattered: and all the Mams and Dads, and all the bairns, agreed: "Nash Trip wor a reight gran day aht."

One year the committee men chartered a whole train from Batley Railway Station all the way to "Brid." It was Brian's first ride on a train, as it was for many of the trippers. The small station was heaving with people when he arrived. The throbbing train, hissing steam, thrumming pulsing engine and long slithering line of carriages disappearing well beyond the limits of the platform, seemed immense and powerful. Just stepping onto the train and making sure you did not fall through the cavernous gap onto the track was a thrilling hilarious adventure. Some children loved the challenge and strode boldly forth; others whimpered for their Mams. Many of the Mams themselves were nervous about boarding while others, including Auntie Louie, were exchanging robust niceties with the committee men, stationed every few yards along the platform, to help fowk and assist the bemused platform guard in ensuring a safe departure.

"Nah then, Louie lass. It's fust time ah've seen top on thi legs. Thas gorra reight gran pair theer."

"Get shifted, thee. Tha's got sum room teh talk. Tha's gorra marth on thee like Burrer's Mill whistle. An what'll thar Rita do wi thee when *ah* tell *er* what *tha's* been sayin teh *me?*"

"Nay, Louie lass. It wor ony a jowk."

"Aye. An that's shut thar gob up, ant it, Billy Arkins? Cum on, Glynne luv. Cum on Brian, owd cock. Ger odd er mi and. Jump. Tha's it. Cum on, owd flower. Les see wee-er weer sittin …"

There was the usual banter and hilarity, heightened for many by the unfamiliar situation of being on a train. But later when they all got back to Batley it was agreed: the train ride was a disaster.

"It did nowt all day but bluddy *chowk* fowk, wi its fumes – startin an endin at bluddy Moo-erly Tunnel. Thick brahn smoo-ek seepin through winders, foower-cin fowk teh keep em shut all way teh Brid an all way back agee-en. Ah cudn't even enjoy a cig …"

Next year, everyone agreed, they'd go back to the coach.

"Yer knaw weer y'are wi a coo-ech – an nor arf!"

After the summer trips, Brian's life once more centred around Chapel Fold and walks to school and local shops. He was becoming aware of a bigger world in as yet unexperienced places beyond the world he knew and he was becoming more and more a listener, an observer of people and the world outside his inner world. His inner world was nervous, fundamentally insecure, increasingly full of his "wrongnesses." He was becoming adept at making himself inconspicuous and from his invisible corner he watched and listened to the world outside. It was a way of escaping his wrong self, this listening and watching. And also, although he did not know it, it was a way of building a new self, through listening, watching, copying, adding onto himself bits that he gleaned from the world outside, not yet quite making them an intrinsic part of his personality.

Healey Junior School gave him a basic education in numeracy and literacy. But the channels that truly taught him about society, history, geography, and who holds power and who does not, were the adults in his family and community; Staincliffe Library books; books at home about Belsen or Pickwick Papers; pictures and headlines in the Daily Herald, Yorkshire Post, Batley News and women's magazines; posh fowk he heard on the BBC Home Service and the posh fowk he sometimes observed in the flesh.

Sometimes extraordinary incidents happened in his life, incidents quite outside his usual world. One day, Queen Elizabeth and Prince Philip visited Batley. The teachers at Healey were thrilled and excited and the children all had to make a small flag which, they were told, they would wave at the royal couple as they paraded in their big posh car through Batley. On the day of the royal visit the whole school walked all the way down to Dark Lane to stand on the corner of Manor Way and wave small flags and cheer the royal car gliding past. The Staincliffe Junior bairns were there and lots of grown-ups too: all lined up on the causa along the whole length of Dark Lane. The adults talked self-importantly about the visit.

"Theer cummin in a big car fro Dowsbry. Theer branchin off t'Alifax Roo-ed onter Track Roo-ed, past Docter Inchcliffe's ouse an noo Irstlands Park an then all way on Dark Lane, dahn Clerk Gree-en, past Cimitry Roo-ed an then on Commercial Stree-ert tert Town All. Thiv purra reight spread on feh't snap. An – ey up! Thiv purra noo lav in, in case *she* needs ter gu. Oo aye, lass. I tell you not a word on a lie theer!"

After a lot of standing around, Mr. Knott and the teachers urged the children to cheer their Queen and within a few seconds a big black car purred past and Brian had a good brief look at Elizabeth, waving and smiling from inside the purring car, and Philip doing the same, only his smile looked more like a half-smile – half-sneer. The adult gossip around him was interesting but Brian was baffled over this business of going to "cheer the Queen." He was disappointed that nothing really happened. Fowk in Batley never said "hooray." It was a strange sound to make and when the bairns all said "hooray" as the car went past, you could tell it did not sound right. It sounded thin and feeble; nothing like the whooping and yelling the bairns made when Roy Rogers galloped over a hill shooting Indians, at Collins Picture House on Satdi mornings; the nearest Batley bairns ever got to "hooraying." None of the grown-ups he knew came to cheer the Queen and after the car disappeared down Clerk Green everyone returned to school and threw away the flags. By the end of the afternoon it was as if nothing special had happened that day. It wasn't half as good as the Nash Trip, or even the Sunday School Trip. In fact it all seemed a bit pointless. It was not too long before he understood that it was Mr. Macmillan, the Prime Minister, who had real power and not the "Bluddy Queen," as Bob called her, then still in his fiery socialist days.

A more exciting thing happened along Dark Lane a few months after the Queen drove by when Brian saw a black-skinned person for the first time. Moira was taking him and David on some errand or other Down Batley. They were standing on the causa on the Staincliffe Estate side of Dark Lane waiting for a slow lorry to go by when Brian spotted a tall, very black African man, wearing a smart suit and hat, carrying what looked like a Bible in his hand, walking down the Purlwell side of Dark Lane opposite. He was astounded by this amazing phenomenon. He laughed, pointed, yelled.

"Ooo! Look ovver theer: it's a blackie!"

He felt an instant sharp stinging blow across the back of his head. Moira had slapped him – hard. She took hold of his arm, gained eye contact and shook him.

"DON'T YOU *EVER* SAY THAT AGEN! How would *you* feel if sumdi said summat like that about *you*? I'm *a-shamed* of you, Brian Erst. I am that."

And with that she marched them across Dark Lane and down toward Purlwell. And Brian cried, not because his head was hurting but because he was mortified; he was deeply ashamed of the terrible, terrible thing he had called another human being. It was around 1957. Fifty years later, as the twenty first century uneasily settles-in, Dark Lane, Purlwell and Mount Pleasant are almost entirely populated by British Asians.

Not long after seeing his first dark skinned man, Brian came downstairs from bed one morning to find a strange visitor sitting on a chair in the scullery. It was a lady: a lady the like of which he had never before seen. It was a crisp Autumn morning and the back door was wide open. Heavy dew coated the back garden grass, scattered with brown curly privet leaves. It was chilly. A mist hung in the air above the dew-carpeted grass outside. And this strange lady was sitting in the scullery looking the very embodiment of chilly Autumn, catching him out and surprising him, after a long hot summer. She was a large lady with rough florid skin on her face and hands, the only parts of her that were not covered in clothes. Her clothes, face and hands seemed coated in Autumn mist and dew. She had a man's flat checked cap on her head and shoulder length light brown curly dusty hair fell from beneath the cap in abundance. She wore an ancient dusty full-length coat the colour of grey earth in the front garden borders during a dry spell and the coat covered her powerful shoulders, chest and hips, underneath. On her feet were heavy black boots, scuffed and dusty and reight worn dahn and she was wearing thick grey socks like the ones Brian wore for school. Her big red chapped hands were wrapped round the chipped white pot of tea, which she held to her raw face, warming it with steam.

Still sleepy, not quite certain whether this apparition in the scullery was a dream or not, Brian hovered in the front hall doorway. The lady did not see him. She was absorbed in holding and sipping the warming tea. Tuthers were still in bed an towder-end had left for work. He began to panic and feel trapped by this strange woman in his house: where was Mam? Then Mary emerged from the outside lav and came through the wide open back scullery door and saw him hiding in the doorway.

"Cum on, Brian. Cum an geh sum brekfest. Geh yehsen sat at table."

Mam pulled him from the doorway into the scullery past the lady, who continued drinking tea, not seeming to see him. He sat at the back room table and Mary gave him a fierce warning look not to say owt daft or say owt out loud about the extraordinary visitor in the scullery.

"What d'yer want? Porridge, er too-est?"

"Porridge, please."

Mary went to the pan on the stove and stirred the porridge before ladling out a bowlful. She brought the bowl to the table instead of telling him to fetch it is-sen. The woman sipped the tea, her big hands wrapped round the pot. Mam ignored her, walking round her, doing scullery jobs, fidgety and nervy. Brian dunked a spoonful of treacle from the Tate and Lyle tin on the table into the porridge bowl, stirred, and started to eat. No matter how hard Mary's warning looks warned him to mind his behaviour, he could not help but stare at the strange lady sitting on the chair in the scullery. Eventually the lady finished her tea and stood up and Mam took the empty pot from her. She towered over Mam as she straightened her clothes from sitting.

"Thank yer, Missis, fer der tea an porridge. Yeh's a good lady 'n' God'll bless yeh."

And Brian marvelled at her thick gravelly voice and strange "country" way of speaking. Her voice was as exotic as her looks. But Mam showed nothing on her face.

"Tha's orreight, luv."

And with that the lady went outside and picked up a sack she had left by the back door. She heaved the sack over her shoulder and disappeared down the passage. And then she was gone, blending into the misty Autumn morning. Brian could see from her fidgety, jerky behaviour that Mam was excited by this strange visitation but he could see she was in no mood to bother with his curious questions, so he continued eating, waiting for Mary to say something, which she surely would eventually. Mary wiped the chair the woman had been sitting on with a damp cloth and brought it back from the scullery to its usual place at the back room dining table. She put the pot and an empty porridge bowl into hot water in the big pot scullery sink and poured Brian a pot of tea and brought it to the table. She sat down opposite and fixed her eyes on him. Mam never sat at the table in the mornings. She always had too much to do. She wagged her finger.

"Doo-ern't you tell yoo-er Dad abaht this. E'll gu mad if he knaws ahve ad a tramp in touse …"

Brian promised he would not say a word. She told him how she had found the tramp.

"Shi wa just standin theer. Int back doorway, when ah cum back frum callin yer out er bed. She's a tramp, yer knaw. The poor soul dus-ent ave no weer teh live Brian. Shi spends all er life trampin from town teh town, gerrin food wheer ivver shi can finnd it, an beggin at fowks back doo-ers."

"Weer dus shi sleep at night time Mam?"

"Well, ahm not shoo-er, luv. In barns – sheds – underneath edges – probably in ower out ouse las neet."

"She might er slept in scullery or on settee in front room, Mam."

"Nay doo-ernt bi ser daft luv. Shi wunt ave cheek teh du that."

But Brian thought to himself it was perfectly possible. Doors were never locked at night and on a warm night the downstairs windows were left wide open, for anyone to climb inside.

"What did yer wipe chair down feh, Mam? An why did yeh tek chair intert scullery?"

"Well, she wah probably full er lice – an ah doo-ernt want you lot gerrin nits in yer air agen. Think on all that trouble we ad wi them bluddy things las time. Shi wouldn't think nowt er bein kept int scullery, yer knaw. Shi's not used ter bein inside. Eh, poo-wer sowl. Thes sum fowk wee-ent ave em near doo-er, yer knaw – includin yeh Dad."

Brian saw from his Mam's satisfied face she was pleased she had been able to give the lady a pot or tea and a bowl of porridge. Then Mam remembered she had jobs to do and everything went back to normal. It was the first – and last – sighting Brian had of a tramp in all his life.

*

When did council house fowk start locking doors at night? Possibly it was around the late 1960s when even poor fowk like the Hirsts were beginning to have things better if not quite "never having had it so good" – as the then Prime Minister, Harold Macmillan, claimed. Certainly it happened *en masse* in the 1980s when a climate of greed and covetousness was becoming the norm in English "society" – which Mrs. Thatcher said she did not believe existed. Mary worked unremittingly grindingly hard from her marriage at eighteen to finally quitting her cleaning job at the Bull in her mid-seventies but she felt sorry for those she saw as worse off than her and she would unhesitatingly, in a spirit that was truly "good," give or do what she could to help. Bob had a hard fatherless childhood. He was physically damaged from hewing in the pit when he was very young and psychologically damaged by war. But for many years he led a sedentary life: staying in bed when he wanted; drinking at the Nash when he felt like it; spending hours poring over the horse racing pages; sending Mary down to the bookies to place his bets; sunbathing in the back garden of his last house at Russell Close; and hours and hours spent in front of the TV, in splendid isolation, with a pot of tea on the table beside his chair, made, stirred and served by Mary. It was Bob, in his old age, not Mary, who embraced the Thatcher ethos of people "earning their keep" and the Tebbit maxim of "getting on your bike" to find work.

Bob's and Mary's lives in their different ways illustrated the suppression and eventual near-extermination of English working class culture which began in England in the 1980s. Many members of the working class were duped into believing they had moved up to the "higher" status of becoming "middle class." These fowk embraced the emphasis on the individual and the ethos of self-aggrandizement which came with the Thatcher era. Since Thatcher, those who already "had it made" tended to sit back and carp about those who did not. The "successful" fowk pocketed anything that came their way as their due reward while the real workers, the Mary's of this world, got on with "earning" a living, in a moral as well as a material sense. The Marys, when they can, help those less fortunate than themselves while many of those who are more "successful" (materially) sneer at the sentimentality of working class people like Mary, dismissing the values inherent in her attitude to the tramp, to the "poor" neighbour without coal at Wainwrights Yard, to "poor" Mrs. Boothroyd in the Chapel Fold bungalow, to "poor" Sid, the pot man at the Bull; and to "poor" Mrs. H., with all her poverty-stricken lasses, just down the road at Woodsome. Or even worse, "successful" fowk just close their eyes to "the poor" and bleat about their own "problems:" having to pay a bit more tax; not being able to take so many holidays since the children came along; or the awful "sacrifices" they have to make paying for their bairns' private education. What "successful" people really mean, when they trumpet their superior "unsentimentality," their "realism," their "sacrifices" is: "Fuck the real workers; we're doing fine on the fruits of their labours."

Brian saw his first beggar in a Verona street in the summer of 1972, fifteen years after the tramp apparition at Chapel Fold. The first sight of a human being crouched on the ground begging shocked him but a frisson of superiority passed through him also: people in his own country did not need to beg – he thought. The first time he came across a beggar in England was in the summer of 1983, some four years into the Thatcher government. The sighting was not in a big city and the beggar was not crouched abjectly on the ground. He saw his first beggar in that pleasant Derbyshire town, Matlock, when he was walking over the River Derwent Bridge, making his way to a shop, or a pub, or a café, or a bank. The path over the bridge was narrower than usual where repairs were taking place. A not particularly ill-dressed young man in his early twenties walked toward Brian and as he walked past he held out his hand and asked for money. Brian shook his head and hurried on to his destination, feeling cold inside. He was horrified and devastated: a beggar, in Matlock, in England, in 1983. The last and only time he had encountered anything like it, in England, was the tramp in the Chapel Fold scullery in 1957, twenty six years earlier.

*

Mary was able to give the tramp tea and porridge but sometimes, to her dismay and despair, she was not always able to find the means or money to give birthday presents and cards to her children during the lean 1950s and 1960s years. (Later in life when she became "well-off" she scrupulously sent cards to every one of her extended family.) Brian was wished a happy birthday by his Mam and siblings when the day came and he might, if someone was flush, be given a few pennies to buy a bag of spogs from the corner shop at the end of Chapel Fold, or he might be given an orange, a rare treat, which he would peel slowly and suck lingeringly, or Mam might bake an extra custard pie, or coconut and jam tarts, or a currant cake, or she might make a bright red jelly and cold sweet custard. There were no cards lined up on the sideboard and winder-bottom, no especially bought presents and no party. Some of the better-off bairns he knew received some or all of these frills. He sometimes imagined he was posh Jennifer or David and on his birthday there was a room full of cards, a table laden with party food and drinks, like Coronation Day, and a sleek bike which he rode and rode, with all his friends on their bikes, round and round and round, in his head. Sometimes he was consumed with the desire to have these birthday treats, especially a party, with everyone there just for him. He would tentatively nag Mary as his birthday approached, knowing his desire for a party was futile and, as he grew older, knowing the pain his pleading caused her. When he persisted in nagging, her reaction was final and predictable: a flat angry reaction and a fury toward him, and perhaps toward herself, that a party was impossibly expensive for her to even consider. On other occasions, when he spoke wonderingly of so-and-so's new bike, or of someone else's big birthday party, if Mary was not too busy and tired, she hugged and cuddled him and told him a hug was as good as any present or party, and he was content and happy with that.

In the 1950s children did not have the pressure of an advertising culture centred on the ever-accumulating consumption of material things that often blights young people's lives today. Brian was briefly envious and covetous when he saw other children with more possessions than him. But it was a transient feeling which soon faded. It was only when he became an adult that he realised how many in the social world he came to inhabit would regard his childhood birthdays as bleak and deprived and his birthdays were indeed "deprived" – but only of *things*. And because he was not used to having *things*, not having them did him no physical or mental harm.

There was one Christmas which turned sour when the younger-end were aged around one, six, seven and eight. It was a hard time for Mary when finding the money to buy even the most basic presents was a grinding worry and some no doubt well-meaning person was told of Mary's plight. Perhaps it was one of the good Quaker souls at the Town Mission? The kindly benefactor, whoever he or she was, sent second-hand toys and gifts to Chapel Fold, just before Christmas Day. The gifts and toys were in good condition but they were not the sort of items Mary would ever buy. Bought new, the gifts were way beyond her pocket. They included a gaudy plastic tricycle in Noddy Book colours, a huge fluffy soft toy and other items that just did not look right in the Hirst house. Mary tried half-heartedly to coax the younger-end to play with the "luvli" Santa presents but they wanted none of it. Even at their age the well-meaning charity of the donor to them felt cold.

Most Christmases during Brian's Junior School years, however, were as wonderful as the Coronation Party and the glistening ice slide in the schoolyard. It was a time well before lower working class children expected expensive and expendable middle-class gifts such as huge plastic tricycles and soft toy animals. Simple things were enough. The preparations and the anticipation came well before Christmas itself with the making of the "spice cake" in October. Mary used her Mam's recipe, which was partly written down, partly word of mouth, and when she lost confidence Elsie came all the way from Batley Carr to help and advise. Spice cake (more commonly known as Christmas cake) consisted of just the fruit loaf itself with no trimmings or outer layers of marzipan and icing. Up to ten spice cakes were made in baking tins the size of a small loaf of bread: enough to last from Christmas Eve to New Year's Day. Mary saved all year to buy the ingredients. During preparations, everyone but Moira and Shirley (who continued the recipe in later years, as did Lynne) was banned from the scullery but you could hear the giggles, curses and moments of high anxiety as Granma, Mam, Shirley and Moira worked on making the cake mixture.

Once the mixture was used up and put in the oven in the bread tins, the children were allowed inside the scullery to run fingers round the big brown pot mixing bowl until it was absolutely clean. Later, the finished spice loaves were taken from the tins and left to cool before being wrapped in layers of greaseproof paper, tied with string or wool, and packed into biscuit tins placed high on the top pantry shelf near the air-brick, where they would "mature" until the first one was opened on Christmas Eve.

Christmas built up gradually after that. There were cribs and nativities at Sunday and Junior schools and another beautiful nativity was laid out near the steps leading from Batley Market Place to the Police Station and War Memorial Park. "Down Batley" glittered with Christmas lights on dark December nights and there was a huge lit-up Christmas tree in front of the Town Hall. On trips down to Nelson's, Brian took extra money to put in the Christmas Club. (Mary squirrelled money away for Christmas Clubs wherever she regularly shopped.) Christmas started properly a day or two before Christmas Eve. A small artificial tree was brought down from a high cupboard shelf upstairs, wrapped in old newspapers, along with a box of baubles and strings of "trimmings" from previous years. David and Brian were allowed to help dress the tree but it was a tense procedure, sometimes ending in a slap from Mary over a broken precious bauble. Brian adored shop-bought trimmings but most years Mary would forego buying trimmings for more important things such as food, and so they made their own trimmings with strips of coloured paper looped into a ring and stuck with wallpaper paste, then strung together before being suspended from the ceilings in the downstairs rooms.

Mary and the older-end told Brian the usual stories about Santa Claus but with John and Malcolm around, doubt soon replaced belief and Mr. Stone put paid to the story completely when he dressed up as Santa Claus at the

Mission Christmas Party and Brian could just tell it was him, not Santa. He did not believe in any of the Santas he saw after that but prudently kept it to himself as the adults and the younger-end seemed to enjoy the pretending, and when he started secondary school, he became part of the adult conspiracy.

"Brian, luv. Tek bairns out fer a walk, will yeh, while ah just get them presents upstairs wrapped up feh Christmas. Ah doo-ernt want em catchin-on abaht Santa."

He enjoyed the conspiracy and keeping the Santa story alive with the younger-end. Right up to the last year at junior school Brian and David were packed off to bed early on Christmas Eve with threats that Santa'd bring them nowt if they did not go to sleep immediately. They knew by then what the game was all about and tried to keep awake, to see Mary sneaking into the bedroom with the Christmas stockings. But sleep always overtook them before she came in with the presents.

On Christmas Day morning they woke early and the green net stockings bought at the Co-op were there on the bed. Emptying the stockings was the start of Christmas Day. The contents were simple: an orange, an apple, a bag of already shelled nuts, and peanuts still in their shells, a chocolate bar, a tube of Smarties, a pair of socks (real shop-bought ones, not ones "frum rags"), a stretch cotton belt with a silvery snake clasp, waxy colouring crayons, a pencil and sharpener, a toy car. After inspecting the contents of the stockings they dashed downstairs. If it was a lean Christmas there might be Dandy and Beano Annuals which they shared, laid out under the synthetic Christmas tree. When Mary's budget was a little more flush, there would be an extra-special present. One year, to his utter joy, Brian was given a Micky Mouse wrist watch which he had nagged over for months. He proudly showed off the watch to other children at school but it broke beyond repair just a few weeks into the New Year. By today's standards his childhood Christmas presents were sparse. He was aware that other children were given more expensive special presents, usually a bike in the case of boys, but the knowledge did not dampen his enjoyment of the gifts he was given and as early as his last year at Junior School he understood the endless scrimping and scraping done by Mary to buy the presents. And perhaps because of this understanding he valued the presents more than some of his better-off friends valued their more expensive gifts. He valued them for the love and care in the giving as much as for what they were in themselves – just *things*.

Christmas Day morning was a blissful time. A fire was lit early in the front room, in addition to the back room fire, and Brian and David lay on the rug ("brodded" by Mary) right in front of the front-room fireplace, munching the stocking treats, reading the shared Beano Annual, getting hotter and hotter from the blazing fire, while Mary prepared Christmas dinner. It was before factory farming and chicken was an expensive dish. Mary bought one chicken a year in those days, a capon from Nelson's especially fattened-up for Christmas. If times were flush, there was a joint of pork as well. Bacon rolls and chipolata sausages were extravagances never reached but Mary served roast and mashed potatoes, three or four vegetables, sage and onion stuffing, apple sauce, and Yorkshire pudding and gravy as a starter – all cooked from scratch. There was no Christmas pudding but there was apple pie and custard and big bottles of pop, or tap water, and after, mince pies and hot steaming tea. There was no alcohol in the house. Fowk went to the Nash for that stuff. Mary thought there was something risqué, something immoral and dissolute, about people who kept drink inside the house although in her seventies and eighties she became partial to a Christmas present of a bottle of advocaat from one or other of her bairns.

As well as fruit and nuts in the stockings there were big bowls of oranges, mandarins, apples – and extra bags of nuts appeared from nowhere. They were rare luxuries. Christmas afternoon was spent wandering between the two main downstairs rooms, nibbling nuts, sucking an orange, listening to the wireless, reading, giggling at Bob farting after eating all that rich food. Then tea time came and everyone was starving and the second feast of the day was laid on the table: a big stand pork pie, cold ham, special Christmas tomatoes, a slab of crumbly sharp cheese, a jar of Branston pickle, plenty of bread and margarine, mustard made from powder and mixed with malt vinegar fiery as a strong curry, home-made pickles made of sliced cucumber and onion in a bowl of salty malt vinegar, more mince pies, a spice loaf cut into slices, and tarts and buns all baked by Mary. Everyone had their favourite. Brian loved pork pie with home-made pickle. Mary oohed over her own mince tarts. And Bob, always sober and relaxed on Christmas Day, loved a slice of spice cake topped with crumbly Wensleydale cheese and Branston pickle, all washed down with tan-strong sweet tea.

Boxing Day was for grown-ups. It was still special with fires in both main downstairs rooms but lit later in the morning "teh save ont coyle." Dinner consisted of chips fried in the fat from the capon and pork, and cold meat and pickle. Tea consisted of potted meat sandwiches (a sign treats were running out) but still with spice cake and mince pies. Sometimes Bob spoiled Boxing Day for Mary by "sloping off teh Nash" before dinner and rolling back drunk in the middle of the afternoon. Then there was a row, with slamming doors, swearing and shouting. After the row calmed, Bob fell asleep, snoring in his front room chair, while Mary curled herself up, miserable, on a chair in the back room and tried to lose herself in magazine stories. Later when he sobered up Bob pleaded with Mary to accompany him on "a session" in the evening, putting on his charm but Mary refused, accusing him of still being half-drunk from dinner time, knowing he would be insensible by the end of the night.

On a good Boxing Day, Bob stayed in during the day and in the evening Mary prepared herself for a rare night out drinking with Bob and their friends, down at Nash, or at a Down Batley pub. With Moira's and Shirley's help, she put on make-up, nylons, a nice skirt and top, a decent coat (belonging to Shirley) and a handbag with not much inside. Bob took great care and time over sprucing himself up, polishing his shoes to a perfect shine, dressing in a suit, an immaculately ironed shirt and a tie. John, Malcolm, Brian and David stood at the front room window with Moira and Shirley, watching the rare sight of Bob and Mary arm in arm, striding down the front path and down Chapel Fold, heading for a "reight good Boxin Neet aht." And later Bob came into the bedroom and crouched by the bed, his breath reeking of beer and tobacco, mumbling loving incomprehensible words to David and Brian.

Auntie Louie could take her drink. In her heyday, she was capable of downing several beers during an evening out at a pub or club. Mary was not a drinker. A couple of halves of mild with a dash of lime was her idea of a "good session." But on Boxing Night she sometimes drank more than she could take and the morning after she would have to lie in bed late – something she *never* normally did – and she was pale, wan and "gipping" all day, much to the amusement of everyone.

Christmas ended the day after Boxing Day when everyone went back to work and everything was normal again. The front room fire was not lit until after teatime and it was back to stews for dinner and salty fat'n'bread teas. When there was only one fire lit downstairs, the bedrooms and front room were cold and clammy and the back room was full of damp clothes piled on chairs, or hanging damp and limp on the creel above the fireplace, or draped on the clothes horse in front of the fire. Brian yearned for warmth. He hated the smell of damp washed clothes filling the air but dared not move the clothes horse from its place in front of the fire for fear of Mary's wrath. Instead he sat on the fireside chair and edged his way around the damp clothes, holding his hands over the fire, capturing some residual warmth.

Then it was New Year's Eve and the last of the spice cakes came out of the pantry and Mary baked a new batch of mince pies. There was a special New Year's Eve tea: tinned salmon, salad, warm boiled eggs, cold meat, chips and home-made pickles. Bob went down to the Nash for the New Year "session" and the older-end went to sophisticated celebrations in Dewsbury, Bradford or Leeds. Mary stayed in with her younger bairns. The fire in the back room was left to smoulder and die down, and a big fire was banked up in the front room, where Mary and the bairns gathered for the night. Mam read endless love books while the bairns played with toys or read the Beano Annual from cover-to-cover again, for the umpteenth time.

Toward the end of Junior School years, David and Brian were given the treat of staying up until midnight. There was still no television in the house and the wireless was turned off in the back room. Nothing actually happened at midnight except the spectacle of a few drunken revellers staggering along Chapel Fold. One year the miracle of snow arrived on New Year's Eve. You could feel it in the air well before it started and by ten o' clock it was falling heavily, and everything outside was covered in white. It was beautiful. Mary was absorbed in a crossword and puzzle book but eventually she became tired of snapping at David and Brian over drawing the curtains back and letting in the cold air. She came to the window to stand with them, gazing in wonder and exclaiming over the transformation of Chapel Fold, and the beauty of the heavy glistening flakes swirling under the yellow street light. Twelve o'clock came and Mary and her bairns stood rooted, gazing out of the window, awestruck and silent.

Industrial units where Healey Juniors once stood

Front garden at Chapel Fold, now a parking spot but Mr. Danes's privet hedge (left) still growing strong

The half-moon crescent at Chapel Fold, barely changed but for trees and fencing

Top of cinder track. Left, Staincliffe Juniors gable end. Right, vicarage garden wall

Brow of Bunkers Hill

Where Bunkers 'piece' used to be

*The secret courtyard, now a car valeting business.
Old trees still there, behind*

Colemans now a cheerful small Asian supermarket

Chip-oyle at end of Chapel Fold

Oldroyds now a small Sainsburys

Formerly Shepleys fruit and veg shop

Formerly Staincliffe Library – fine stonework still in evidence

Formerly Batley Town Mission

Coloured glass window at the Mission

*Formerly the Wheatcroft Snicket area –
now a mosque and madrassa*

Batley Baths and Fox's Biscuits

SENIORS – AND A FIERCE GROWING LAD

Brian moved up to Healey Seniors in September 1958. Malcolm and Frank Wilson told him scare stories just before his first day started.

"Yer'll 'ave ter watch it. All fest yeers geh ther eds shuvved dahn lav bowls. An then lav's flushed all ovver yer ed. An watch Mr. Smith. Ee's a reight un. Ee'll slipper yer fer breethin, ee will!"

The school was due to close the following August and be replaced by the brand new Batley Boys High School. There was an atmosphere of cheerful chaos at Healey Seniors. The teachers and older boys were in limbo and de-mob happy, anticipating the big move, and first years knew they would not *properly* start "big school" until the new school opened in September 1959. The scare stories came to nothing. Older boys ignored first years and existed in a separate world. The all-male teachers at Healey were a mixed bag and Brian was more interested in their various personalities than he was in lessons. Most of them were young compared with his teachers at Juniors. There was a huge and terrifying physics teacher whose favourite game was to roar at boys in corridors, ordering them to walk on the right as he mowed down anyone moving an inch from the designated side. He terrified Brian and put him off physics completely. The biology teacher (aptly called Mr. Bunny) was strict and scathing but Brian liked the subject, which seemed to consist entirely of pollination and photosynthesis and he came top in the end-of-year test. He hated PE and joined the sissies, feeling on safer ground with them than with sporty lads. The geography teacher was no disciplinarian and lessons consisted of mass misbehaviour, the teacher bellowing louder and louder but to no avail – the chaos just escalated. Brian hated it but giggled nervously, afraid to detach himself entirely from the universal indiscipline for fear he might be branded "morngy." (A softie.) It was his first taste of how unruly and potentially wild a group of boys can be, even though he came from a family full of boys. The history teacher, Mr. Smith, did not look much older than the senior boys but he had iron control. He was tall, distant, severe and never smiled or softened. Brian enjoyed the silence of history but took little in, focusing on avoiding landing in trouble with the scary teacher, rather than the content of lessons.

English was taught by Mr. Margetts who was also his form teacher. He liked Mr. Margetts. He was older than the other teachers with children of his own and he knew how to talk to, and engage with, eleven and twelve year old boys. English consisted of Mr. Margetts talking to the boys about themselves and their experiences, or reading long plays aloud. Brian was a fluent reader with a high clear voice and diction and Mr. Margetts often picked him out to read star parts. Had he not done this, Brian would have stayed quiet, invisible, creating his own inner world within the world of the English classroom. Mr. Margetts once rescued Brian from a summer hail storm and gave him a lift home in his light beige Hillman van. Brian loved the Hillman. It was smarter than Barry's old Austin. The engine made a lovely quiet purring noise and Mr. Margetts told him all about the gear stick as he drove. He asked Brian questions about himself and his family and Brian chatted happily. He felt secure, having an adult's undivided attention, without the threat of other lads around, and he made things up when he wanted to conceal something from his teacher:

"Mi Dad works in an office an' he's gorra car. An' mi Mam works in a dress shop Down Dewsbury, Sir."

It was the early days of what would become a lifelong habit of telling lies about himself and his family: lies which gave him balm and calmed his fears and shames. Mr. Margetts listened to him carefully but Brian saw the doubt in his face at some of his replies. Teachers in 1958 were expected to pass on knowledge and skills and keep good discipline, and pastoral care was something many secondary teachers simply did not do. But some teachers took the pastoral role seriously and Mr. Margetts was the first of two or three crucial teachers in Brian's secondary school years who worked systematically and hard at helping him in his personal development, ensuring the successes he eventually achieved in schooling.

The shadowy shames and fears which inhabited his mind from infancy continued to haunt him at this stage. His cousin Glynne was in Brian's class which pleased them both at first, before the stereotyping began. Brian read aloud in English confidently and happily: Glynne was shy and overcome by nerves when asked to read aloud. Brian detested sports and woodwork, convinced he was hopeless: Glynne loved rugby and woodwork and was taking boxing lessons in a local club. The intense closeness between the cousins began to fade. They saw only their differences from that time on, right up to Glynne's death six years later. Brian was becoming more and more adept at masking his feelings and was beginning to create a new persona, to escape from the boy he was; the boy he thought he should not be. He enjoyed play-reading in English and was not self-conscious about reading aloud in class. It gave him the opportunity to try out different voices and accents. He was beginning to learn he could make himself popular with other lads and avoid being branded a sissy by mimicking the voices and gestures of teachers and other kids, and showing-off his growing repertoire of accents. He thought of becoming an actor when he grew up and the human voice in all its variety of tone, timbre, accent, depth and range, fascinated him. Exploring his own vocal skills was a way of escaping, of hiding, from his inner fears and shames. He was beginning to learn about subterfuge and adaptability in social interactions. He was becoming skilled at moving from one group of lads to another when it suited his needs. He sought the security of the sissies in PE, where he felt threatened. But he was happy to abandon the sissies in the playground and in lessons other than PE, mixing instead with "normal" lads, entertaining them with his acting and voice skills.

On the surface Brian was happy at Healey Seniors. He was quiet, gentle and polite toward his peers and even more so with adults. He disliked aggressive loud machismo boys and bad behaviour in class frightened him. But more than fear, it was behaviour he could not comprehend or share and so he kept a distance between himself and the badly behaved boys, only superficially joining in, in order to appear "normal" and not stand out. He was already skilled at making himself invisible when he was unsure, or when he was in a situation he found threatening, and he was beginning to learn ways of making himself popular. But underneath the surface, the all-boys and all-male teacher school alienated and repelled him. There was always a feeling deep inside him of his wrongness, his "Mary-Ann-ness." And the layers of fears and shames about himself, and the relative poverty of his family, isolated him from being part of the mainstream ethos at Healey Seniors.

Brian formed a tentative friendship with another outsider in his class. Rodney was one of the few boys in Brian's class who had attended Staincliffe Juniors and failed the eleven-plus exam. He was a frail boy with a fragile personality. Another boy or teacher only had to look at him and he was overwhelmed by blushes and a nervous giggle. He had an older brother and elderly straight-laced Methodist parents who over-protected him from the outside world. He lived in a late eighteenth century cottage in Old Heckmondwike, a district less than a mile from Staincliffe Estate, which still retained its rural pre-industrial character. Brian persuaded the malleable Rodney to invite him home after school one day. He was curious to see where he lived. It was another world from the red-brick Staincliffe Council Estate. You reached Rodney's stone cottage via a long unmade lane and beyond the cottage was a gate and stile leading to a nearby farm. All hell was let loose when Brian and Rodney reached the lane that afternoon. A huge pink sow had just escaped from her sty and was determinedly rolling down the lane toward the main road. Rodney's older brother was in charge of managing the crisis. He seemed to appear from nowhere and brusquely thrust a dustbin lid into Brian's hands and an old wash rubbing board into Rodney's.

"Cum on, lads. Elp mi get this divvle back tert sty. Bang that lid as ard as tha can an kee-erp mowvin terward er. An if shi charges, use lid ent washing boo-erd, ter ward er off."

For Rodney and his big brother it was a fairly normal occurrence. For Brian, the cacophony made by the banging and yelling, and the sow's ear-piercing screams and sheer menacing size, was both terrifying and exciting. Somehow the three of them forced the sow back into her sty. Chapel Fold seemed like another world when he returned home to tell Mam all about the sow adventure.

*

It is lunch break on a hot summer day at Healey Seniors. The pupils have been allowed onto the playing fields, rather than being confined inside the small yard at the front of the school. Some are playing improvised cricket, others ball games; some are sitting on the grass in groups; talking, laughing, arguing; others are swaggering around, looking for a victim to persecute. Alone, Brian lies on his stomach on the grass, which is warm, moist and pungent beneath him. He is pre-pubescent and knows nothing about sex. He does not even know the word. But lying on the grass there are pleasurable warm sensations coming from his penis. He is perfectly happy on his own with the warm grassy earth and bodily sensations beneath: his head full of vague dreamy thoughts.

He gazes around and catches sight of a lad in his class. The lad is sporty, big and burly, and there is talk of him being a potential star in rugby, the most important game in the working class male community of Batley. He is popular and admired by other lads in a way Brian knows *he* can never be admired in this all-male world. He watches the boy running around playing with other boys. He admires the boy, wishing he could play with him, be his friend, knowing this can never be because of this difference in himself which he deeply feels. The lad stops his game. He runs around the field, pushing and jostling others. He sees Brian lying on the grass and runs over and falls on top of him, pinning him down, challenging Brian to fling him off. Brian does not resist. He likes the weight, the feeling, of the other boy's body on top of him. The big lad wants to wrestle. After a second or two of challenging Brian's passivity the boy loses interest, jumps up and runs off. Brian stays where he is, alone, wishing he could play with the other boy, on his terms. There is a nascent yearning inside him for the touch of the other boy's body and there is sadness about what he feels can never be. There is the fear of being mocked or rejected for what he feels, always lurking, even in the middle of pleasant thoughts and sensations.

There was another threat at Healey Seniors quite separate from being called a sissy or fowk finding out shaming things about his family. The threat was in the shape of a boy his own age; a boy at the new St John Fisher Roman Catholic Secondary School in Dewsbury; a school which had a tough reputation when it first opened, a year or so earlier. A new council estate was being built where once there were fields between Healey Seniors and the top of Bunkers Hill. The new estate provided a good short cut from school to Chapel Fold. To reach the new estate, Brian first had to leave Healey Seniors by the back entrance and cross a new road to a muddy footpath on the other side. Walking along the footpath on his way home, Brian would spot the John Fisher boy coming toward him. He was a small wiry boy with a fierce scowl and an ugly little scrunched-up monkey face and hair which had the look of a well-used Brillo pad. Brian guessed he had antagonised the boy in some way – perhaps by staring at his fearsome appearance? Every afternoon the monkey-boy took to glaring at him fiercely and threateningly, stiffening as he came closer. Brian had no appetite for a confrontation and obligingly stepped off the footpath, averting his eyes from the boy and allowing him to charge by, knowing the boy wanted to mow him down.

One afternoon Brian knew "summat was up" as soon as he spotted the boy's approach. He was marching toward Brian rather as a bull paces: head down, ready to charge. When he drew nearer, charge he did at Brian, who did not step aside quickly enough. The boy knocked him to the ground and stood over him with fists raised, waiting for him to struggle up and retaliate. Brian however had no interest in saving his honour or in provoking further ignominy. He was more amazed and puzzled by this unprovoked attack than angry and he just lay there, wondering what the boy would do next. His passive response bemused the boy who waited a few more seconds, still standing over him, before walking off. After that the boy still looked angry with the world but to Brian's astonishment he took to saying "ey up" to him in a friendly voice each afternoon, as Brian stood aside to let him pass.

It was Brian's first experience of the utter irrationality, the madness of a sort, that a testosterone charge can induce in men – and in fierce growing boys. It intrigued and puzzled him because it was not something he ever experienced in himself: this purely physical manifestation of anger and aggression. He was as capable as any other boy of anger and sudden fierce outbursts of temper, but his outbursts had an emotional base and invariably they were re-active and defensive, unlike the fierce boy's pro-active aggression. His encounter with the boy was another early example of his growing sense of *difference* between himself and most other lads he knew. Brian *coped* at Healey Seniors. He coped with the experience of being thrown into a diversity of boys and male teachers as best as he knew how. A mixed-sex secondary school would have suited his personality more, where he might have had the comfort, security and support of the opposite sex: props for his nervous personality; props he received at home from Mam, Shirley and Moira. He was happier and more at ease at home in the company of females.

It was during that year at Healey Seniors when Mary became seriously worried about Brian's persistent bed-wetting. She took him to Dr. Hinchcliffe who diagnosed a weak bladder, or so Mary said. But Brian had his suspicions. He still shared a bed with David, who hated waking up in the morning to a wet, pee-smelly bed. After seeing Dr Hinchcliffe, Mary seemed calm about his bed-wetting although he knew the extra washing of bed sheets galled and burdened her. Dr Hinchcliff advised Mary to wake him every night, a couple of hours after he fell asleep, and take him to the bathroom to pee and in this way cure him of bed-wetting. With Shirley's and

Moira's agreement, Mary decreed he was to sleep with his two older sisters in their double bed in the small back bedroom and they would wake him and send him to the bathroom when they came up to the room at their later bedtime. The arrangement lasted a few weeks and the bed-wetting temporarily stopped. But it was not a happy situation. Shirley and Moira were young women by then and it cannot have been something they enjoyed, having a younger brother sharing their bed. Brian hated it. His big sisters seemed gigantic and he woke in the night, squashed and squeezed in the middle, with hard elbows and knees digging into him and he cried out and moaned, feeling suffocated. Eventually single beds were bought for the middle lads which solved the problem of Brian's bed-wetting habit affecting David. The beds were signs of an improvement in the material circumstances of life at Chapel Fold. The move to his next school would mark an even greater improvement in Brian's prospects.

*Former Healey Secondary Modern School,
now Healey Juniors*

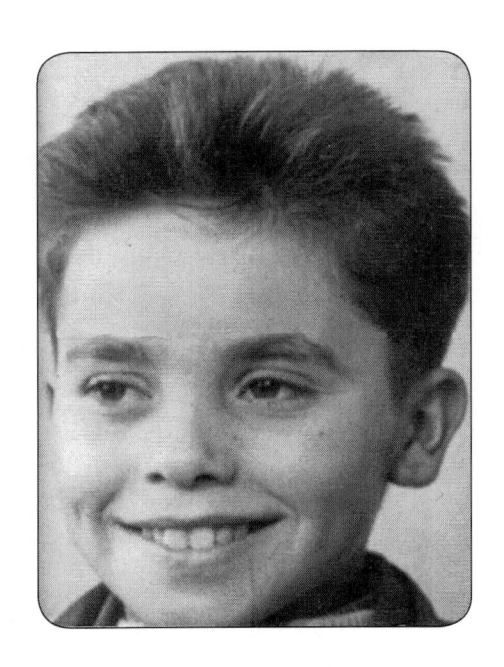

Brian aged 11

AHM GUNNER BI A TEE-CHER, WHEN AH GROW UP!

Before Batley High School opened in September 1959, letters arrived at Chapel Fold from the new headmaster giving his full name at a time when teachers preferred more impersonal, formal titles. Mary was interested. Malcolm was determined.

"Mmm. Nah then. New edmasters name's 'George Christopher Locke.' Them's nice names, ant thi?"

"Ahm not stoppin-on et new school. Ahm leavin, soon as ah can, teh bi a bilder, me."

The letter gave details of the compulsory uniform for first and second years. The uniform excited Brian and David – and worried Mary. The two boys had never attended a school where a uniform was expected and wearing these smart new clothes gave them and the new school an instant status and importance. To Brian the uniform was a visible sign his life was changing. He felt he was moving from one world to another. Older boys who did not intend to "stay-on" after reaching their fifteenth birthday, which included Malcolm, were exempted from wearing the uniform. Finding the money to buy two sets of uniforms, let alone three, was a real worry for Mary but aided by West Riding Education Committee clothing grants, and her usual scrimping and scraping, she managed to kit David and Brian out in full uniform.

The well-off Mams bought the uniform from recommended outfitters shops in Batley and Dewsbury, with the badge already sewn on the blazer. The poorer Mams like Mary bought blazers from cheaper outlets and sewed or glued the badges onto the blazer pockets themselves. The new school badge was a great hit with the younger boys. It had a white rearing centaur and underneath was the school motto: "Wisdom and Strength." It was the centaur the boys liked, not the dull words underneath. The older Hirst siblings all had a tale to tell about a teacher they respected and admired; someone they felt had taken a personal interest in them. These teachers tended to gain their pupils trust, respect and admiration in an unobtrusive understated Yorkshire way. George Locke was different. His first letter to parents showed he was a teacher prepared to wear his idealism, aspirations and passionate belief in a certain kind of education, on his sleeve. This unusual open communication from a head teacher pricked the old-uns' interest and added to Brian's excitement about going to the new school. He could barely wait for the start of term in September.

The brand new school did not disappoint when September came. It was huge, consisting of a three level block of classrooms, a large assembly hall-cum-theatre, a giant gymnasium, a dining area and kitchens, and separate teaching wings for science and technical subjects. The cheerful chaos of Healey Secondary Modern in its final year was replaced with a highly structured and organised school; a school which was saying to the nearly thirteen year-old Brian: "This place is important; what we do here is important; *you* are important: we can do wonders for you." This ethos and atmosphere in the early days at Batley High thrilled him, sending shivers down his spine. He began to think he was important in his own right at school for the first time. He began to dare to think he could become the someone else he wanted to be, if he succeeded in this new school, though his thoughts were fuzzy about the exact nature of this "future Brian" he wanted to become.

He loved the way morning assemblies at Batley High were organized; with military precision and ceremonial spectacle. Years later, when he became a secondary school teacher himself, he realised how carefully designed those assemblies were in keeping nearly a thousand eleven to eighteen year-old boys in order and uplifting and enthusing them at the start of the school day. Every class had its place in the assembly hall with first years at the front and sixth-formers at the back. Form teachers imposed silence on their classes before leading them from classrooms to allocated spaces in the hall each morning. Teachers stood near their own class, making sure they settled down in an orderly and silent manner. Miscreants were silenced or, more rarely, excluded. Mr. Rodwell, the music master, wore his graduate gown while sitting at an upright piano to the side of the stage at the front of the hall busily arranging music scores. Sweeping classical orchestral music was played from a gramophone operated by a sixth-former at the side of the stage as the assembly filed in and out. Brian had no idea who wrote the music but he loved the grand sweeping sounds. He loved those first few minutes of assembly, sitting on the floor, listening to the music while waiting for the hall to fill with pupils and teachers. Later in life he discovered and explored some of the works of Sibelius, Smetana, Dvorak, Grieg, Holst. They sounded familiar. Then he remembered. He had first heard them in Batley High assemblies, aged twelve.

Mr. Parkin, the Deputy Head, stood at the front of the stage watching boys file in. He had been head of the now-closed Batley Technical School (where Shirley had once been a pupil) and was liked and respected by the older "ex-tech" lads. Brian thought he looked like an ageing sombre eagle with his academic gown, beaked nose and thick lensed spectacles. His demeanour and appearance added to the ceremony. Sometimes Mr. Parkin led the assembly and on those mornings Harry Schofield, the Senior Master, stood at the front of the stage as boys filed in, looking fierce and contemptuous as only he could. Mr. Schofield was among a minority of graduate teachers in the school but chose not to wear a gown for assembly. When the whole school was assembled and silent, with just the sound of sweeping strings, or surging timpani, or triumphal brass, Mr. Locke appeared at the rear entrance doors, clutching books and papers in his hands. He dashed down the central aisle, his gown sweeping behind him in his own jet stream of movement, and bounded onto the stage to the lectern, while Mr. Parkin went to sit at the side, and the sixth-former stopped the music at a suitable pause and assembly began.

The main assembly rarely lived up to its grandiose start. It consisted of singing a hymn or two, the words of which Brian never forgot, like most of his generation – religiously inclined or not – who sang (or croaked) daily a dozen or so hymns throughout schooling. There was also a bible reading, read by a pupil or a teacher, and then a homily from Mr. Locke or Mr. Parkin, and assembly finished with the day's announcements before the ceremonial exit to the first lesson of the day. George Locke was at his best giving announcements, when his commitment, enthusiasm and dedication to the success of the school and its pupils came to the fore. He was in his forties; a slight wiry man with a shiny tanned bald head who exuded energy and passion about the job he was doing. His strange drawling voice and accent, with odd rises and dips and languid expansions of syllables, intrigued Brian as much as his energy and enthusiasm inspired him.

When Mr. Parkin took assembly his entrance was more stately: calm and sedate, contrasting sharply with Mr. Locke's sheer drive. Mr. Parkin could tell a good tale. In one of those early assemblies Brian was transfixed by a tale he told of driving throughout the night all the way from Yorkshire down to Cornwall – a dark midwinter night in the middle of the dark years of the war. He did not need to say which war: there was only one war then: the Second World War which had only ended in Europe fourteen years before; a war in which many Batley High Dads, and teachers, had taken an active part. He described driving with vehicle and street lights switched off, past buildings and towns darkened by blackouts, and the fear and disorientation of a journey where road signs did not exist. He spoke about flashes of light in the sky and booming thuds from defences in the cities he drove around. He held the assembly spellbound that morning and Brian was filled with respect for this man, talking so fluently, persuasively and naturally of his wartime experiences.

George Locke made a point of speaking to every first to third year class during the first few weeks of term. It was no mean feat as there were eight or more classes in each of the three year groups. Brian was placed in the second-to-top stream in the second year and soon it was the turn of his class to wait behind after assembly for the pep talk from Mr. Locke. It stimulated interest from the start. Once the hall was empty of all the other classes and teachers, Mr. Locke came bounding down from the stage to where the class was sitting waiting. Unusually, he asked the class to stand and gather round him. In those days pupils did not stand around a teacher, and certainly not a headmaster: they sat on the floor and looked up, or they sat behind a desk and looked at the teacher behind his desk. If they were behaving badly or the teacher was in a bad mood, they were made to stand behind desks with hands on heads while reprimands and threats were meted out, until given permission to put down hands and sit. Gathering around a teacher in a standing position was a non-verbal sign of something different happening that morning: it was saying the boys were important to Mr. Locke: he wanted to talk *with* them on equal terms, not *at* them.

He began by discussing the school badge which he knew was popular among the pupils, telling them about the centaur's symbolism and its relation to the motto and how he wanted them to follow the motto – to be strong and wise. He already knew some of the boys and chatted with them about previous schools, hobbies and favourite sports. He told them how much he liked hiking in the country and rock-climbing and doing something called mountaineering. He talked about what it felt like to do something you liked, how good it felt to achieve something: scoring a goal, painting a picture, climbing a mountain. This vibrant charismatic man broke down the nervous distance Brian habitually put up between himself and the alien world of boys and men at school. He was enjoying the conversation. It excited and interested him and he wanted to join in. Mr. Locke asked the boys what *they* wanted to do when they grew up. He told them they could do *anything* – be a mountaineer, play for Batley at rugby, be a doctor, a soldier. Brian was filled with enthusiasm and put his hand up, bursting to speak. Mr. Locke fixed his gaze on Brian:

"Ye-ees? You, boy-ee? What would you-oo like to do-oo?"

"Sir, sir. Ahm gunner bi a *tee-cher*, when ah grow up!"

"Goo-ud. I'm sure yo-oll succe-ed. Ne-ext boy?"

Mr. Locke did not mock or laugh at what he had said. Instead, he took what Brian had said for granted. But Brian noticed fatty Watty, who lived in a posh house down Purlwell near the rugby grounds, sneering down his nose at him as if to say:

"Oo dyer think you are, Esty? Sayin yehll be a teacher an yeh Mam working in rag-oyle."

But at that moment he did not care what fat slobby Watty thought: Mr. Locke believed him. It was a seminal moment. It was tantamount to changing his future, just uttering those words to Mr. Locke – at that particular moment of his life. He had said he wanted to be a teacher on the spur of that moment; it was the only posh job he could think of. But he *knew* once he said it he was never going down the pit, or become a builder, or a soldier, or a fitter, like all the older males in his family. He told his Mam and Moira when he got home that night what he had said to Mr. Locke and Moira said "Why not?" and Mam said "Well, um? Aye, owd lad. Why not?" And he could see they were both a bit doubtful he could do it – but they also looked interested. The idea that he was going to do something different, something no one in the family had done before him – be a teacher and stay on at school – frothed in his head during all that first term at Batley High until eventually, in his mind at least, the idea became a fixed certainty.

During the first term Brian was friendly with Ray Stevens, insofar as a nervous introvert such as he could be friends with the extroverted, sometimes outrageous Ray. But Ray had calm days and in that mood he was a good listener: receptive and sensitive. One late October afternoon, several weeks after they both started at Batley High, the two boys walked home together from school. When they reached Mount Pleasant rugby grounds they sat down on a bench and looked down at the Bradford Road snaking through the valley below. It was 1959 and many of the mills and rag-oyles were still functioning. The air was beginning to chill autumnally and you could smell coal smoke coming from the mill chimneys and rows of terraced houses below. The two boys shivered on the bench. Ray was in a quiet, receptive mood.

"When ower class saw Mr. Locke, ah towd him ahm gunner bi a teecher when ah grow up. An I am, an all! An ahll tell yer summat else. When ah leave school ter bi a teecher, ahm *never, never* cummin back ter this *shitty* town!"

"Shitty" was a word Ray often used in a way that always made Brian laugh, although he did not like saying the word out loud himself. But he knew he meant it, beyond the drama of the moment and impressing Ray. He knew then he could be different if he wanted. He could be like Jennifer at Juniors and the glasses boy at Infants; like Pip in *Great Expectations*. It was an important moment in his life. Teaching could be a means of escaping the sense of diminishment, the sense of being nowt but a little Mary-Ann that constantly plagued him deep inside.

Brian loved big spaces, new sights and small things transforming from one thing to another: watching rain swirl down a drain in a cobbled snicket; seeing the beauty of the Pennine landscape at Battyford; observing the Wolds through the window of the Club Trip coach; mixing powder paint and making a new colour; crumbling a small piece of earth into fine powder. Now he was on the edge of a different kind of transformation: a transforming of his own social status; a conscious, systematic transforming of his personality, manners and behaviour. But he knew his Mam and family would not like him sneering at Batley, the town to which he belonged, and so at home he only said he wanted to be a teacher.

School became important to Brian during his first year at Batley High but it was not at the *centre* of his life: Chapel Fold, his family, his neighbours, were still the real centre. It was during that year that he came to puberty. He still had no knowledge of sex beyond his immediate bodily sensations. Sex was a subject his older siblings and adults in the family were tight lipped about. Brian conflated this family rectitude over sex with dirtiness and shame. He thought sex was something you kept in the shadows, although it was obvious sex was *happening* among the old-uns. His oldest niece Linda was born just before his tenth birthday. His nephew Christopher arrived not long after he reached eleven. Michael came six months after

Christopher. And Shirley's first child Julie arrived when he was thirteen. He knew about pregnancy, contractions, labour, childbirth and the pros and cons of breast feeding. They were topics Mary, Shirley, Moira and Sheila openly discussed. But as for the sex act which started all this: it was never mentioned.

Sex, for Brian at this stage in his life, manifested itself in the bantam cock mounting the hens in the pen behind the outhouse. Sex was two dogs appearing one day on the small green opposite the house at Chapel Fold, engaged in fierce and painful copulation. Brian watched from behind the front room window with fascination and horror as the big dog struggled to extricate himself from inside the small bitch after the sex. They seemed to be stuck together and the male could not withdraw. They dragged each other around in ignominious circles, both animals yelping and crying with pain until they finally separated. Sex was lying on his stomach on his bunk bed, pressing down his weight on his penis and enjoying the sensations from the swelling beneath. He enjoyed this activity but he was also ashamed of indulging it. He kept it secret, never discussing it with anyone. It did not occur to him until some while later that David, Glynne, Malcolm and John were all going through similar experiences. None of them ever spoke to him about sex. The nearest anyone came to talking to him about it was Young Bob – that day in the bantam pen.

Not long after his thirteenth birthday, sex became real and actual. He was lying on his stomach on the bed one afternoon thinking about a boy he had played with earlier that day and the swelling turned into an exquisite scary throb which in turn turned into a tumescent explosion, consuming him in frightening pleasure. He often went to play with the boy whose image was in his mind on the day of his first ejaculation. The boy had a large collection of toy cars which Brian coveted. In the early days of their friendship, Brian and the boy would lie on the path outside the boy's house, racing the cars, making-up commentaries and sound effects of screaming brakes, crashing gears and scorching tyres exploding. Or they lay on the fireside rug in the front room, reading the boy's collection of comics. The boy knew Brian coveted the toy cars and comics and he enjoyed the power of ownership. He sometimes teased Brian, refusing to let him share a comic or play with a favourite car until Brian threatened to leave, in a real temper. Then the boy would relent, not wanting him to go. Brian understood the power game the boy was playing but he was playing his own power game in threatening to withdraw his friendship. He was sexually attracted to the boy but tried to keep it secret. He could not say why, but he suspected there was something wrong about his feelings.

In the early days of the friendship they had mock fights and trials of strength which the other boy usually won, being taller, heavier and stronger. As the friendship developed they often played in the boy's bedroom, which he had all to himself – a privilege Brian also coveted. During school holidays they played there for hours at a time. The boy's parents were out at work and they had the run of the house. Toy cars and comics were forgotten. Instead they wrestled and mock fought. Brian found the physical contact sexually thrilling. He liked being pinned down on the bed or on the floor, lying underneath the boy straddled on top of him. The boy was not as sexually developed as Brian nor was he as emotionally complex. He seemed to enjoy having Brian's company and winning the wrestling matches – and sometimes exercising the more subtle power over Brian which his ownership of the toys, comics and having his own bedroom gave him. His pleasure in the physical contact did not seem as intense as Brian's. No matter how hard Brian tried to conceal it, he was in a state of constant sexual excitement while they wrestled, but the boy seemed oblivious of this. Brian was initially comfortable with the relationship because he felt in control. The boy wanted his company. He enjoyed the power of possessing things Brian coveted and he enjoyed his physical dominance. Meanwhile Brian played a deeper game, which the other boy only vaguely apprehended, by concealing and suppressing as best he could the intense sexual pleasure the physical contact between them gave him.

As time passed the boy became more sexually aware. He took to lying on top of Brian, thrusting, telling him he was "fucking" him. Brian thrilled to this but he was confused. He knew about "fucking" by now. But it was only something Mams and Dads did: in secret. The paradox troubled him. The other boy seemed less troubled. He wanted Brian to show him his private parts but Brian was reluctant. He was afraid of going as far as exposing his body and losing the concealment clothes gave him. He did not fully understand why but he threatened to withdraw his friendship when the boy persisted in his demands. One day, after a long wrestling match in the bedroom, Brian went to the bathroom to pee. The boy sneaked in and without Brian realising, watched him peeing into the bowl, from behind. Brian was angry when he turned and saw the boy staring at his private parts but the boy was unrepentant. He had spied the beginnings of Brian's pubic hair growth and wanted to look more closely and talk about the hair. Brian at that moment *hated* the pubic hairs and did not want the boy to see them. The hair down there disgusted him: he felt it was wiry, dirty, nasty. He was furious and confused by his inner feelings and he took those feelings out on the boy. He stormed off, saying he no longer wanted to play, vowing to himself he would never go to the boy's house again.

Shortly after this incident, on a hot day, Brian, David and Glynne were lying on the flat concrete outhouse roof, sunbathing. They had stripped off shirts to use as headrests against the hard hot concrete of the roof and were lying on their stomachs enjoying the sun on their backs. Brian heard someone scrambling onto the outhouse window ledge below and climbing onto the roof. He looked up lazily and saw it was the boy, and before he could stop him, the boy fell on top of him and began to thrust. The others watched, curious. Brian was horrified, embarrassed and angry. The boy was publicly doing what they normally did in secret. He was behaving like those dogs on the green. Everyone was watching. He yelled at the boy and struggled to get him off. The boy leapt up, startled by Brian's sudden real anger and fled, scrambling down from the outhouse roof and disappearing. The others looked on, approving the way Brian had dispatched the boy and, to his immense relief, they made no comment over what happened. After this incident, Brian avoided all contact with the boy. The friendship ended. It was the closest he ever came to what would now be called a gay relationship, in a physical sexual sense. Brian's rejection of the boy's attempts to take the relationship further was the beginning of what was to become a dogged lifelong repression of his sexuality and a rigid avoidance of physical contact with others of his own sex, smothering his yearnings and desires inside. He became what is now called a "non-active gay" and he maintained that celibacy for a lifetime.

Until puberty, Brian had coped with situations where he was put under the spotlight at school. He liked reading aloud in Mr. Margett's English lessons at Healey and, if he thought he knew the answer, he was not embarrassed about putting his hand up in class and showing off his knowledge. Similarly he was an open talkative child at home and only became guarded and unsure of himself when Bob was around. He changed when puberty came. He became self-conscious and nervous about speaking out in class, or being singled out to read aloud. He loved words and finding new words but he hated the new subject of French, where he spent his time terrified the teacher was going to make him speak these strange new words out loud: in front of everyone. (Thirteen is a terrible age to introduce a child to his or her first new language. The younger, the better.) The French teacher's discipline was insecure. His teaching method involved introducing the class to new grammar and vocabulary and then ordering individual pupils to repeat words, phrases and simple sentences out loud. Pupils made terrible mistakes and were unable to wrap their Yorkshire lips round these strange new sounds:

Teacher: "Je m'apell est..." He points at his victim: "You boy, it's your turn now."

Victim boy: "Em er, geh mapple er – Ronald, Sir."

This method caused jeering and disruption which the teacher could never quite control. The thought of being exposed to any kind of ridicule from other boys terrified Brian so he spent French lessons looking out of the window, composing his face into a vague and somewhere-else expression, pretending utter surprise and ignorance when the teacher asked him to repeat a new word or phrase. He tried making himself invisible, not moving or talking to anyone and often the teacher did not notice him, being more involved with the noisier lads which suited Brian perfectly. He escaped having to speak the language out loud due to the teacher's unawareness of boys as individuals. The French teacher fell for Brian's trickery and left him alone, dismissing him as a dizzy idiot. These were stratagems Brian used all his life after: hiding himself behind a carefully crafted outward persona; making himself invisible; deflecting revealing himself to others.

He used the same tactics in PE: acting gormless, being invisible, but in any case the PE teachers were only interested in potential sporting stars and so he easily escaped their notice. Football players in the early 1960s were not the super-stars and super-earners they are now. Out of season, Leeds United players occasionally coached football at Batley High. It was a way of supplementing modest incomes and talent-spotting future players. Football meant nothing to Brian except terror of being laughed at for his inability to kick or throw a ball with any degree of skill. Jack Charlton, then a young Leeds United player, coached football at Batley High for a few weeks in 1961 when Brian was in the third year. The keen football fans were excited about Charlton and even Brian had heard of him. Every boy was given fifteen minutes, in a small group, of coaching from Charlton and if a boy showed potential he would receive more intensive coaching in future lessons. Brian reluctantly trooped off with an enthusiastic group to the area of the playing fields where Charlton was waiting. He had his plan already worked out: he would deliberately "cock it up" and be rapidly sent off the sports field by the local hero footballer and that would be that. Charlton was a big tough looking man who was only interested in coaching the most talented boys. As soon as teachers were out of earshot he made it abundantly clear what he thought of football duffers:

"Why-ee, man. Ye's bluddy yoos-less. Away-ee. Goo on. Gerrof tha bluddy fee-eld now. S'os ah can con-cen-tra-et on tha utthers."

Science lessons were almost as bad as PE. Brian was taught physics and chemistry in the second and third years but not biology and these "hard sciences" mystified and scared him. Technical drawing mystified him also. So in all these subjects he played the same tricks as in French and PE – gazing out of the widow, feigning gormlessness, trying to become invisible. These tactics were his way of enduring the lessons that scared him. He learnt virtually nothing and had no memory of the content of those lessons later in life.

During the first term at Batley High pupils were introduced to the basics of woodwork and metalwork before being placed for the next two years in one of these two "practical" subjects. Brian prayed he would be put in the woodwork group but that was not to be. The woodwork teacher was ancient. He wore a brown overall and wandered around the woodwork shop, rambling on about vices, joints and saws. Hammers and saws were tools Brian found impossible to handle but the teacher hardly noticed. He only really noticed the boys who took naturally to the tool-centred ethos of the woodwork shop. Occasionally he noticed Brian or another incompetent and in broad Yorkshire he would exclaim:

"Weer d'yer think y'are, lad? On yeh fatther's YOT?"

His manner was mild and harmless and the boys giggled and imitated him behind his back. The irony of the woodwork teacher's favourite reprimand only occurred to Brian many years later. What would the teacher have said, had he known the true circumstances of Brian's "fatther?"

The metalwork teacher was a Scottish monster who kept control through a sadistic reign of terror. He was small and slight. Even some of the second year lads were taller. He saw his slight physique as a potential handicap with adolescent lads – who sometimes like to square-up to smaller adult males – and this was what made him so ruthless. The boys soon learned to stand to rigid attention at the beginning of lessons next to the vices ranged along the work benches while the Scottish devil prowled around in his tight-fitting white overall smeared with grey grease, looking for the slightest flicker of levity on faces – before he attacked. He would pick up an object – a screwdriver, a file, a piece of metal – and throw it at the culprit who dared smile or whisper. If the pupil under attack was close enough he cuffed him hard across the back of the head and came up close, face-to-face, sneering up at his (usually taller) victim, daring him to so much as blink.

"Ah'm nae hevin' nae nen-sense frem yae, lad-deh. Ender-stond?"

And his victim would nod, and Nae Nen-sense would leer in triumph, and the lesson would proceed, with frequent pouncings for no reason other than to assert control. It astonished Brian how calmly most boys coped with this creature. Many of his classmates had a real love for the subject. They loved being given a piece of metal to wedge into a vice and having a file in their hands to work on the metal; to shape it into a poker or some other object. "Mr. Nae-nen-sense" totally, utterly, terrified Brian. Vices, files, lumps of metal, and those incomprehensible machines, lathes, terrified him too. Metalwork was a black nightmare with a devilish monster at its centre and he shook violently, sickly nervous sweat pouring down his face, from beginning to end of the metalwork lessons until eventually even Devil-nae-nen-sense noticed, and softened his approach – toward Brian. But it was no good. As far as Brian was concerned, metalwork was a nightmare with a monster at its heart. He managed, in two years, to make an approximation of a poker which he took home to be laughed over, in the nicest way, by all the family. It was paradise when the end of year nine came and metalwork and Nae-nen-sense left his life.

The maths teacher, Mr. Lister, was also a small man but he was kindly and wanted above all else to introduce boys to the beauty, logic and meaning of his beloved subject. He had a nasty temper when riled which Brian only saw once. He was in the third year, walking down a corridor in the main classroom block where a group of big fifth years were waiting noisily outside the maths room. Mr. Lister emerged from inside the room and his appearance immediately silenced most of the class. But a tall boy did or said something which infuriated small Mr. Lister and he reached up and smacked the boy hard across the cheek. Everyone heard the harsh slap and there was a tense silence in the corridor for just a second or two before the tall boy apologized and the tension dissipated.

Brian liked Mr. Lister and, until he moved to Batley High, he liked maths which until then consisted of arithmetic. Mr. Lister taught maths, not arithmetic. He introduced the class to algebra, logarithms and other abstract things. Brian was more mystified by maths than by everything else that mystified him in those first two years at Batley High. Technical drawing, physics – even metalwork – made sense compared with maths. It astonished Brian that other boys in his class loved Mr. Lister's maths lessons and it exacerbated further his growing sense of his difference. The ease with which other boys seemed to tackle maths compounded Brian's misery about his wrongness. He convinced himself he was stupid and tried the usual tactics: gazing out of the window; being invisible. But Mr. Lister was too good a teacher to let this happen. He was on a crusade to convert all boys to the beauty of maths and when he saw Brian was struggling he paid him close personal attention, leaning over him, his breath reeking of tobacco, patiently explaining, trying to get him to see the beauty and logic of the current topic. It was no good. Maths made Brian tremble and sweat with fear. He shut himself off. He wanted maths to go away; leave him alone. Eventually even kindly Mr. Lister had to retreat, realising his precious maths might reduce Brian to nothing. He made a huge concession which knocked his professional pride. He allowed Brian to continue with arithmetic, and decimals and fractions, which made sense to him, while the rest of the class pursued more abstract tasks.

Brian liked art lessons above everything. The art room had none of the threats or mysterious array of equipment that so terrified him in sports, science, technical drawing and metalwork – and it had none of the baffling abstraction of maths. He felt at home with paint brushes, charcoal, crayons and sketching pencils; with shaping clay in his hands and with the pottery wheel but was alienated and repelled by test tubes, bats and balls, T-squares, files and vices, and endless pages of logarithms. He was fascinated in art lessons by concepts such as perspective, depth and composition and could not wait to try them out, whereas concepts of expansion and contraction in physics, algebraic formulas, angles in TD, and simple mechanisms such as joints and brackets in metalwork, baffled and perplexed him. Perhaps it was something to do with the Mary-Ann-ness, the wrongness, he had by now convinced himself was intrinsic in his nature. Perhaps he equated the subjects he loathed with the hard masculinity he was convinced he did not have. Art was softer, more pliable, in *his* mind at least.

The art teacher, Mr. Palmer, fascinated him as much as the subject he taught. He was one of the few teachers who taught on an intellectual level rather than doling out rigid pedagogy. He was courageous enough to tackle difficult subjects, such as the human body, in an open unembarrassed way. He had a strong London accent and was nicknamed "Harry App" on account of the way he pronounced "hurry up." Imposing discipline bored him. Pupils tried to rile him by mocking his accent, his thick-lens glasses, his gangling gait, but he had his own way of dealing with this.

"Now yew jast listen to me, yang mayne. When yew've got yowsewf a Bee Aiy in Foine Aart like me, then yew can scorff!"

It worked. The mockery lessened and some of the class wanted to know about these strange things, "a BA" and "fine arts," and Mr. Palmer was happy to explain and even admit he was not a god who knew everything related to his subject, telling them his "theory" side was stronger than his "practical." It delighted Brian how Mr. Palmer would hold up a picture to the art class showing naked women and men and coolly talk about shape, form, foreground and background. Or he would show a picture of a lipstick advertisement and discuss phallic symbolism, stimulating real curiosity among many in the class. Brian was intrigued about this thing called "a degree." When the first Speech Day was held he looked at the staff list on the programme and saw only a handful of teachers – Mr. Locke, Mr. Parkin, Mr. Schofield, Mr. Palmer, Mr. Margetts, Mr.Rodwell had "BA" or "BSc" or "BMus" after their names and he decided when he became a teacher he would be one of those.

He loved art lessons most when it came to the time of settling down with a task, especially when it involved using charcoal for preliminary sketching, usually in preparation for a painting. All his senses were fully engaged when using charcoal: it had a burnt-ashes smell; it rested in the hand like a living thing; it made wonderful soft swishing sounds when applied to paper, and you could rub it in with your fingers, or rapidly touch a line, to make it narrower or wider – and then miracle, the sketch appeared on the page! Mr. Palmer left his pupils alone during these sessions, watching what they were doing but rarely interfering. He gave pupils that precious commodity – time – to work on the task. And Brian loved it. He loved the shapes gradually appearing on the paper and the fact that it did not matter if it went wrong, provided you saw your mistake and rectified it. He loved being able to rest a minute and look out of the window. He loved the way Mr. Palmer encouraged boys to wander round and look at what others were doing, with none of the tense underlying competitiveness of other lessons.

Mr. Mangham, who taught English, was Brian's favourite teacher in those first two years. Like George Christopher Locke, he always signed his full name on the end-of-year report: Ian Leslie Mangham. He left Batley High after two years and English lessons were never again the sheer fun they had been with him. Mr. Mangham and Mr. Palmer were great friends. They lodged in the same big house, Up Purlwell. Brian often saw them walking to and from school together. (Few teachers then owned cars and certainly not young newly qualified teachers.) Mr. Palmer was tall and willowy whereas Mr. Mangham was average height and squarely built. They were always talking non-stop and laughing at the other's jokes whenever he saw them walking to and from school. He wished he could transport himself invisibly into their conversations which he thought must be the epitome of erudition and wit.

Gradually during those first two years art took second place to English in Brian's favourite subjects and it was all because of Mr. Mangham. He was like Mr. Palmer in one respect. He told pupils personal things about himself, something teachers did not generally do at that time. He could have told his classes he was a Martian and they would have lapped it up, so much did they like him. He told them Batley High was his first teaching post after leaving Bretton Hall College where he had just completed three years training in teaching English and Drama. Mr. Mangham introduced Brian to the pleasure of writing stories and he felt a real joy and thrill when his stories were praised. He was not embarrassed about reading them aloud to the class, simply because Mr. Mangham said they were good stories and no one dreamt of questioning his judgment.

Mr. Mangham encouraged pupils to talk and do role plays, activities which were new to them. Brian desperately wanted to impress Mr. Mangham when he gave pupils the task of preparing a short talk on a favourite subject or hobby. Most chose sport or a practical hobby. Brian hated sports and had no hobbies except reading. However, part of the mythology among the boys concerning Mr. Mangham was that he was "A Communist," which impressed Brian greatly, even though he was unsure what a Communist was. He decided to give a talk on the Russian Revolution of 1917 – a tall order for a fourteen year-old who knew nothing about history beyond some basics on the Romans and Tudors. But he pressed on, researching in the school and Staincliffe libraries. It was all about workers revolting against a ruler who had the peculiar title of "Tzar," which Brian pronounced "Te-zar." Mr. Mangham always had a satirical smile on his face, as if inside he was laughing at how insane the whole world outside himself was. The enigmatic secretive smile intrigued and captivated Brian. He wanted to know his secrets; share his private thoughts. He smiled as Brian gave his talk and praised it at the end, telling him "Te-zar" was pronounced "Zar" but in such a non-correcting, matter-of-fact way that no one laughed at the mistake.

It was the laughter and sheer enjoyment of English lessons that Brian loved. Much better than story writing, role plays, giving talks, were those occasions when Mr. Mangham suddenly announced he was bored. Whenever he said this, the whole class pricked up their ears, waiting for the fun to begin. His storeroom door was situated to the side at the front of the classroom, just to the left of the blackboard. It was full of props for drama lessons. In one of his bored moods, Ian would wander inside the store room and after a few seconds the class would hear strange sounds coming from inside: thuds, bumps, growling, howling, sneering and ghostly WHOOOS. The noises provoked waves of laughter. He could have continued making mad noises from inside his storeroom the whole lesson and the class would have laughed and laughed. But then came a few seconds of silence, giving pupils time to catch breaths, anticipating what might be coming next. And then he would emerge from the store room, using various props. One day he wore a pan on his head, the handle stretched out behind, a moustache charcoaled on his face, his hand up by his forehead in a rigid salute, a fanatical manic look in his eye, and he goose-stepped, backward and forward, across the front of the classroom till the class howled with laughter. His antics were utterly wonderful moments for crypto-anarchic early adolescent children. It was years before Monty Python and Basil Fawlty and here was this wonderful teacher, pre-figuring all that.

Very few teachers can do it, but Mr. Mangham could whip his pupils into frenzies of rolling laughter and still stay in control. Sometimes the hilarity went too far but he had a vigilant eye for unacceptable disorder and could switch from acting the clown to a strict po-faced teacher, in seconds. When the class saw he was serious they sat to attention. Brian was nervous and uncomfortable about bad behaviour in lessons such as French, where the teacher often lost control. He did not want to be part of it and hated seeing the teacher trembling and shouting, humiliated. The certainty that it would never happen in English enabled him to enjoy the levity, the fun moments, to the full. Part of the frisson the boys got from Mr. Mangham's antics was that they were complicit in an element of rebellion. The older more formal established teachers disliked his methods and were not beyond trying to undermine him. Harry Schofield, who was a formidable disciplinarian, threw open the door one day in the middle of a fun session, pretending he did not know Mr. Mangham was there with the "rioting" class. He was about to quell the class but Ian pre-empted him:

"SILENCE! NOW!"

And instantly the class fell silent. Harry was visibly crestfallen, bemused by the game Ian was playing. Nothing was ever said explicitly but the boys loved taking part in their young English teacher's game of sticking two fingers up at stuffy establishment colleagues. It was probably his refusal to fit into a conventionally run school that led him to leave after two years, to Brian's huge disappointment. English was never such fun again.

Batley High was not entirely centred around lessons and teachers during those first two years. The school was officially opened by Sir John Hunt, a mountaineer colleague of Sir Edmund Hillary. The choice of John Hunt was George Locke's. Mr. Locke was passionate about outdoor activities and believed boys could be made into men through participating in them. He encouraged pupils to take part in the Duke of Edinburgh Award Scheme. Those pupils such as Brian who avoided the "D of E" did not escape outdoor activities however, as every pupil was expected to spend a week at the school's Summer Camp at Penmaenmawr in North Wales. George Locke made sure that grants and subsidies were made available to poorer parents, thus enabling their children to experience Summer Camp. The camp was spread over the last six weeks of the summer term and virtually every pupil and every teacher took part.

Brian had ambivalent feelings about Summer Camp. On the one hand, he was excited at the thought of travelling to this new place with its strange Welsh name, and also at the thought of not sleeping at home. (Apart from the New Brighton B+B holiday with Shirley and David, it would be his first experience of life away from home and Batley.) On the other hand, he was nervous and unsure. He feared the week might turn out to be just one long PE lesson and was worried about sleeping in a tent with several other boys and the possibility that he might humiliate himself by wetting the bed – something that still occasionally happened at home.

The trip to Penmaenmawr turned out to be both ordinary and extraordinary. It was a normal school day when the time came for Brian to attend School Camp, but instead of wearing school uniform and carrying his satchel on the long walk to school, he found himself dressed in khaki shorts and a casual shirt, carrying a heavy cardboard suitcase full of clothes and sundry items to sustain him for a week away from home. It was similarly disorientating at school, where instead of attending routine lessons, he found himself boarding Fred Lyles's coach which, once it was loaded with boys and luggage, rumbled slowly away from school. He could see pupils in classrooms in the main block looking wistfully at the coach through windows, wishing it was their week to go to camp. It was cool and cloudy weather that day and Brian was initially too nervous to heed the journey. But the allure of a new landscape captured his attention when the coach reached the road beyond Chester and wound its way around the North Wales coast to Penmaenmawr. The weather was solid grey with a persistent warm drizzle. It was a sombre start to the holiday. The landscape looked grey: grey sky; grey drizzle; grey slate quarries; grey stone on high hillsides. Even the sheep scattered across the hills looked grey and the grass itself, mixed with scree, looked greeny-grey.

The drizzle stopped after the first day but the weather stayed cool and grey. Summer Camp was not one long PE lesson and Brian enjoyed it, although he knew he was an outsider in this world of male teachers and boys. Most boys and men teachers seemed to enjoy just getting on with things: securing tent poles; organising games, quizzes, competitions; digging latrine trenches in the far corner of the field; making beds; polishing walking boots; preparing a meal in the kitchen tent. They did not talk to each other in a conversational sense. The talk was perfunctory, transactional and monosyllabic: "Pass me that hammer," "Move that bench," "Go and wash your hands." He missed the gossip, the varied conversation, of the women in his family, whereas other boys seemed happy with the grunt, curt, almost wordless world of camp. He thought it was another sign of his *difference* from most other boys. To cope with this thought, he did what he was already adept at doing: he kept himself on the edge of things; made himself invisible when he felt threatened; presented a dreamy outside veneer to mask his inner feelings. But he did enjoy the long hilly walks and climbing a stony path to the summit of Mount Snowdon. The vistas and hills impressed him but they did not move him emotionally as did the hills and contours of Battyford, or the view below from Mount Pleasant, or the Yorkshire Wolds on the way to the coast. The North Wales landscape left him cold emotionally: it left him feeling separate. Yorkshire Pennine country enfolded him; he felt emotionally part of it, as if he were inside another's embracing arms.

He attended school camp at a time when he was becoming increasingly aware of sex. While panting up a steep path on a hillside near Conway in the middle of a line of boys struggling to keep up with Mr. Locke striding out in the lead, Brian would gaze furtively at the muscular legs of the tall boy in front, longing for something he thought he did not have, boyness, before looking guiltily away, knowing it was "wrong" to admire and desire another boy's body. Meanwhile Mr. Locke, dressed in baggy khaki shorts, green anorak, big brown climbing boots and thick socks, his copper brown calves pounding the hill, his bald head shining like a beacon up front, was urging them on.

"Come alo-ong bo-oys, not fa-aar n-ow."

Ray Stevens had none of Brian's inhibitions. He was called a fairy and a puff and a queer by the macho boys and it did not seem to affect him. He carried on behaving and speaking as he always did. One afternoon Brian entered the big canvas sleeping tent he shared with several others. Ray and a little gang of three boys were already inside the tent. Ray was lying on his back on a bunk bed making small whimpering sounds. One of the three boys was lying on top of him while the other two boys sat nearby watching. They were all fully dressed but the boy on top had unfastened his shorts. Nothing else happened: just this frieze of four boys. Brian lay down on his stomach on his own bunk bed. He was aroused by the situation and yearned for one of the two watchers, to whom he was attracted, to come and lie on top of *him*. But he was unnoticed, as if he really were invisible. Soon the tent filled with other boys returning from a hike and the boy on top hastily fastened his shorts and left the tent, with his two friends in tow, leaving Ray lying on the bed. It was a frustrating dilemma for Brian: this deep attraction to the physique of other boys inside, but outside this dreamy distant boy he made himself out to be. It made him forever a secret spectator of the other developing boys around him, never a participant.

One afternoon not long before summer camp he was dawdling home from school with his closest brother David. Generally pupils in different year groups – even brothers – did not mix on walks to and from school. But Brian often attached himself to David and his friends on those long morning and afternoon school walks. It was a means of contact with non-sissy boys. He did not have to make direct contact himself and face the terrifying risk of rejection or mockery; instead he just became an appendage, as it were, of his "normal" younger brother. On this particular afternoon David tagged onto another boy in Brian's year nicknamed "Thorpy" and Brian followed. The three boys wandered up Wheatcroft Snicket munching Thorpy's sherbert lemons which he was happy to share with the two brothers. Thorpy had a greasy pale face, alive with red adolescent spots, and the beginnings of a beard, which matched his dark swarthy hair. He talked in a deep confident voice, as if he were already a middle-aged man. David was desperate to know something.

"Ey up, Thorpy. Is it true what Smithy in ma class sez? Du Dads stick ther willy up Mams' – em – *things* – ter mek babbies."

"Yer. Coorse it is Dave owd lad. Ah saw mi dad doin it ont sofa wi mi Mam las week. Thi thowt ah wor i bed. Yer shud er seen mi Dad's prick. It wah that big. An mi Mam's – er – shhh – *cunt* – ad airs all round -"

"Ooo, eurr! Shurrup Thorpy. Doo-ernt tell us any moo-er. It's *orrible*."

Brian was not as interested in the question as David. It was remote to him, what Mams and Dads did with each other, but he listened carefully in silent distant spectator mode, occasionally participating in the conversation for appearances sake. He joined David, pretending to be horrified and appalled at what Thorpy told them. The two brothers swore they would never, ever, perform such a mucky act, Brian being much more adamant than David. He learned then, and accepted, what normal penetrative heterosexual sex involved in essence. But he also knew then, that day up Wheatcroft listening to Thorpy, that heterosexual sex was something which was never likely to involve *him*.

Although he was becoming more and more aware of sex and sometimes was consumed by another lad, he froze when it came to acting upon or revealing his sexual feeling. Homosexual acts between consenting adults over the age of twenty one did not become legal in England until 1967, when Brian was twenty. Homosexuality was a profoundly taboo subject in his early adolescent world of the 1960s. In his early years at Batley High he heard words like "puff" and "pansy" and "queer" said disparagingly at best and with utter contempt and hatred at worst. It put him in a state of frozen terror to think he might be a puff, a pansy, a queer, and have these names applied to him. He deeply feared being looked down on and, even worse, being subjected to hatred, and so he stayed on the sidelines when sex reared its head, feigning indifference outside while inside trying to work it out, trying to fathom it.

From his earliest days at Batley High he avoided using the crowded toilets at break and lunch times. He held himself back until he reached home or he asked to be excused from a lesson, when he was sure the toilets would be empty of other pupils. He was not aware of any systematic open homophobic bullying or harassment at school but sometimes he observed a surge of excitement, some pushing and shoving at break times when the "on-duty" teachers were nowhere to be seen. Boys would suddenly form into a small mob with a scared victim in their midst, doing something furtive and bad inside the toilets. Brian's response to this scary behaviour was to move as far away as possible from the mob. Later he heard whispers about "cocks" and "sucking" (the term "blow-job" was quite unknown then) from the swaggering machismo boys. But he shut his mind off from what they said, distancing himself, not wanting to know.

Sometimes, walking back home from school, he could not hold back his need to urinate any longer and he used the Market Place public toilets which stank from the pool of piss permanently swirling over the floor. He hurriedly urinated, anxious to escape the smell but he also took a sneaky look at the wall above the urinals and at the doors of the toilet stalls, where every available space was full of messages and drawings – in pencil, chalk, ink, or carved and scratched into the plaster and woodwork. There were drawings of female genitalia and the names and telephone numbers of girls who were "good for a shag." But he was more intrigued, puzzled, and ultimately repelled by the drawings and messages relating to gay sex, which focused on the size of people's cocks and "cock sucking." Disgust and repulsion at what the messages were saying about male sex overcame his intrigue and curiosity and he hurried off, shutting the messages and drawings out of his consciousness, not connecting them with his own sexual desires and fantasies, which were as much about his emotional needs as they were about sex.

More than anything at this early stage of adolescence, bafflement predominated in his feelings and thoughts on sex. He was aware of his sexual feelings for other boys but was reluctant to act upon them – except the brief physical-sexual friendship with the "toy car and comics" boy. During school break times he liked to stand on his own, leaning against the practical block wall. It was a quiet area which did not become too crowded or full of threatening macho lads playing ball, chasing, having mock fighting games. It was the area where quiet loners stood, or boys stood in pairs, playing conkers, swapping cigarette cards, earnestly discussing hobbies and passions. It was a nerds and loners area. He stood on the edge listening, amused by the passions and conversations around him. One boy had begun his secondary education at Batley Grammar but had not fitted in and was transferred to Batley High. He had a round freckly face and wore thick lensed specs and had untidy and unusually long light ginger hair. He talked non-stop and fluently about the genius of someone called Buddy Holly. This was 1961/1962, when the only popular music Brian knew was what he heard on the Light Programme on the wireless at home, which rarely went beyond Lonnie Donegan and skiffle in modernity, or he listened to Moira's and Shirley's LPs of Frank Sinatra and Ella Fitzgerald performing Cole Porter lyrics, with backing from Nelson Riddle's Big Band. The Buddy Holly boy amused him and he was impressed with his fluency and intelligence. When the conversations bored him, he would observe the activities of other boys around, secretly picking out the ones he fancied. Sometimes, a more "normal" lad, Alan, left his ball or chasing game and came to talk with Brian. Alan was the taller and he liked to stand close with his legs wide apart, his hands pressed against the wall behind Brian's head, talking inconsequentially, challenging Brian to respond to his physical presence. Occasionally he wrapped his arms around Brian, holding him tightly in a bear hug. They were agonising encounters, for Brian. He was aroused but frozen, terrified of the wrongness of his feelings, not realising Alan might have feelings the same as him. So he stood frozen against the wall, not responding, waiting for Alan to become bored with his passivity and go away.

Another boy, friendly and handsomely blond and popular, sometimes came to Brian's table in art lessons, leaning over him from behind, pressing his weight on his back.

"Ey up, Ersty. Ah like way yeh've used charcoal fer is face theer. It's great."

Brian was again aroused but frozen. He responded monosyllabically, feigning boredom or mild irritation until the blond boy lost interest and left him alone. These encounters left him stirred, baffled, afraid. He feared if he responded and showed his sexual feelings these normal-seeming boys would see what a little Mary-Ann he was and be disgusted by him. He was sure they would turn their backs on him and wipe him out of their lives. How could he tell if *they* felt the same feelings as him? He could not. Was it wrong to feel the way he felt? The voice of his community said: "Yes. It most certainly is." What would happen if he showed how he felt? Rejection, he was sure.

Brian was able and confident in swimming and gymnastics. He liked these individual activities, where he could explore the capabilities of his own developing body on his own, without the threat of being ridiculed and belittled over his nervous pansy ways – a threat always present in team games. He began to shine in gymnastics and even "Siggy Sykes," the Head of PE, praised him. He found it easy to jump over boxes and stand on his hands and somersault his body and land firmly on his feet. There was one gymnastics lesson where a group of boys gathered around to watch him perform.

"Ey up, Ersty, At's a brill andstand."

"Yer, well. Look ar im. E's goh reight bild fer it, ant e?"

At home he was the tubbiest of his four immediate siblings although he was not overweight or obese. John, Malcolm and David were of a wirier build than him and he was teased and called "fatty" by them, just as he sometimes called David "four eyes" in his glasses period, or John "ginger nut" – when well out of his fist's reach. The admiration in the gym lesson secretly pleased him but it bothered him too. It did not fit the self-image by now firmly fixed in his head that he was a fatty and a sissy – and on a deeper, unarticulated level, he wanted to admire, not be admired. The role of passive outsider on the edge of physical activities was where he felt secure. Being at the centre of admiring attention bothered him. From then on, he deliberately started to play down his gymnastic skills, becoming awkward and reluctant in order to escape the limelight. He scurried to the edges from where he could admire rather than be himself the focus of admiration. His reluctance was partly caused by the terror of rejection. It was fear and confusion within himself over his "wrong feeling" of sexual attraction toward other boys. He was terrified of these feelings becoming exposed, even in his quiet place on the edges, let alone at the centre of peer group attention.

He detested the changing room culture in the gym and swimming baths. He disliked the competitiveness over physique and strength and, on a more implied inchoate level, the competing over sexual prowess. He loathed the boys who were visibly excited in the changing rooms, running around with knotted towels and flicking them on other boys' bums and genitals. A nerdy boy told him one morning break about "sadism." He took an instant dislike to the notion but on a deeper level was attracted to it, as we often are toward things we fear, and the boys in the changing rooms to him personified that tendency. He was profoundly nervous in the changing room about exposure; not just exposure of his body to the gaze of others but exposure of his wrong self, his Mary-Ann-ness, and so he huddled on the bench dressing and undressing as quickly as he could, careful to cover his private parts and shutting himself off from those who enjoyed exposing themselves and exposing others – the ones who loved grabbing at other boys' concealing towels after the showers, and pulling them off to show what the towels hid. On one occasion in the gym changing rooms a sporty but sensible and popular lad, not normally known for bullying, who Brian liked from a distance, suddenly approached him.

"What's up wi yeh, Bri? Why d'yer allus put thi shet on afore yer pants? Ah yer tryin ter ide summat?"

"Yer. e allus dus that, dunt e?"

"Yeh, e dus…"

Brian was confused and bemused by this attack: the boy and his followers seemed to want to see his body but they were not sissies. A similar thing happened in the changing cubicles at Batley Baths when a "normal" boy took great delight in climbing the cubicle wall next to his, poking his head over the top and grinning, catching him unawares.

"Got yer, Esty. Ats a nice cock. Whoa, e's blushin."

Brian did not understand the relaxed but competitive pleasure that "normal" boys seemed to get from showing their bodies off to each other. It was something he felt he could not share because of what was inside him; because of the fear that his wrongness might come humiliatingly tumbling out for all the world to see if he joined in. But although he was often solitary, threatened, uncomfortable, in the all-male ethos and culture at Batley High, he did seek out a few friends, or they sought him out. The friendships did not run deep. The foundations were insecure. Sports and the outdoor activities culture of the school drew many boys together to make deep friendships. Others loved making things in practical subjects or were grabbed by science and maths and shared these pleasures, and even the oddballs shared arcane knowledge of their passions, hobbies and obsessions. It was his sissiness and nervousness that brought him together with a few other boys. Ray Stevens was the closest he came to having a "best friend." Ray was a mixture of shocking outrageousness and deep vulnerability at the extremes and Brian avoided him when he was at either pole. But between the extremes he was funny, witty and generous. Unlike other boys, he was willing to tell some of his innermost secrets.

"Ah ate bein a lad. Ah wish ad been born a lass. Ey up, Bri. Can yer see mi weerin lipstick? Mmm! Luvly lips ant thi? An ah ate ower bluddy Kev an is pissin rugby. E can stick is bluddy rugby ball up is shitarse!"

It was a kind of catharsis – of feelings in himself left unsaid – for Brian, listening to another boy confessing these things. When Ray was in a stable serious mood, talking to him was as good as talking to the women in his family – with the added bonus that he could talk to Ray in an oblique way about sex; something he was too embarrassed to discuss with the older women in his life and something they never discussed directly with him. But even in their most intimate conversations, Brian and Ray never spoke directly about their own sexual feelings. The taboo around gayness then was too deep. It was a non-subject: there was no lexicon, no grammar, for gayness, except insults and derision, so it went unsaid; blotted out; negated; only adding to the sense of negation boys such as Brian and Ray already felt about their sexual natures, preventing a full frank friendship developing.

Another boy in Brian's friendship circle was more emphatically effeminate than Ray and was also a more angry and aggressive personality. He was paranoid over being mocked and teased. Even at this shy introverted stage of his life Brian loved showing off his mimicry skills to small audiences and his talents as a mimic made him popular with mainstream straight boys. Brian made the mistake one day of mimicking the paranoid boy at the end of the last afternoon lesson, when they were alone in Mr. Mangham's empty English classroom.

"Ooo, ah *luv* green, me. It's mi *fayvrit* culler. Ahm buyin a *green* frock ternite."

"Piss off you, Erst."

The boy flew into a temper and lunged at Brian, knocking chairs from the tops of desks where they had been placed to give the school cleaners easier access to the floor. The falling chairs made a terrific racket in the empty classroom and the caretaker heard the noise from outside, where he was cleaning a corridor. He came in and saw the disarray and promptly marched the two boys to the Headmaster. Mr. Locke was furious, calling them "Nau-au-ty ba-ad bo-oys," his usual phrase for miscreants, which Brian sometimes mimicked when teachers weren't around, to raise an easy laugh from other lads. He was aware of Mr. Locke's dislike of the other boy's mannerisms and felt he became tainted ever after in Mr. Locke's eyes, by association. He was wary of Mr. Locke after that, making himself invisible if he could in his presence, or becoming absolutely impassive. And after the chairs incident he avoided the volatile boy.

By the time he was reaching the end of the second year Brian was only at ease at home with the women in the family or when entirely alone with his imagination, thoughts and feelings. There were occasions when he had the house to himself and he would sneak into Moira's and Shirley's bedroom and undress down to his underpants (which he was wearing by now) and select from the wardrobe a skirt and a blouse or a dress and a pair of high heeled shoes. And then he carefully dressed himself in his sisters' clothes. He would then wobble to the mirror and stare at his image, wondering in a vague way what it must be like to be a girl. Or he would turn his body around quickly, making the skirt or the dress swirl, admiring the effect in the mirror with the total narcissism of a thirteen year old boy.

The phase of dressing in his big sisters' clothes and wondering about being a girl did not last long. Girls his own age were distant creatures with whom he had virtually no contact at all. Batley Girls Grammar School was half-way up Field Hill on the other side of the road from his own school and seeing the girls walking up and down the hill in the mornings and afternoons was the nearest he came to girls his own age. He knew nothing about girls and dressing in female clothing gave him no real pleasure, imaginative stimulation, or transformation. After a while his secret game lost its allure: it gave him nothing like the pleasure, stimulation and transformation he gained from writing a story, or sketching with charcoal, or reading.

During the third year Brian became more adept at creating a role for himself among his peers. He was nervous, troubled, guilty and ashamed about his inner sexual feelings and what he felt was his wrongness and he avoided close contact with other boys, apart from Ray, the paranoid boy and one or two other nervous misfits. But unlike Ray and the others, he was becoming more and more skilled at concealing his nature and feelings. He was skilled at making himself invisible but when circumstances forced him into the limelight he was equally skilled in adopting a persona which the normal boys liked and respected. The persona he cloaked himself in was that of a boy who was a good mimic; a boy who could imitate teachers and other kids, bringing out their oddities and absurdities in his mimicry, to the amusement of his small audiences. He was also gradually adopting a new voice. It was not exactly a posh voice, like Jennifer's at Juniors, but it was moving steadily away from the broad Batley Yorkshire of his family into something more like Educated Northern and this, along with his ever expanding vocabulary, gave him a certain status with other lads. It gave him distance, so they did not notice his queerness, his ineptitude at practical skills, maths, science and sports, or his nervous sense of his wrongness. His new voice also concealed his family's relative poverty about which he was becoming more acutely aware. The new voice was less Yorkshire-sounding than most other lads and it gave him distance and simultaneously enabled him to blend in more easily with the upper working class and middle class boys who were in the majority in the higher streams at Batley High.

He was not aware of it at the time, being too preoccupied with his inner troubles, but his good looks and short sturdy physique also gave him status among his peers. Although they rarely admitted it the "normal" majority were sharply aware of their ranking in the good looks pecking order. Looks were important to them in attracting the opposite sex and good looks helped establish their place among their own-sex peers. At fourteen, Brian was entirely focused on his own concealments; on developing a persona which would enable him to feel comfortable in the world of school; a world which ignored and misunderstood his sexual nature. He did not realise the normal boys also concealed inner anxieties – especially about looks – underneath the tough gritty Yorkshire exterior they routinely adopted and were expected to adopt by family and community alike.

Brian had no contact with females around his own age and no interest in them sexually. In a mixed-sex school he would undoubtedly have made close platonic friendships with girls. He was comfortable, happy and relaxed with the older women he knew and although he never broached his inner anxieties in a direct way he was at least able to express his ideas, hopes and ambitions to them. Had the chance to make friends with girls arisen he might have been able to express to someone his own age – someone other than himself – his growing sense of his own nature and personality and in doing so relieve some of his inner anxiety and develop his true and natural self. But the opportunity to know girls his own age did not arise and so he rigidly pursued his efforts to conceal his real self behind a crafted persona; he worked hard on making his true self invisible to others. He was already burying his real self out of sight of the world at the age of fourteen.

At home Brian was finding his own niche in the ever growing family. He felt trapped and stifled by the weight of his four older heterosexual brothers and four heterosexual younger brothers, not to mention Bob. He was the middle one of nine brothers. He was the queer one trapped in the centre of a sandwich of normal ones all around him. There was always an unease in Brian toward Bob and toward the unbending maleness of his brothers, to varying degrees. By the time he reached fourteen the women in his family included Mary, Louie, Granma, Shirley, Moira, Sheila and Dot. They were all, in different ways, strong and assertive personalities and more than capable of holding their own in a male-majority family. Mary, and to a less extent Louie and Granma, provided Brian with rock-solid unqualified love and support. He was Mary's bairn, Louie's nephew, Granma's granbairn, and that was enough for them. Moira and Shirley gave him the same unqualified love and they inspired him with the successes they were making of their own lives. They gave him encouragement and support to pursue his idea of staying-on at school to become a teacher and their support influenced Mary who might, left to herself and to the mindset of her generation and class, have otherwise routinely expected him to leave school at fifteen to become a builder, a miner, or a mill worker. Sheila was an articulate conversationalist and Brian loved the hours spent listening to her, joining in when she paused for breath. Dot was nearest to him in age and to some extent in development and temperament. She was six years older and still growing, searching for her place in the world and for identity, and a strong bond grew between them.

Brian soaked himself in the domestic female part of his extended family where he felt safe and secure from the otherwise male world in which he lived. He became indispensable to Mary who was running the home and caring for Barry's two bairns and sometimes Shirley's, Moira's and Young Bob's bairns too. He helped her with chores in the house – cooking, washing up, cleaning the gas cooker, scrubbing floors, running errands, entertaining Michael and the other bairns, making beds. One day while tidying a brother's bed he felt something soft and gluey on his fingers. It was semen. It was the first sign he had that his brothers had sexual bodies like his and it shocked him rigid. But after the shocking realisation, it left him feeling sad that he and his brothers never talked to each other about sex.

All of Brian's older six siblings left school to become wage-earners at fifteen. Brian, as a non-wage earner, made himself indispensable to his married siblings and their spouses by becoming a reliable and always available baby-sitter and helper. He welcomed the chance to earn money. He was happy to push Shirley's two daughters in their big stately Silver Cross Royal Blue pram (which could not be folded up and stored on a bus) all the way from Staincliffe to Birstall so that Shirley could catch the bus home with her heavy shopping bags after her visits to Chapel Fold. Shirley's pram was a big purring Jaguar or Rover and he was the driver passing through rolling vistas of beautiful countryside. From the arrival of Barry's Linda when he was aged ten, followed in quick succession by the births of Christopher, Michael, Julie and Shirley's Linda – and a non-stop line of nephews and nieces after – Brian thought nothing of being called to hold a feed bottle to a bairn, or entertain one, or bounce one on his lap, or walk one down the front passage and round the back garden, or push one in a pram or Tansad around Staincliffe Estate and beyond. He threw himself into all this as an escape from his inner self, from the fundamentally alien male world around him; in school, in the family and in the wider Batley community.

It was during the third year that he became baby-sitter-in-chief for Shirley and Jimmy and he kept that role for a further four years until he reached eighteen and left Batley for college. He grew close to Shirley and Jimmy. There was more space for him to be himself in the small family at Birstall than there was at Chapel Fold and although his inner anxieties were never a topic of discussion, conversations with Shirley and with Jimmy expanded his mind and gave him confidence to express his own ideas and hopes in a relatively uninhibited way; something that was difficult to achieve in the crowded, competitive and often broodingly angry world of Chapel Fold.

At the end of year nine when he was nearing fifteen Brian accompanied Shirley and her family on a one-week holiday to Filey. His brother-in-law Jimmy had two sisters and three much older half-sisters. One of Jimmy's half-sisters, Edie, married Alf, who owned an ancient van which he converted himself into a rudimentary motor caravan with fitted benches and a small table. With Edie in tow, Alf transported them all in his van to Filey. It was Brian's first sighting of Edie and Alf, though he had heard about them from Shirley and Jimmy, who made him laugh with their satirical accounts of this fractious, prickly and distinctly oddball couple. It was an hilarious start to the holiday on a boiling hot August day. The eighty mile journey took hours. The main roads of England were extremely congested in the 1950s and 1960s even though car-owners among the lower working classes were still scarce. Alf dared not drive the van faster than 30mph and even then the engine kept boiling over and frequent radiator water top-up stops were made.

Edie and Alf were in their early-fifties at the time (1961) but their lifestyle, speech and mannerisms were rooted well into the previous century. Edie was a tiny nutmeg brown woman with angry jet black Irish eyes. She never used make-up and wore the plainest, drabbest clothes and shoes imaginable. Alf was small and wiry with inward vivid blue eyes and a shiny red sunburned bald head. The couple lived in a permanent state of relentless warfare. Alf's sole tactic of attack was to totally ignore Edie, acting as if she were not there, and throughout the long journey he only spoke to Jimmy in little staccato bursts of speech and only about the van's engine problems. Edie seethed and hissed with irritation, anger, rage at Alf and she directed all her attacks on him through Shirley or Jimmy. (She once told Shirley she and Alf *never* spoke directly to each other when they were alone.) Brian was accustomed to broad Batley-speak but Alf and Edie spoke a much older, almost pre-industrial form of Yorkshire dialect which has now almost entirely disappeared except in the remoter parts of North and East Yorkshire:

EDIE: "Sherr-li, lass. Tha nors. Ah towd Alf teh wee-er is noo shet this morr-nin. Burr as e tekkn any gorm? As e buggery!"

ALF: "Tha see-ers, Jimmy lad. It's yon gaskit thee-er. Bugger's worn reet dahn."

Brian could barely suppress his laughter. It was not so much the couple themselves or their speech that made him want to laugh, it was that he had heard it all before in Shirley's and Jimmy's imitations. The humour in the situation was trying to keep a straight face through it all and watching Shirley and Jimmy valiantly trying to keep straight faces too.

He loved the week in Filey. They stayed in a large rambling flat in a huge Edwardian house on The Crescent owned by a woman Moira had worked with at Filey Butlins Holiday Camp. They could be themselves in the flat with no snooty fellow guests looking down on them. The rooms in the flat were vast with enormous high ceilings and windows and, to his intense pleasure, Brian had a bedroom to himself. He kept the sash window open all night and listened to the seagulls and the surging suck and exhalation of the sea tide from just a few yards away. Some evenings Shirley and Jimmy went to a nearby pub and he baby-sat in the vast flat, reading and munching sweets while sitting on the big window sill in the living room, smelling the sea outside and listening intently to its sibilant sounds. Mornings in the flat were marvellous with Jimmy invariably cheerful and busy in the kitchen, cooking a big breakfast. His speciality was caramel brown fried onion, with bacon, egg, sausage and tomatoes which Brian thought was wonderful and Shirley sniffed at.

"Ahm not ser sure wi shud be avin onions fer brekfest, Jimmy."

Brian spent daytimes on the beach when the thunderstorms were not rumbling. He sunbathed when the sun came out or shivered with towels wrapped round his shoulders when the sun went in. Or he entertained Julie and Linda, or dug the sand with their tin toy buckets and spades, making sandcastles for them to marvel at. Or he laughed at Jimmy's jokes and "sarky" comments about other sunbathers around.

"Ell fiy-er. Look at yon fella's belly, ovver theer. By! Ee musta supped a few tankers-ful er Tetleys in is time!"

It was a week of drifting for Brian; drifting through sandy days. The week was an island, aeons away from Chapel Fold, school and the inside turbulence of a homosexual adolescent in an uncomprehending world. There was stability and happiness in Brian's life when he was at Shirley's and Jimmy's and when he was with Mam, Moira, Sheila or Dot. But he was most at peace when he was alone and solitary and surprisingly, in that large family, the opportunities of being alone were plentiful. David was more gregarious, more at ease and comfortable in the world outside home, where he spent much of his leisure time and his frequent outings from home often enabled Brian to have the bedroom they shared to himself. Money was always scarce. Quite often Mary literally did not have a penny to spare and it was inconceivable to expect anything from Bob. Brian welcomed his two shillings baby-sitting fee from Jimmy but he always needed more, not just for spogs and crisps but to buy small items of equipment for school, such as a newly fashionable biro, then gradually re-placing the bits of stick with a tin nib on the end routinely given to pupils at school who did not own their own fountain pens. A real status symbol at the time among his peers was a Parker fountain pen and he longed to own one. But he knew the only way he could own a Parker was to buy one himself.

David had the confidence, encouraged by Mary, to go to the newsagent down Mount Pleasant and ask if a paper boy was needed and, to his delight, he was immediately offered a job. Brian was too nervous to ask, certain he would not cope and convinced he would be considered too timid to do the job. As usual Mam stepped in.

"David, owd lad. Ask et paper shop if thiv gorra a round gooin spare for ower Brian. Yer naw worr e's like. Too bluddy shy ter ask fer is-sen."

If David had not asked Brian would have stayed jobless. Mam was right. He did not have the courage to ask himself. He enjoyed working on the early morning paper round although at the beginning there was a big hindrance in the shape of Sam, the black half-corgi family pet, who Bob insisted should accompany Brian on his round. "Pet" was hardly the word to sum up Sam's cantankerous malign spirit. He persistently behaved disgracefully, ignoring Brian's commands to keep close by – picking fights with other dogs right within their very own territorial patches as Brian pushed papers through letter boxes.

"Mam! Ahm not tekkin ower Sam wi me no more ont paper round. He's gunner lose mi mi job, he is."

"No, luv. Yer reight. E's a bluddy nuisance, an nor arf. You goo on yer own from termorrer luv. An what are you lookin at, sour puss? It's about time yer took him fer is bluddy walks yersen, Bob. E's *yoor* bluddy dog. Insted er leavin it teh yeh bairns."

He enjoyed the early morning paper round much more without Sam, delivering papers like the *Times* and

Telegraph to private houses near Chapel Fold. The big detached houses had long front drives with garages to the side and endless-seeming back gardens. He enjoyed the solitude, glad of the chance to be alone with his dreams and hopes. He had lost the capacity of his younger self, just absorbing the immediate physical world and the fascinating transformations that endlessly occur around you when you look closely. His focus of interest was becoming more social. He was interested in the kind of lives the people might lead in the houses where he delivered the newspapers. He read the front pages, learning who Harold Macmillan was, and Selwyn Lloyd, and the meaning of Conservative and Labour, although the world of national politics was all very distant from his world. The quiet solitary space at the beginning of the day was when he first began to see himself quite consciously as an outsider. It was a space in which he could think and try to work out what it meant: being an "outsider." He dreamed and yearned and planned how he would change his life when he grew up. He would have his own car, a big house, a professional job – and maybe even a wife and children, though at the back of his mind he knew the latter would most likely not happen.

He thought how he and his world were gradually changing. He was moving from one place of being to another. There was still no television or telephone at home and Bob would never own a car but Barry owned all three of these desirable status symbols and Shirley was rapidly catching up. His mind was filled with these reflections on his changing world. He was making that massive change we all make from childhood to adolescence. He was earning money now, enough to buy a Parker fountain pen (and the bottle of "Quink" ink that went with it) and he bought small items of clothing with the money he earned: socks, underpants, cheap polo neck sweaters from Dewsbury market stalls and copious quantities of spogs and crisps which he gobbled voraciously. He was on the way to doing something no one in his immediate family had done: staying on at school after the minimum school leaving age of fifteen. It was July 1961 when he reached the end of the third year. He was four months away from his fifteenth birthday. He was wearing the same uniform as other boys at school with the help of clothing grants from the West Riding County Council and he was eating school dinners with better-off boys than him although *his* dinners were free. He was wearing underpants now and bed-wetting less and fewer of his clothes "kem frum rags." He had been on school camp (aided by another WRCC grant) and was about to go to Filey for a whole week long – "Wi Sherrli an Jimmy in Alf's van." Soon he was going to move away from shitty old Batley. He was going to be a teacher.

The nerds and loners corner at Batley High

*School photo –
Brian aged 14*

"SOCIAL MOBILITY" AND "DIFFERENCE"

Metalwork, science, maths and technical drawing were left behind when Brian started O level courses in English, English Literature, History, Geography, Divinity and Art in September 1961. He continued to endure the dreaded compulsory weekly PE lesson and there was also a compulsory Careers lesson each week. If the current "balanced object" of the National Curriculum in the GCSE years had existed in 1961, with its mix of compulsory maths, English, a technical subject and a science, Brian would have rejected "staying on." Instead, he would have chosen to leave school at the end of his first term in the fourth year, just three weeks after his fifteenth birthday, to go and work down pit, in mill, in a shop, or in a bottom-ladder office job. English, PE and Careers were compulsory in the GCE fourth and fifth year streams at Batley High in 1961. English was the only "academic" subject considered vital for every boy to take, right up to leaving school, PE helped keep the body fit and healthy and Careers was compulsory because many boys did not survive the O Level course and dropped out of school to go into the world of work and earn some brass. Brian would not have coped with compulsory science, maths and technology. Continuing those subjects would have meant prolonging the "torture" he experienced in his first two years at Batley High. On top of this, none of the adult members of his family had the time, or in some cases the knowledge, to help him with these subjects. His oldest two male siblings, Barry and Bob, had the knowledge, both being good at technical subjects and maths, but they had not themselves taken O Levels, and besides this, they were too busy leading their own lives.

The teachers who helped Brian choose his O level subjects knew him well. They did not need endless tick box forms to know his strengths and vulnerabilities. They knew him through human contact and observation and they judged him capable of passing some subjects at O level with good grades. They knew his strong and weak subjects. They knew if he was forced to take subjects he hated and feared he would shrink into himself, no matter how much attention they gave him, and he would leave school at fifteen without O Levels or any other qualifications. (The short-lived "CSE" was not introduced into schools until some years after and O level was the only formal qualification available in general subjects during the early 1960s. There was also an RSA exam, suited to technical and scientifically minded pupils.) The school did however insist on pupils taking a minimum of six O level subjects. Brian would have been happier not taking geography but he reluctantly accepted the need to take it in order to meet the minimum six-subject rule. There were many pupils in his year who were strong in maths, science and technology but weak in English. They were not as fortunate as Brian. In theory, they could not gain a maths, science or engineering place in higher education without O Level English and so were forced to study it. The school focused on individual strengths primarily. Technical and science-minded boys came out with top grades in their strong subjects at O level, most of them also succeeding in gaining an O Level in English. Others gained just a scrape pass in English, after three or four attempts. There were some who, on the strength of their high science, maths and technology grades at O and A Level, gained higher education places in those subjects, without passing the "required" O Level English. Many of those "boys" are now no doubt coming to the end of long successful careers in science and engineering, despite their lack of an O Level in English – a lack which would horrify today's rigid, inflexible-minded, curriculum-makers and enforcers.

The school ensured a reasonable spread of subjects in insisting pupils study a minimum of six O Levels but fundamentally the system was there to fit the child rather than the child fitting the system. Putting the child's capabilities first meant that children from disadvantaged backgrounds, such as Brian, were given a good helping hand onto the first step of the educational ladder beyond the minimum school leaving age. Children from more advantaged backgrounds who happened to be weak at English, or maths, or science, were also *helped*, rather than hindered, in the child-first system. There is powerful evidence that many children, especially those from disadvantaged backgrounds or those with pronounced weaknesses in particular areas of knowledge and skills, "fail" in the de-personalised, over-systematised educational regime of today, compared with the child-centred ethos in enlightened schools such as Batley High in its early years. You only have to look nowadays at the numbers of disaffected young males on street corners, many trapped in the drugs culture, and single girls pushing prams around our town centres, most of them in the "disadvantaged" class, to *see* the evidence. Many lower working class children in the 1960s succeeded in going on to further and higher education. Far fewer from today's "disadvantaged" groups manage to reach the same educational level that significant numbers of disadvantaged children reached in the 1960s.

*

None of these conundrums were in Brian's mind when he started O Levels. He was just happy to shed the trembling fear and confusion he felt in the physics and chemistry labs, the humiliating incomprehension of the maths room and the sheer terror of the mad Scotsman's metalwork shop, with its whirring lathes, vicious vices and cold nauseous smells of oil and metal. He was a homosexual adolescent in an all-male aggressively heterosexual school. The pervasive sense within him of wrongness, of being different, of being an outsider, and the deep anxiety which this constantly caused, deepened during the O Level years. But he felt more at home, more confident about himself and his capabilities in the English, history and divinity classrooms, and in the "comfort" of the art room, than he did in the maths and science rooms, or in the nightmare of the metalwork shop. And to his surprise, he sometimes enjoyed geography, his most "scientific" subject, when it involved learning the position of countries and oceans on the globe.

But the best thing of all about starting the fourth year was making a new real friend: someone he could be himself with: someone with whom he could share his inner turbulence, hopes and fears. Batley High already had an excellent reputation, only two years after it opened. The school appealed to working and middle class aspirational parents from all around the West Riding Heavy Woollen District. These were usually parents whose sons had failed the eleven plus; parents who were desperate for a secondary school which would provide their boy with good O and A Levels and maybe even help him gain a place in higher education. Several new boys joined the school in Brian's fourth year. Two of them were placed in his registration group and in some of his subject classes. Brian was well versed by now at spotting "posh fowk" – who he was now learning to call "middle class" – from a mile off and he saw immediately that both new boys in his class were middle class, but not high up in that league. They both spoke with Yorkshire accents but not "broad Batley." They used the definite article, for example, rather than t'ubiquitous "absent definite article" of Batley-speak. Both boys, it turned out, had spent three years at a small private day school of dubious quality in their home town near Batley and their parents had withdrawn them, favouring instead the good quality education offered by George Locke at Batley High, a Local Education Authority school run by the West Riding County Council under the leadership of its progressive and nationally admired Chief Education Officer, Alex Clegg, who was later awarded a knighthood.

Billy and Philip were both tall and thin. Billy was blond and sporty; good looking, in a fey way. He played "soft" sports such as tennis, cricket and football and so he was never included in the in-crowd of serious rugby players at Batley High. He wanted to be a PE teacher but was plagued by serious asthma and what seemed to be a permanent heavy cold. Both boys were nervous types in different ways and they were initially shocked and uncomfortable, confronted by the aggressive straight culture of the dominant majority at Batley High – when teachers were not around. Brian warmed to both new boys immediately when he saw how nervous and uncomfortable they were, suddenly finding themselves plunged into the Batley High culture. Billy was tall and lithe. Philip was tall, gangly, and seriously un-coordinated physically, and wore glasses, and had bad facial acne. The first thing Philip told Brian was how he detested all sports, especially rugby. Brian liked Billy's quiet shy personality and his way of hovering somewhere between the mainstream culture and the nerdy loner end of school life and they remained quite good occasional friends for the next four years. Brian and Philip immediately fell into a close friendship.

Philip soon became Brian's first real friend of his own age and sex. The nearest he came to the friendship he had with Philip were the relationships he had with his older sisters and sisters-in-law, where he could be more fully himself than he could with the male members of his family and the vast majority of straight boys at school. His friendship with Philip immediately offered more than his existing friendships with Ray and the paranoid boy; with the clever nerds; with the mainstream machismo boys who befriended him. From the start, being with Philip, listening to him, watching him, talking to him, was like being both with himself and simultaneously being with someone very different. It was an absorbing, fascinating, stretching and deeply comforting new experience for Brian: real friendship with another boy.

The friendship was intensely verbal from the start. The two boys chattered ceaselessly, often to the irritation of teachers and to the bemusement of other boys watching them together. They chattered throughout the morning registration session. They chattered when walking down corridors to assembly. They chattered during lessons, when they could. They chattered throughout break and lunch times. They chattered about everything: their families, their homes, the differences in their backgrounds. Philip was the only child of a senior civil servant father and a college secretary mother. He lived in a modest terraced Victorian house in his home town but his father was well-off enough to buy a brand new car every two years and the family took holidays in upmarket hotels in Scarborough or Bournemouth. Philip's uncle had a BA in English and was the Headmaster of a suburban school in his university town, a school even bigger than Batley High. In contrast, Brian had Uncle James. Brian was intrigued by the idea of having no siblings constantly bothering you and a whole bedroom all to yourself and a "graduate" headmaster uncle. Philip was equally fascinated by the size of Brian's family and told Brian how he had always longed for siblings. In a garrulous, uninhibited, endless stream of chatter they each educated the other about a different social strata and it stretched them personally and socially as well as giving them great pleasure and satisfaction.

It was not long before they confided more intimate things to each other. They discussed their dislike and fear of the dominant culture of the boys and many of the staff at Batley High, and the intolerance and even hatred which prevailed of anyone, such as Ray, who dared be openly different. They discovered they had a great deal in common in the difficult relationships they had with their fathers and the deep love and affection they felt for their mothers. They discovered they shared the same fundamental problem with their fathers: a profound sense of not being loved, of not living up to the manly expectations their fathers had of them. Philip's father nagged him constantly and was often snide and witheringly scathing about his unsportiness and his sometimes "nancy-boy" ways, whereas Brian's father rarely spoke to him at all, although looks said everything.

They talked about sex. Philip was more willing to talk about his sexuality and his attraction to his own sex, whereas Brian held back longer before revealing to Philip his own sexuality – his profound sense of shame inhibiting him from talking easily about sex. Brian was invited to stay for weekends at Philip's home. They shared Philip's bedroom, each in a single bed with just a small bedside table between them. Brian saved up enough money from baby-sitting and paper round fees to buy a brand new pair of pyjamas, especially to wear for his first weekend visit to Philip's house. On the first night they lay in their separate beds on their sides, facing each other, with only the small table between, and talked well into the early hours about their similar – and differing – sexual feelings and orientation.

As well as similarities, there were marked differences in Brian's and Philip's personalities and aptitudes, and the differences prevented the relationship from becoming too inward and self-referencing. Their differences kept a balance of distance between them and created a mutual respect for the other's strengths and separateness. Philip was good at maths and sciences and, apart from English and English Literature, where they constantly vied with each other to come out with top marks in the class, they studied different subjects. Brian was happy to listen to Philip's problems with algebra or his difficulties with the rugby-playing lout he was forced to sit next to in maths. Philip listened to Brian's problems with geography and sometimes his problems coping with a troublesome boy who was made by the teacher to sit on the empty seat next to him in divinity lessons.

By the age of sixteen Brian was skilled at projecting a persona to the rest of the world behind which he kept secrets, and observed, learning to simulate the ways of the world out there in his outward demeanour and manner. Nowadays we have the vocabulary to describe this sort of behaviour. He was becoming more and more adept at being "a straight-acting gay boy." He had developed his own ways of surviving the dominant culture of the school. He was skilled at cool sardonic glances aimed at potentially aggressive enemies, knowing this was a good ploy in distracting them from making physical or verbal attacks upon him. He was skilled at avoiding eye-contact with really dangerous boys and at protecting his own space from intruders. When necessary he would use verbal wit and mimicry to protect himself from attack and from the exposure of his inner self which he constantly feared.

In the English class Brian and Philip were scared of a notorious bully who used his physical strength to dominate and humiliate boys weaker than him. Brian detested the bully-boy's hangers-on, who got away with bullying, knowing they were protected by their leader. He particularly loathed a thin, weedy, squeaky-voiced acolyte whose favourite trick was to snatch Brian's pen, ruler, text book – or another item – from his desk as he walked past on some pretext to the teacher for being out of his seat. The weed did this once too often when the English teacher left the classroom for several minutes – and Brian snapped. He leapt from his seat and snatched back the item the boy had taken.

"Get lost, Smithy. That's *my* bluddy ruler, not yours. Moron!"

He glared directly into Smithy's face, daring him to retaliate. The teacher's reappearance gave Smithy the excuse to go back to his seat but Brian noted the fear in his beady little watery black eyes and it was something he learnt to do from that time: stand up to threats and face enemies down. It gave him a frisson of pleasure when he realised Smithy was scared of his own strong stocky frame and even though a physical contest was the last thing he wanted, he learnt he could draw on his physique and his good looks to protect himself.

Philip was naturally more transparent than Brian. He was several inches taller but weak and gangily thin and the class bully and his hangers-on terrified him. He had his own tactics for dealing with the more threatening elements of life at Batley High. Whenever he looked in danger of attack or threat he deliberately posed, deliberately exaggerated, the gormless grinning gangly idiot with the posh voice.

"Oy, thee! Gerrart en mi fuckin roo-ed, will yeh?"

"Oh, I say. So sorry. Was I in your way? I didn't realise. I'll move, shall I?"

The ploy invariably worked. It deflected the tough boys and made their attacks on him pointless: what was the point of attacking someone who was already a gibbering idiot anyway? Philip had learnt well from years spent deflecting his father's verbal attacks. When not under threat from alien life forms at Batley High, Philip was a more extrovert character than Brian. He was fascinated by theatre and films and what was left of the music hall tradition at Leeds

City of Variety Theatre. He revelled in telling Brian which artists in the shows he saw were "queers" but it was a world that repelled Brian, who was already looking for something "deeper," something more "intellectual," from entertainment. But he listened, sceptically-intrigued, to Philip's showbiz gossip.

Brian got to know Philip's parents during weekends spent at their house. They were pleasant toward him although there was always a slight distance. He suspected the distance was connected to what they knew of his family background, which fascinated Philip, who utterly lacked class snobbery. Despite the distancing he could see they were pleased their nervy only child had made a close friend of a seemingly ordinary Batley High lad, even though the lad was thoroughly working class.

A Parents Evening was held in year eleven and Brian accompanied Mary, helping her find her way around the school to see the different teachers, each in their own domain. As they approached the main doors of the school, he saw Philip's parents emerging. He smiled, ready to turn on the charm, and pointed them out to Mary. He was pleased, but a little apprehensive also, at the idea of introducing his Mam to his best friend's parents. They all met just outside the doors. Brian and Mary smiled, ready to talk. But Philip's Dad looked at the ground and shuffled past, as if Mary and Brian were not there and his "Mum" swept past, ostentatiously ignoring Mary, briefly smiling at Brian and murmering a greeting. And off they scuttled to the car park. Mary said nothing and her face was blank but she knew it was a brush-off. To Brian, it was a repeat of those patronising fowk in the New Brighton B&B all over again, only this time it was worse because by now he was old enough to know exactly what was happening: it was class snobbery at its most petty and mean and it sickened him to the core.

The incident set off a whole train of thoughts and resolutions inside him as he sat outside various classrooms waiting for his Mam to come out from talking to his teachers. He decided he would never introduce her to middle class friends and their parents again. He could not bear the hurt she must have felt and he hated how bad it made him feel. He felt both he and Mary had been stabbed, wounded. He decided he would not tell Philip about it. It was not about him. It was about his parents. Furthermore he knew Philip was desperate to spend a weekend at Chapel Fold and meet his family, and Brian was desperate for him not to. He knew Philip would manipulate the situation to push for a visit even more, to prove *he* at least did not care about Brian's class background. He thought bleakly, starkly, about the difference in dress and appearance between his Mam, and Philip's Mum. Mary was working at Percy Walkers at the time and she had washed off the day's grime with Fairy Household Soap and put a frock on, underneath a plain coat. She wore comfortable old flat shoes which were nice for walking the long mile from Chapel Fold to Batley High, after a hard day at work, and she carried just her purse with a few coins inside, and perhaps a hanky in her pocket. Philip's Mum wore heavy make-up and smelled of perfume. She wore a hat with a couple of feathers sticking from it; a waist-length brown fur coat; a tight fitting tweedy skirt; rich brown leather high heel shoes and a smart leather handbag draped over one arm.

Brian decided he was impervious to Philip's parents and their petty class values: *he* was just a fussy fat bald manager with an inflated sense of his own importance and a petty tyrant in his little home empire: *she* was pathetic and completely enslaved to the fat bald tyrant, giggling like an idiot at his constant snide attacks on her, then crying like a baby to Philip when *he* was out of the house. He decided his "Mam" was worth a million of Philip's "Mum" and he was going to be especially nice to her on the long walk back home. He loved his Mam and that would never change. He loved her *umbilically* – his current vogue word – and that was just a fact! But he decided then and there that nobody; not Philip's Mum, *nobody* was ever going to look down on *him* like *they'd* looked down on his Mam. He would not give people the chance. He would do everything he could to make sure it never happened. He did not know what this "everything" was that he was going to do to protect himself from class snobbery – and hatred from others over his sexual nature – which he axiomatically and entirely illogically conflated with his social class. All he knew was how to conceal these features within himself – by disguising, slowly wiping out, his natural speech and accent and slowly suffocating his sexual feelings under the false exterior he presented to the world of being a "normal" heterosexual boy.

Mam enjoyed her chat with his teachers. They were all "luvli an said nowt too nasty" about him. She was in a good mood on the way back, gossiping about this and that and not mentioning the brief encounter with Philip's parents. She splashed out on chips for him and a fish cake for herself from a chip shop *en route* from school to home and they ate from the opened wrapping paper as they ambled home:

"Ooo, batter on this fish cakes a bit moist. What's yeh chips like, Brian?"

Later that night in bed he brooded over Philip's parents and shame filled him when he remembered an incident a couple of years earlier. He was walking with a group of boys just after school, along Commercial Street, Down Batley. He did not know the boys well and they knew nothing about his home or family. Suddenly he saw Mam walking out of the Thrift Stores, dressed as she had been tonight and carrying heavy bags of groceries. He was sure she had seen him but he pretended he had not seen her and continued walking past, feigning total fascination in what another boy was saying to him. Had Mam seen him and realised that he had seen her? He was sure she had. He was abjectly ashamed now of ignoring her, of cutting her out, realising the hurt he might have caused. It was before he became familiar with the early paintings of Van Gogh (*The Potato Eaters* phase); Brecht's Mother Courage; the working class females in the novels of D.H. Lawrence; the poetry and characters in Crabbe's *Parish*. From such works as these he learned about working class women's stoicism, irrepressibility and their indomitable spirit; qualities which Mary had in plenty. But that night he also saw and understood her generosity of spirit and tolerance in the face of meanness, and wished he could be the same.

Underneath the grinning gangly exterior, a steely dogged manipulative will lurked inside Philip and eventually he had his way about staying-over on a Saturday night at Chapel Fold. Mam and the younger-end were intrigued by the idea of this posh lad's visit. Bob also seemed interested and a little amused. Perhaps he was pleased his strangely sensitive, sometimes fragile middle son had at last found a proper friend he seemed to care about. It was not a girlfriend but at least it was a friend. The visit was carefully orchestrated. The oldest four siblings were already married and living in their own homes. Malcolm was away in the army. David was staying-over at the home of a friend as he often did at weekends and Philip would sleep in his bed. And miracle of miracles, John agreed to sleep on the sofa downstairs for the night. That just left the four youngest and his parents to fill the remaining three bedrooms. Easy!

Philip arrived for Saturday tea and loved being climbed over by the younger-end. His obvious lack of skill in handling small children tickled everyone. The kids were packed off to bed early. John left for his clubs and pubs (and girls) dressed in his best Saturday going-out clothes.

Just before Bob and Mary left for a night at the Nash, Bob astonished Brian by presenting him with two bottles of beer.

"Ere yare, lads. Get that dahn thi sens. It's a reight good bitter is Tetleys."

"What the bluddy ell ah yow up teh, Bob. Fancy! Gi'in em beer."

"Goo an shite, Mary. It's what lads do: sup beer!"

They supped the miraculous Tetleys and talked when at last they were on their own. The talk was desultory on Brian's part. Philip was eager to discover everything he could about the Hirst family life, while Brian was anxious just to get the whole weekend over without mishap. It all went well for the rest of the evening up to Bob and Mary returning – and Bob surprisingly quite sober. But then, to Brian's deep chagrin, John returned, rolling drunk, after everyone was in bed. Everyone at Chapel Fold heard him – singing at the top of his voice all down the street and into the house; having a party all on his own. Brian tried his best to laugh it off but he was mortified. He convinced himself that the bastard was doing it on purpose: there was a *price* to pay for him giving up his bed for the night. Philip, however, loved it.

"So *that's* what it's like, having an older brother who works down a mine!"

The friendship with Philip was the only thing Brian enjoyed about the two O Level years. He endured and coped with everything else. The friendship remained strong although Philip had a fuller life than Brian outside school. Brian had the family, baby-sitting, his paper round, Chapel Fold and the occasional weekend at Philip's house. Philip enjoyed regular weekend trips to "shows" in Leeds, Bradford, Wakefield, Sheffield and sometimes even London. He went on his own or with his mother and her work friends. Philip loved ballroom dancing and often partnered girls from his Mum's office in the dance halls around Wakefield. He loved ten-pin bowling and became more and more involved with the younger crowd of girls in his Mum's office: with one girl in particular near the end of the fifth year. Philip did his best to persuade Brian to join him at the bowling alley, promising him a girl, a friend of his friend, to make up a foursome. Brian struggled to raise the money and the wardrobe. The idea of mixing with girls scared him but he did join Philip and his girlfriend, Clare and her friend Alice on an evening at the bowling alley. He enjoyed the bowling game but was utterly lost about how to behave toward Alice. She was from another world and meant nothing to him. Brian was sad when Philip decided not to stay on to take A Levels. He gained a job at sixteen in local government administration in Leeds working on a new miraculous thing called a "computer," after passing the required 'O' Levels in maths, sciences and English. They remained good friends, meeting each other often throughout Brian's sixth-form years, but after that the friendship gradually faded.

The friendship with Philip and meeting his parents gave Brian more confidence socially and made him a more relaxed and confident person at school. But taking 'O' Levels had its difficulties. He was doing something no one in the family had ever done: he was staying on at school full-time after the minimum school leaving age. All his older siblings had taken apprenticeships after they left school at fifteen but the apprenticeships were combined with working and earning a wage and their training was done on-the-job and on one-day release at Technical School and did not often involve homework. Homework was difficult. There was a sense at Chapel Fold it was something bairns did, not a grown lad who was old enough to work. Finding a quiet space and a surface to do the work was problematic. Mary did her best to give Brian the space and quiet he needed to do the homework but sometimes a baby needed entertaining, or feeding, or taken back home, or an errand needed running, or the washing up done, or the gas cooker cleaned and it was Brian, as the oldest child in the family not earning his keep and not doing a "real" job, who had these tasks thrust on him, or more accurately, it was Brian who willingly took on these jobs, often without being asked. He wanted to prove to his Mam how much he appreciated the support she was giving him in staying on at school.

At school the aggressive all-male culture dominated and Brian continued to feel undermined, alienated and an outsider. But things were beginning to change, slightly. A female drama teacher, Margaret Millicent Isherwood, was appointed to the teaching staff. Miss Isherwood was disabled and could only walk by using crutches or a wheelchair. She parked her disabled person's adapted Ford Popular car right in front of the school's main entrance doors to save her struggling from the staff car park into the main teaching block. She had a formidable reputation for strict discipline and even the most macho boys were scared of her. Occasionally Brian heard her speaking when giving a drama announcement in assembly. She had wonderful BBC elocution (with a hint of Yorkshire) and a lovely high modulated timbre to her voice. Many years later he heard her voice again on a BBC Radio Four programme. He was unsurprised to hear that this strong woman he once knew as the drama teacher at Batley High had become headmistress of a much more solidly middle class school in the Harrogate area.

He generally found O Level lessons uninspiring and the sense of threat around him was always there. The O Level was not just a new thing for Brian: it was new for many of the teachers also, especially those on the arts and humanities side of the curriculum. Most of the science and technical teachers at the school had formerly taught at Batley Tech and were experienced and well qualified to teach to A Level in their subjects, and there was the added bonus of enthusiasm among the majority of boys for these subjects. There was not the same confidence and enthusiasm, either among boys or among some of the teachers, in the humanities and arts. A staffing problem occurred in the English department during Brian's O Level course and for several weeks his favourite subject became a farce when supply teachers were brought in to cover English lessons. One was a very elderly man brought out of retirement temporarily. The class was told he had an Oxford MA in classics. He was also a well known Labour Town Councillor: a pillar of the Batley community. He was a hopeless teacher, cheerful enough, but totally disconnected from the boys and it did not help that he was small in height and had a large pot belly. Many of the boys towered over him. Brian's skin pricked and stung with embarrassment and shame as the subject he loved was reduced to this elderly man rambling on, chuckling to himself as he wrote things on the blackboard – while the boys talked among themselves and totally ignored him. The next supply teacher was if anything even worse. He was British Asian (still a very rare phenomenon in Batley in the early 1960s) and had a strong Asian-English accent which the ruder boys whooped at and ridiculed and which the better behaved boys struggled to understand. He carried a battered brown brief case. It looked as if it had travelled the world over many times. Brian was intrigued and then disgusted and contemptuous to read the faded embossed gold letters on the front of the brief case, showing the teacher's name followed by "BA (Calcutta, Failed)." The British Asian teacher "taught" the O Level English class for a matter of a week or two but the lessons were bedlam, the teacher yelling at pupils in incomprehensible English and the majority of boys braying back, provoking him to yell even louder. The only moments of peace and sanity were when Harry Schofield, or Mr. Parkin, and once even Mr. Locke, appeared at the door and imposed silence, taking one or two of the worst behaved boys out, in the hope the chaos might subside.

Eventually a permanent English teacher was appointed. He was young and new to O level teaching and nervous about it, and not at all confident about the capabilities of Brian's class in sitting O levels in English language and literature. He did not inspire or generate much interest but plodded doggedly on with the set texts for literature and with the component parts of the language course, spoon-feeding the pupils rather than encouraging them to learn for themselves. Later in life Brian remembered very little about his O Level English and English literature lessons, or the texts studied. He loved the *sound* of his first introduction to the language of Shakespeare, in the set text, *Macbeth*, and he enthusiastically learned whole passages off by heart, not so much because he understood them or was even particularly interested in what they were saying but just for the sound of the language. He enjoyed the occasional chance to write a story, even though the story was one-hour timed, in preparation for passing the composition element in the O level exam. English was enjoyable most at this stage through sitting next to Philip: making a raft of their friendship in the middle of an always potentially hostile ocean around them – and he enjoyed competing with him for the highest marks, too.

George Locke taught geography O level, the nearest Brian got to taking a "science" subject. For that reason alone it was the one subject he disliked – a dislike which insidiously eroded his confidence. He loved poring over maps and by the age of fifteen he had a good grasp of the shape of the British Isles and the whole of Western Europe (before 1989). He could draw the maps from memory with a good approximation of shape and where the capital cities were situated. He loved imagining, wondering, as he pored over maps. What must it be like to see the Arc de Triumph? The Vatican? The canals of Amsterdam? What must it *feel* like to be on top of the Alps? To work in a vineyard in the south of France? To roam the wilderness of the Scottish Highlands?

George Locke had no time for this fanciful sort of nonsense from "Yo-oung Hi- er-st" and was often visibly irritated with Brian's vagueness and dreaminess in the geography class, and the way he shrank away from the hard facts of the course. He took real offence at Brian's lack of enthusiasm for his own precious teaching subject. Brian's handwriting skills had never been good. His junior school teachers and Mary blamed his left-handedness or, as Mary put it, his "cack-handedness." George Locke could not stand Brian's childish, ugly, semi-printed, un-joined-up scrawl and made him stay behind at the end of lessons and write pages and pages of letter formation exercises at the back of his geography exercise books. Brian suspected it was as much about Mr. Locke punishing him for not enjoying geography as it was about his poor handwriting.

Mr. Locke sometimes veered away from O level and discussed massive world-important subjects such as global over-population, conservation, over-consumption and in-built obsolescence, and what could be done to eradicate these problems and make the world a better, safer place. He had the confidence to talk about these big abstractions with fourteen to sixteen year-old boys who by and large lived in a very narrow world. The issues he raised fascinated and intrigued Brian and perhaps more importantly gave him a sense that such issues were part of *his* world, not the exclusive possession of "middle and upper class" fowk. Mr. Locke had the good sense and confidence to know that these discussions were just as important educationally for the boys in his care as passing an O level in geography.

True to form also, Mr. Palmer continued introducing new concepts, techniques and artists, in the O level art class. After an introductory short outline on a particular technique or artist, he would stand right back and let pupils work out these new ideas and artists for themselves, encouraging them to try out the new learning in their own work. Frustratingly for Brian, Mr. Palmer tended to be detached, analytical, cerebral, about the work his pupils produced, simply pointing out their success – or failure – in trying out a new technique or idea; never personalising his comments, never seeming to offer help and certainly never spoon-feeding. At the time Brian did not understand his art teacher's motives – and Mr. Palmer was certainly never going to talk about it openly – but he genuinely believed his job was to bring new ideas, new images, new knowledge of Western Art to the attention of his pupils: it was up to them what they did with the new things he introduced. He would not have stood out at a progressive school in the private sector, or even perhaps at a highly academic public school, but he was an oddity at Batley High and it was only much later in life that Brian realised what a brave and innovative teacher he was.

Nowadays schools have carefully devised structures in their staffing to ensure that the personal and social needs, as well as the academic needs, of children are met, which teachers refer to as "pastoral" work. No such structure existed at Batley High in the early 1960s but the pastoral needs of pupils were not neglected. Form teachers took it as read that part of their job was to take care of the personal and social needs of pupils. Although he was not always aware of it directly at the time, and was resentful and touchy about it when he was aware of it, two teachers in particular took a close interest in Brian's personal needs during his O Level years: Derek Whitehead, his form teacher and O level divinity teacher, and Harry Schofield, his O level history teacher, who was also Senior Master (third in charge) at the school.

Derek Whitehead was the opposite of detached cerebral Mr. Palmer. He was volatile and excitable and could veer in a matter of seconds between righteous fury and a relaxed friendly jocularity toward his pupils. Unlike most teachers he took a close open interest in the personalities of his pupils and was often perceptive and insightful about the trouble and turmoil many of the adolescent boys were going through. But intertwined with these psychology skills, he could be sarcastic, waspish and harsh if a pupil antagonised him in some way, intentionally or not. Teaching divinity to O level was a new experience for him and he was sometimes anxious about his ability to do it properly. It did not help that the divinity O Level groups were small in number and because of tight timetabling constraints he had to double up his fourth and fifth year groups in some lessons and then try as best as he could to manage the problems which that situation caused. A typical lesson with Mr. Whitehead might consist of him teaching a new topic to fifth years while fourth years got on with revising the previous lesson. Sometimes he would veer off the lesson into a personal interrogation of a pupil. In one lesson, he quizzed poor shy blushing Rodney (the boy Brian once helped coral the wandering sow) about his family's religious beliefs. How he knew about Rodney's family was a mystery to Brian and to Rodney himself. Rodney's parents were strict Methodists but every year they attended Christmas midnight mass at Staincliffe Parish Church. How, Mr. Whitehead wanted to know, could they reconcile their "strict" Methodism with attending a Church of England service each year? Rodney was a nervous inarticulate boy at the best of times and he simply clamped up, his face blushing scarlet while Mr. Whitehead worked himself up into a temper over the matter. Brian suspected Mr. Whitehead knew just as much about the Hirst family as he knew about Rodney's family but he also understood how fiercely sensitive Brian was about his background and refrained from pushing him in the same way he pushed Rodney. He showed more understanding of Brian's family background than other middle class teachers at the school.

By the time Brian reached the fifth year he was becoming more and more interested in fashion trends and he often dreamed of wearing all the smartest gear. Sometimes he wore John's latest pair of fashionable shoes to school in order to be "with-it," sneaking the shoes back inside the bedroom cupboard before John returned home from his pit shift. The plastic corridor tiles laid down at the new Batley High were susceptible to scuff marks which could only be erased with difficulty by the cleaners and so a rule was strictly imposed that all pupils must wear "pumps" (the 1960s version of trainers) inside the school building, the soles of which did not mark the corridor tiles as badly as leather shoe soles. Every boy had his own designated coat hook in the cloakrooms and also a basket beneath the cloakroom benches in which outdoor shoes were left throughout the school day. Brian arrived at the cloakroom one afternoon to find John's latest Italian winkle-pickers had disappeared: some sneaky bastard had stolen them from his wire basket. It was a major crisis. John had paid good money from his earnings for the shoes and there was no way Brian could raise the money to buy a replacement pair. There would be hell to pay when John found out. Mr. Whitehead was on cloakroom duty the day John's shoes were stolen. He was sympathetic when Brian told him what had happened and understood what a disaster it was for him. It was like losing that ten bob note down Wheatcroft when he was ten, all over again. Mr. Whitehead was livid with righteous anger against the unknown thief, vowing he would hunt him down and ensure he was punished – a promise which, alas, never came to fruition. Later, to Brian's relief, when John was told what had happened he took it calmly. It "tickled him pink" that he was now in a position to own shoes which others less well off than him coveted.

There was a disturbed troublesome fourth year pupil in the divinity group when Brian was in the fifth year. He was the sort of boy who stirred up trouble among his own age group, leading to fierce arguments or fights and when this happened he became obsessed about the current conflict with his contemporaries. He turned on teachers, too, when really roused. Derek Whitehead had a simple way of dealing with him: he made the boy sit next to Brian, who made no objection. Brian was indifferent to, and detached from, the trivial fights and arguments between the boy and his peers. The boy was intelligent and likeable (and good looking), underneath his fierce exterior belligerence. The cool sardonic persona Brian adopted toward him worked perfectly in calming him down and pacifying him. They barely exchanged a word in all the lessons they sat next to each other but the boy seemed happy and at peace sitting there. He spent much of the lesson with his hand down his trousers, which Brian chose diplomatically to ignore, secretly marvelling at his persistence and staying-power in the masturbatory region. It was a clever move on Derek Whitehead's part: he really understood the personalities and chemistry of the boys he taught.

There was a sizeable age gap between Mr. Whitehead and Mr. Schofield but they were great friends. One of them often appeared in the other's lesson and the lesson was temporarily abandoned while they had long chats and jokes together, often just audibly criticizing other members of staff, including Mr. Locke, whom they both seemed to dislike. They would rebuke any boy who dared show he was listening to their "private" conversation. Sometimes they played a game where one of them pretended to spot a particular pupil in the class and the two of them then proceeded to have a conversation about that pupil's peculiarities and peccadilloes. The comments sometimes came quite close to the bone and the jokiness could be seen as a form of bullying or abuse but it also showed how well they both knew their pupils. They did it once to Brian, near the end of the fifth year.

"Mmm. Is that young Hirst, over there? He can be a noisy awkward so-and-so can't he?"

"Oh yes. He's a devil. I really 'ave ter watch him!"

It really angered Brian. It was not what they were saying that infuriated him, which was trivial. It was the unfairness. They were mocking his extreme shyness and reserve when at school. He could sometimes be moody and touchy toward teachers but it was the only time in his six years at the school that he openly showed anger toward them. He felt himself boiling inside and was aware how it made him blush. But he tried to control the anger in order to speak calmly. His voice trembled but the words came out.

"Excuse me, sir? Would yer mind not talkin about me like that? With everybody listnin."

And after that, the conversations about the pupils between the two teachers stopped.

Harry Schofield was in his fifties, older than most of Brian's other teachers. He had a reputation of being a strict but effective teacher. History O level with Harry was a popular option purely because the final results were always so good. The first thing he said to Brian's O level history group at the start of the fourth year was that he guaranteed a top grade to all those who worked hard, learnt the notes and followed instructions on how to answer examination questions. He was right. Most of the boys worked hard at history. They dared not do anything else. They learnt Harry's notes by heart and followed instructions on taking the exam and all were rewarded with grades 1 to 4, the equivalent of GCSE grades A and B today, including Brian, who gained the highest grade 1. Mr. Schofield appeared to dislike his work at Batley High and even more he seemed to dislike boys. He sat sprawled at his desk during lessons, unsmiling, bored, irritable, fierce, angry

– and sometimes just perceptibly amused. He droned on, drilling a passive and always subdued class through the course, which essentially consisted of the Tudor Period and the movement from the Medieval World to the Age of Enlightenment, although the big picture tended to be lost in learning the detail. Occasionally Mr. Schofield veered from the strict details of the syllabus when a particular topic would fire his interest and then history would really come alive. But the norm was dreary rote learning and rigid training in jumping over the examination hurdles. It was only later, when Brian moved on to sixth form, that he understood how interested and concerned Mr. Schofield was in his welfare and progress and how much support he was prepared to give him in getting where he wanted to go, underneath that fierce, bored, contemptuous-seeming exterior.

A major crisis occurred toward the end of the fourth year which threatened Brian's plans to become a teacher. It was thanks largely to Mr. Whitehead and Mr. Schofield that the crisis was surmounted. A few weeks before the end of the summer term Mary told him, with a sad heart, he would have to leave school and find a job. There was not enough money coming into the household to keep him at school. Bob had no interest in Brian's educational ambitions. As far as he was concerned there was not a problem: Brian should have left school at Christmas and gone out into the world and earned some brass, just as he had to in 1926 when he reached the age of fourteen. And now was the time to face reality. Mary put the situation to Brian starkly: if he wanted to stay fed and clothed and sheltered, then he had to go to work and earn a wage. Brian was devastated and cried himself to sleep that night but within a matter of days he accepted what he thought was inevitable and started to think of the sort of work he could do. He desperately did not want building, or mining, or shop work. He still kept in occasional touch with Ray and the paranoid boy, who were both by now working at the bottom of the ladder in local men's outfitters shops, and the covert "queerness" they hinted went on in their workplaces repelled him. With Moira's help he slogged his way through "office jobs" in the vacancies columns of the Batley News and the Yorkshire Post. He had no idea what "office jobs" involved but it seemed the best option available, for him.

Mary contacted Derek Whitehead in his role of form tutor to appraise him of the situation and with Harry Schofield's backing, Derek went into top gear to ensure Brian stayed on at school. With real concern and regret, he told Mary it was a shame, as Brian was a bright lad who could really do well. Mary had not been told this before explicitly and it jolted and surprised her. She rarely questioned a teacher's judgment on any of her children – because teachers were educated fowk who were supposed to know what they were talking about. She still thought of Brian's abilities in the terms of the junior school teacher who swung him round by the hair and called him "a bright spark." She had told Mary that Brian was an "average lad" who would do all right but would never get too far in life. (Aged ninety three, when she was visiting Brian in Scarborough one day with Shirley, Mary told him what the junior school teacher had said about his abilities and how she wished she could show *her* what was what now! Brian was startled by her vehemence: it rather went in the face of his own stereotyping of Mary as a stoical working class woman who spent her life passively accepting fate. Complete nonsense of course. How could she have survived what she did survive all those years without steel in her soul and frequent questioning of "fate," behind her apparent passive acceptance of things as they are in the world?)

Derek enrolled Harry Schofield into solving the crisis and between them the two teachers discovered that WRCC clothing grants were available which Mary had not taken advantage of. They were also aware of Brian's paper round and baby-sitting incomes and they told Mary he was legally old enough now to work full-time during school holidays, when he could boost the family income. Mr. Whitehead promised Mary that he and Harry Schofield – and George Locke himself – would do all they could to find Brian a holiday job. After Mary's talk with Mr. Whitehead, it was settled: Brian would, after all, stay on at school.

*

Is there a lesson here for the problem of the standstill in "social mobility" for the "underclass" which has occurred in England since the 1980s? Perhaps there is. Nowadays every problem in our education system (if it can be dignified by the word "system" – more a scrum of disparate ideas and ideologies) is tackled with detailed "schemes," which usually involve tick boxes, targets and league tables. Often these schemes and mechanisms seem to have little impact on disadvantaged children. Perhaps the problem is due to "social mobility" being conceived as an objective thing, with a definite shape and definite features, and the "solution" to educational problems which spring from this way of thinking is to change the shape of the objective thing, social mobility, and update and tweak it, to make it more effective. "Social mobility" is surely more about living actual people undergoing a process in their very lives, rather than an "object out there." Social mobility is about people like the fifteen year old Brian not wanting to be a miner but wanting to be a teacher and his mother wanting to do her best to support him, and teachers like Derek Whitehead recognizing and knowing his talents, knowing the boy, and committed to pulling out the stops, in collaboration with his mother, to help him achieve his ambitions. The *process* of Brian's setting out on the road to social mobility was an inspirational headmaster who planted an idea in his head and a mother and a few teachers who supported him unstintingly: teachers who really knew him, the actual real boy, and his capabilities: teachers who, for all their human flaws and imperfections, were willing him on. It worked for Brian and for many more lower working class children like him at that juncture of English history when they became socially mobile. It was done by human processes first – a motivated boy, a supportive mother, actively engaged teachers – and objective structures second – clothing grants, free dinners, the opportunity to work and earn money during school holidays.

*

As it happened, it was Moira who found Brian a full-time summer holiday job at the end of the fourth year, at the Rest Assured bedding factory in Birstall where she was then working as a wages clerk. Brian was four months away from his sixteenth birthday when he started the summer job at Rest Assured at the end of July 1962. Work began at 8.00am and finished at 5.00pm five days a week, with time-and-a-half overtime on Saturday mornings, and it lasted the whole six-week school "holiday." During his first day at Rest Assured Brian spotted a boy who had been in a lower stream in his year at Batley High. The boy had already been working full-time since January and would more than likely be working at the bedding factory for many years to come. Brian and the boy nodded on the first day but the boy already looked like a man, in another world from school, and during the whole six weeks they kept their distance, the boy being a "real worker" now and Brian being in another world – a "student-worker."

The makers of the National Curriculum and social mobility experts would admire the huge factory floor at Rest Assured. It was a perfect "object," with its clear component parts all laid out, right through the whole process of making a bed mattress. First came the parts that made up the bed, from ready assembled interior springs, to huge rolls of flock for stuffing, to rolls of patterned, variously coloured cloths for covers and edges. Then came the assembly platforms where mattress frames were put together, springs laid out and stuffing arranged around them. Next came the giant overhead sewing machines, operated by women, who sewed the finished covering and edging together. And finally came the transport and wrapping department, where the newly made mattresses and bases were encased in huge plastic bags before being carried outside and loaded onto lorries, and then delivered to bed shops all over Britain. There were managers and workers in each section, from bringing the raw materials in, to taking the finished products out, and there was a general factory floor manager, Wilf, who oversaw all section managers. The sales and administration managers and clerks were based "upstairs" in a cluster of offices, some of which had large wall-to-wall grimy windows overlooking the factory floor below.

There were toilets but no canteen. A tea-lady came round with a drinks and food trolley during breaks. Sometimes camaraderie broke out between workers, and the mechanical objective process of bed-manufacture was interrupted by fun sessions, against which the managers would briefly and benevolently turned a blind eye. The "fun" usually took the form of a sex war between the men doing the lifting and assembling jobs and the women operating the giant sewing machines. But on the whole the objective rigid system of assembling and manufacturing the beds came first and the workers involved in operating the system came second. There was a personnel manager who looked after the basic personal and social needs of workers, from the big boss, down to casual workers such as Brian: arranging time off for a funeral, or a maternity visit to see the wife and the new babby, for example. Rest Assured was not an inhuman place but nor was it designed primarily with workers in mind: it was designed to produce bed mattresses and that objective took precedence over everything else.

Brian worked in the packing and transport section. He spent the whole six weeks, five and a half days each week, packing anything from a lightweight single bed mattress or bed base, to heavy king size mattresses, sliding them inside huge polythene bags then carrying the item to the loading bay where the drivers hauled them into the big Rest Assured lorries. The packing and transport department was a little world all on its own. It consisted of a large oblong table covered in smooth shiny stainless steel which was waist-height and just big enough to lay out anything from small singles to big king-size mattresses and bases. Underneath the big table was stored all the equipment needed to pack the products and just beyond the packing table was a small dingy windowless room which doubled up as the transport manager's office, and store room, where extra supplies of polythene bags and other packing equipment was kept. Several people worked in the department including: Cyril Burns, the package and transport manager, Brian and Joe, the full-time packers, and three or four lorry-drivers. Brian spent all day every day in this small area, mainly in the company of Joe and sometimes the lorry-drivers, when they were not delivering mattresses to countrywide bed shops.

The drivers were friendly toward Brian and Joe and sometimes helped with the packing when there was a rush. But Brian did not know them well. It did not take him long, however, to realise there was a state of permanent warfare between the drivers and Mr. Burns. On the surface it was about mishaps in the delivery schedules or drivers taking too long to deliver but underneath it was really about Cyril's utter inability to people-manage and the drivers' resentment over his blundering, blustering, petty dictatorial ways. Joe and Cyril could not have been more different, both physically and temperamentally. Joe was Maltese. He was in his late-twenties with a wife and three children. He just about reached five foot and was wiry and muscular with dark Mediterranean skin, black curly hair and intense, glittering black eyes. He spoke educated English, with a slight Yorkshire edge, as well as Maltese and Italian. He was a quietly spoken, intelligently thoughtful young man who treated everyone, including Brian, with unwavering kindness and respect. Cyril Burns was in his late-forties. He wore heavy rimmed glasses and had a Hitlerian moustache and dark black greasy balding hair with runs of pink angry scalp showing through. He was well over six-foot with enormous awkward feet and the permanent physical gait of Basil Fawlty on a really manic day. Joe commanded respect from everyone and Cyril kept calm and distant in his dealings with him. To Brian's relief, Cyril barely recognized his existence, leaving him entirely in Joe's capable kind hands throughout his time at Rest Assured. Cyril had been a police constable until retirement at forty, before working at Rest Assured. He had an over-inflated sense of his own importance and abilities and spent all his working days in a state of rage, from mild to all-consuming, against everyone else at the factory who not only failed to recognise his shining genius but constantly mocked, contradicted or openly laughed at his physical oddness and his utter inability to relate to people in anything like an acceptable way.

While Cyril raged and careered and blundered in the background, and the drivers joked and argued, and the rest of the factory went about its usual business, Brian spent all day standing at one side of the big packing table, with Joe standing opposite. The completed mattresses and bed bases were brought down from the main factory floor and propped around the transport office, waiting to be packed and Joe quickly taught Brian how to pick up a mattress without breaking his back in the process.

"Peek it ep in de meed-el, Bri-aan. So yoo ave equal weight on eech side. Like thees. See? Is eezy like thees."

Doing it that way was "eezy" to Joe but to Brian it was back-breaking. Joe did not tease or mock Brian's first hopeless attempts; instead he gently and patiently taught him how to lift and carry with the least exertion, although it never became less than a big physical effort on Brian's part. Once the item was lifted on to the table, Brian and Joe, standing at their opposite sides of the big stainless steel table, brushed the product down on both sides, removing any remaining threads and debris left over from the manufacturing process. Then a big polythene bag was pulled from beneath the table and Brian soon learned how to slide the mattress inside, in tandem with Joe. Once the plastic cover was in place the item was sealed with tape from a huge industrial roll and either Brian or Joe then carried it to the loading platform, Joe taking more than his fair share of this physically most demanding part of the process. Brian learnt how to carry mattresses with relative ease and eventually he became adept at flipping a mattress over from one side to the other, in the brushing-down stage of the work. But bed bases were a different matter, especially the king size frames. He hated the big staple machine which was used to pin protective cardboard pieces round the bed base corners, and carrying the bases out to the loading platform was a nightmare, the heavy weight, rigid shape and wooden frame digging into his shoulder and hands.

There were days when Joe retreated inside himself, becoming silent and withdrawn before he opened-up to Brian.

"That Ceeril. Ee is so petee. Sometimes Briaan ah reeli ate heem. Oh Briaan. I ave three keeds an a wife ter keep, on thees little monee I earn. Briaan, Briaan. What am I dooin ere? In thees terrible cold place. Batlee. Sometimes I ate eet. Why I diden stay home an study, an go to university, oh, I don know. Thees terreeble contree only wan my labour. Not my brain."

On these occasions Brian realised how much of a child he was, far removed from the worries and difficulties that this grown man he worked with faced. But usually Joe was bright, cheerful and happy and Brian liked working with him. The relationship was a little like that with Philip. They talked and talked, or rather Joe talked and talked and Brian, skilled as he was at self-effacement, at disappearing in the company of others, listened and learned, absorbing much of what Joe said.

"Briaan, I reespec you. You are a clever fellah. Very brainee I theenk. Oh, an education! It ees such a good theeng. Work hard Briaan. An then you weell do anytheen you wan. In Malta I have a young brother. I leeve school early to work so Edooardo can go to university in Eetaly for doctor training. Briaan! Soon. My brother weel bee a DOCTOR!"

As the six long weeks ground on, Joe confided more and more to Brian, spilling out his life and soul and his family's and Malta's history. Joe's life experiences were vast and deep compared with Brian's. He thought about life, the universe, everything, in philosophical and complex ways, whereas Brian was only just beginning to touch the surface of the meaning of living. Joe had an emotional depth and a transparency about his emotions the like of which Brian had never experienced from an older man. The men in his Batley-world were universally taciturn and reticent. As he absorbed Joe's world more and more, Brian became overwhelmed by it. He was full of an inchoate misery and fury at how unjust Joe's life was and felt a deep sense of his own inadequacy to help him find a better life. Sometimes he felt suffocated by the intensity of this Mediterranean workmate and his deep emotions and intellect, which he only half-understood. He wanted to close his ears and be at home listening to the gossip of the women in the family, or back at school chatting with Philip about the trivial childish things that absorbed them. He was humbled by Joe from the start.

"Joe. Ah wish you'd stop tellin me how clever I am. Ahm not. Compared ter you. God! Yer speak *three* languages – an you know so much compared ter me."

It did not stop Joe's multi-layered outpourings; they just became deeper and more and more intense. With the callowness of a fifteen-year-old, Brian was glad to escape Joe when his time at Rest Assured came to an end, little realising how the experience of working with Joe had affected him, transforming him, moving him on, from the introverted fragile child he had been before, to someone who was beginning to look out to the world, and to hate it and love it with all its pitfalls and promises, and look into himself, his emotions, his ideas, with greater maturity and clarity than before. But it was not only Joe who transformed Brian that summer. The experience of being a real wage-earner working in a physically demanding and exhausting job also changed him. He looked forward to Friday afternoons when Moira, in her role of wages clerk, came down from the offices to hand out the brown paper wage envelopes to the factory floor workers. He liked giving the wage packet to Mary and seeing the pleasure it gave her in her eyes, sorting his "spend" from her "keep." He enjoyed buying clothes, a new leather school satchel, a Parker pen and a wristwatch, with the money he had worked hard to earn. He was not interested in beer but he started smoking that summer, quickly becoming addicted to nicotine, an addiction that would increase and intensify over another thirty two years.

Working at Rest Assured brought the fifteen-year-old Brian into close contact with the miseries and rewards of the adult world. But working there was also a *physical* shock: it was an assault on his young growing body. There were no chairs for the factory floor workers at Rest Assured and having to stand several hours each day, with just short intermissions when he found a place to sit, was exhausting. His feet, legs and back burned and ached by the end of the working day and he dreaded the short walk from the factory to the bus stop, praying the bus would not be too full, so he could find a seat, yearning for the moment when he could just sit. Mary cooked him a proper "tea" while he was a proper worker, instead of the fat'n'bread teas he ate during term-time. He enjoyed the new-found privilege of eating a worker's tea but steak and chips, or ham and egg salad, were spoiled by an overwhelming desire to sleep as soon as he arrived home from work. During term times he often sat up till midnight, reading downstairs while everyone else slept. And even when he went upstairs to bed he would perch on the bedroom windowsill, into the early hours, watching the street under the orange glow of streetlamps with occasional cars, late night people, family cats and dogs passing by outside: observing from his secret perch, allowing his mind to drift and dream. Now, he could not wait for sleep. By ten he was undressing for bed, feeling the bruises on his shoulders and upper arms, feeling his whole body thudding with aching muscles. And as soon as he lay down, he fell into instant oblivion until seven the following morning when Mary, from the bottom of the stairs, shouted him out of bed to begin another day's work.

When September and the start of the fifth year came, it seemed strange to lie in bed until eight and do nothing more strenuous than carry his new satchel on the long walk to school. He was glad to be re-united with Philip and resume secret adolescent intimacies, in place of the intensity and seriousness of Joe. He missed earning a wage and the luxuries it brought to his life, such as travelling on buses instead of walking. He went back reluctantly to free school dinners, fat'n'bread teas, walking everywhere, and rarely having the money to buy new clothes and other wanted items. But he also missed the factory. It took weeks to rid himself of the smells inside his nostrils of polythene packaging and bales of bed covering. He missed the touch of silky luxury mattresses under his hands and even missed the hard graft of hauling a base on his shoulder, the new-smelling wood frame digging into his flesh.

His English teacher asked him to write about the summer job for a new school magazine. He dashed off a long rambling enactive piece, pouring out his impressions and experiences of working at Rest Assured and satirising Cyril, who he had grown to hate over the six weeks of working under him. The teacher praised the piece but did not include it in the magazine, telling him it was too scurrilous. He had always kept himself apart from the petty hierarchies and rivalries forever rife among his peers, and he had never been the sort of boy to cheek or defy a teacher, but he now found himself looking at boys and teachers with new eyes. He saw how trivial, petty and stupid boys could be – and teachers too – and the institutionality of school life began to bore him profoundly. As the year progressed he became more and more impatient for school to end. He dreamed of escaping to that magical place: the future.

He slipped back into his old routines: school, babysitting, helping in the house, paper round. But added to his routines now was his smoking habit. Increasingly, he took time off school as he became more bored and weary of its routines and culture. Mary worried over his school absences but did not protest too much when he pretended he had another migraine. They both knew the migraine was fictitious but kept the knowledge to themselves. Mary was working at Percy Walkers and during his days off school Brian took over much of the running of the house: cleaning, cooking and shopping, thus relieving her of some of the exhausting work burden she would otherwise have had to carry. The excitement and pleasure of the fourth year, taking subjects which he largely enjoyed and making a real friend, diminished in the fifth year. He did the bare minimum of the required O level work. Added to the alienation he had always felt about the culture of Batley High, school now bored him to the core. He lived more and more in his own world: day-dreaming about the future, imagining the time when he would escape from school, Chapel Fold and Batley. He took more and more time off school. He felt safe on his own at home during school hours, having the run of the house to himself, alone with his dreams. There were more and more times when he craved money and the independence, clothes, better food and ability to purchase cigarettes, that earning a wage would give him. But at Rest Assured he had seen the world of work he would most likely end up in if he did leave school now, and his desire for something else, something better, overcame – but only just – thoughts of leaving school for work and earning a wage.

At sixteen he was heartily sick of the world he knew and lived in. It was many years later before he fully realised how hard, in a material as well as an emotional sense, his life then was. There was a bitterly cold spell in November 1962. Money was scarce for buying extra coal above the allowance Bob received as an ex-miner, and the house inside seemed as cold as the weather outside. During the day a coal fire was kept banked up in the back room. It provided virtually no heat for the rest of the house but it heated the water and helped dry the endless washing permanently hung on a four-bar wooden "creel," stretching across the ceiling above the fire place, with more damp washing hung on a clothes-horse in front of the fire. The house stank of damp clothes that November. The dampness seemed to seep into everything, including the family's bones and respiratory systems and the house reverberated with hacking coughs, sneezes and wet sniffly noses.

There was some relief in the evening after tea when Bob started another coal fire in the front room. Everyone was ordered to stand to one side while he plunged a small metal hand shovel into the back room fire, heaping it up with burning smoking coals. He then made a mad dash from the back room, to the kitchen, to the hall, to the front room, where he emptied the burning coal from the shovel into the grate, thus starting the new fire. It involved negotiating three doorways and tight corners. Mary hated him doing it but mercifully the red hot coal never spilled and the house did not go up in the burning conflagration she feared it would. It gave extra heat in the house during the few hours between teatime and bedtime, as well as providing the family with an escape from the stink of damp clothes and steam in the back room.

There was a vicious spell of dense yellow smog that November and one evening Brian dragged himself from the warmth of the front room fire to brave the smog on an errand. Once outside on the street, he could only see blurred shapes a few feet around him. Beyond, the whole world was wrapped in cold yellow silence with just the headlights of an occasional car cautiously crawling along Chapel Fold. The smog was sulphureous, acrid, bitterly cold and it seeped through his inadequate clothes into his bones. He had never felt so cold. He was in the habit of smoking three or four cigarettes a day by now. It was more than he could afford, and some were stolen from John, or "cadged" from another older sibling, or from Dot. The smog, combined with his smoking habit, got to his chest, making him hack-up big gobbets of thick, foul-tasting yellow mucus which he spat onto the freezing grass in front of the bungalow where Mrs. Owl lived. He bitterly hated Batley and Chapel Fold that evening and his despondency continued in bed that night. The icy smog seemed to creep into the bedroom and no matter how high he piled the bed with overcoats, layering them above the worn old army blankets and faded candlewick spread, he shivered through the night, hearing and feeling the yellow phlegm rattling and wheezing in his lungs. Life that evening was awful.

A few days later the smog disappeared. The weather stayed cold and wintry but clear blue skies and sunshine filled the day followed by cold black-clear skies at night. There was a geography field trip to the Yorkshire Dales at the end of November which, with the help of WRCC grants, Brian was able to join. A group of twenty or so pupils, Mr. Locke and another geography teacher stayed in the Friends Meeting House hostel at Airton, just a couple of miles down the River Aire from Malham. The bitter cold he had felt earlier in the month, both outside and within, disappeared. He fell madly in love with the Dales. It was his first trip to proper countryside at a quiet time of the year, just before tourism became a mass industry in Britain, with all the despoliation and crowding of the countryside it has brought.

Apart from Battyford, the field trip to the Dales was Brian's first experience of the Yorkshire countryside. He loved Malham Tarn and Gordale Scar and every place he saw during that short field trip. To Mr. Locke's irritation, he took little heed of the geography and geology he was supposed to be absorbing. He was too much in love with motherly shaped hills, drystone walls, sheep, rich green fields, and the deep blueness of Autumn skies, to care about the tedious facts of geography and geology. He loved the hostel at Airton and he loved the small village itself, wrapped in the Aire valley beside the fast, clear-sparkling river. He enjoyed breakfasts and evenings spent in the warm hostel in the company of the other lads, who all seemed absorbed in the geography and were on best behaviour under the watchful eyes of Mr. Locke and Mr. Kitson, the kindly geography teacher. He enjoyed the experience of copying up the day's work during the allotted hour in the evenings in a companionable and workmanlike silence – conditions which were impossible at the always crowded house at Chapel Fold. But most of all he loved the night sky. He could not wait to stand outside alone, after prep was done, and gaze at the firmament above. He had never seen anything like it: this dazzle of endless, deep glittering silver on a background of black. It made him gasp with wonder, amazement, joy. It was an experience he never forgot.

When the summer came and O level exams began, Brian was filled with nervous dread. The happy innocence and ignorance of his junior school years were long gone. He knew these examinations would shape his future and he was convinced he had not worked hard enough to pass. He regretted cutting his mind off from lessons he disliked and taking so much time off school. The first examination filled him with nervous palpitations and his head and palms ran with hot sticky sweat, even though it was his "best" subject, English language. He sweated his way through the exam, too full of fear and dread to know what he was writing, worrying and labouring over trivial technical details and rushing and forgetting to take care with handwriting. After that, the remaining examinations passed in a blur and it was the end of term and he was back at Rest Assured with Joe and Cyril, for another long "summer holiday."

Brian's O level results arrived at Batley High one day in late August 1963. There was no telephone yet at Chapel Fold, or fridge, or television, or twin-tub washing machine, and so unlike Philip, who telephoned the school to receive his results, Brian took a day off from Rest Assured to collect his results from school personally. He failed geography with the equivalent of a D grade today, as he expected, and gained the equivalent of GCSE grade A today, in history and English literature and grade B in Divinity and Art. But these passed his eyes in a blur. All he saw on the result sheet was his fail grade 7 (equivalent to GCSE grade D) in English language. He had arranged to discuss his results with Derek Whitehead and Harry Schofield, who had both come in to school especially to meet him and several other pupils hoping to join the sixth form to take A levels. He was convinced he would not be able to join the sixth-form as he had failed to gain the necessary minimum of five O level passes at grades 1 to 6 (A to C today). To his surprise, both teachers were pleased and impressed with his results. They told him the English language results had been poor all round and that he could re-take it in November and still embark on A levels. He wanted to take English, history, divinity and art at A Level and was told everything would be done to get him onto the courses he was interested in when he returned to Batley High to start sixth form. He told Mary, his sisters and sisters-in-law about failing English but glossed it over by telling them how impressed his teachers were with his other grades. They were unflaggingly proud of him, especially Mary, and they wanted him to go on to A levels. It looked like there was still a good chance he was going to become a teacher.

Brian aged 16

Formerly Percy Walkers rag-oyle

Mary with Michael

Fomerly Rest Assured front offices

Friends Meeting House at Airton

The River Aire below Airton

THAT WORD! BUTLINS; A DEATH

Not all the A level courses Brian wanted to take were set up for him on his return to school in September 1963. He was to take A level history at Batley Grammar, and A level English literature and O level general studies and O level English Language re-sit at Batley High. No A level courses in art or divinity were available at either his own school or at Batley Grammar School. If he gained at least grade 6 (a low grade C) in the English language re-sit, the five O levels he would then have were enough to gain him a place at a teacher training college. With a further two good A Level grades there was a chance of a university place although not on an English degree course, where an O level in Latin was required, though universities sometimes turned a blind eye here in cases of students with good A level grades, or those with strong references, not to mention the relaxation of rules at top universities when it came to admitting pupils from the "right" sort of schools.

It was unusual in 1963 to find a non-selective school where pupils were encouraged and supported in staying-on after the statutory minimum leaving age of fifteen, including some such as Brian from the lowest socio-economic class. In many parts of England in 1963 there was a strict line drawn between grammar schools and secondary moderns. Each lived in its own world and had its own values and often these schools had nothing to do with each other. This was more or less the case in Batley before Batley High opened in 1959 with George Locke as its head and with the dynamic, innovative and socially-democratic Alec Clegg in charge of education in WRCC schools. Not only was Brian fortunate enough to go to a secondary school which encouraged and supported him in staying on till he was eighteeen but his school also collaborated with the two Batley Grammar Schools in providing a full range of A level courses for pupils at all three schools.

Batley High School – or rather, "Batley Business and Enterprise College," as it is now called – is built on top of a hill overlooking the town and high Pennine hills beyond to the west. The school is situated in the middle of Field Hill and Carlinghow Hill. In Brian's days at the school, the Girls' Grammar was situated half-way up Field Hill and the Boys' Grammar stood half-way up Carlinghow Hill. Walking betweeen the three schools was a matter of minutes. Pupils from the two Grammar Schools took O and A level courses in technical drawing, metalwork and woodwork at Batley High, the grammar schools having neither staff nor facilities to provide these courses themselves. Batley High pupils took A Levels at Batley Boys Grammar in subjects where the numbers were insufficient to make a course viable at the High School, or in subjects where teachers were insufficiently qualified or experienced at teaching A level and similarly, Batley Grammar girls took A level sciences at the boys Grammar School.

Twenty years later in the 1980s, when education in England became a football game for politicians and their lackeys (mostly played with crass ineptitude) the idea of collaborative curriculum consortiums between schools and "beacon schools" was being trumpeted, as if these ideas had never been thought of before. Years earlier, in 1963, Batley High and the town's two Grammar Schools were quietly and efficiently working collaboratively together:

with no help from politicians or educational "experts." In today's educational world of rigidly "objective" targets and aims, where you cannot take such-and-such a course without achieving such-and-such exam passes at such-and-such grades, Brian's progress into the sixth form, and his actual sixth form study programme, would be looked upon as at best inadequate and at worst unacceptable. His O levels were narrow in scope. He stopped taking maths, science, technology and a modern language after the third year, when he was fourteen. All of these subjects are now considered vital until the age of sixteen under the national curriculum. His two A level and one O level sixth form course was equally limited. There is no question that Brian's education did narrow once he began O levels and in later years he came to regret the gaps in his education, especially in maths, science and modern languages. But thankfully for him he went to a secondary modern school which, unlike most at the time, was prepared to go beyond offering its pupils only a basic utilitarian, vocational curriculum; a school which had the imagination to put the child first and systems and objectives second.

Brian's secondary education after the age of fourteen was personalised, *ad hoc* and improvisatory but it moved him in the direction he wanted to go and eventually it gave him social mobility and the confidence and basic educational grounding to move out of the socio-economic confines of his family and community. How many of today's children, with backgrounds comparable to Brian's in the 1960s, have dropped out of school, bemused and forced through National Curriculum "objectives" and "targets" which make no sense to them: children who have no learning support networks outside school; no pushy aspirational parents to help them comprehend and handle the "objectives"? How many "Brians" today are condemned to social *immobility* and "failure" by a mentality among those who govern and run education which puts objective targets first and the individual profiles and socio-economic circumstances of children second?

*

None of these issues were on Brian's mind when he started sixth form in September 1963, three months before his seventeenth birthday. His main preoccupation was worry about how he would cope at school without Philip. He barely knew anyone in the sixth form and this exacerbated his sense of being an outsider and intensified his by now embedded sense of his "difference." A new head of English and A level teacher, Mr. Parkinson, was appointed at Batley High when Brian began sixth form in September 1963. The previous head of department, Mr. Hoyle, who only taught the very top sets and had therefore never taught Brian, was a flamboyant character who paraded around the school in colourful trendy clothes and hummed jazz tunes to himself and seemed full of his own cleverness and intellectuality. On a bad day he was known to fly into rages against insolent boys and sometimes he leaped over his desk, knocking furniture and boys out of the way, in order to get his hands on the insurrectionist who was his target. Mr. Parkinson was more subdued and conventional. At the start of the course, he told the A level English literature group a little about himself. His previous post had been at a Leeds grammar school and he had a Leeds University degree in English. Brian was disappointed with the small English A level group of half a dozen boys. He seemed to be the only one who was taking English out of a genuine interest in reading and a real eagerness to learn more about English literature. The other students seemed to be taking it as a fill-in, an unwelcome extra subject to top-up the other subjects they were taking – subjects where their real interests lay. Mr. Parkinson seemed as disappointed as Brian, confronted with this lacklustre A level English group at Batley High.

Only one other pupil in the whole year group, and at that a new boy, had chosen to take A level history and so Brian and the new boy would study history at Batley Grammar, just two hundred yards down Carlinghow Hill. Harry Schofield presented Brian and the new boy with several hefty A Level tomes each – the basic and background reading for the course. Harry was disappointed that insufficient numbers of students had opted for history at Batley High, thus robbing him of the chance to teach A level. He gruffly presented the text books and said little about the course but spoke at length about the expense of the books and how he hoped they would be well used and well looked after. Brian was nervous about the new boy and even more nervous about the upcoming ordeal of joining a whole new group of pupils down at the Grammar School.

Mr. Parkinson was Brian's form tutor during both sixth form years. At the start of the lower sixth he told the form about O level General Studies which they would all be taking as a background general education to their A level courses. It would be taught by several different teachers including Mr. Parkinson himself, who would concentrate on things called "current affairs and culture" and Mr. Palmer who would focus on "the arts" and Mr. Calvert, the head of science, who would focus on science and something called "technology." General Studies would be taught in a group of pupils comprising both lower and upper sixth boys, most studying science and technical subjects at A Level. Brian barely knew these boys, a fact which added to his general sense of nervous trepidation about embarking on this last stage of his six years at Batley High. At the end of his first day in the lower sixth form, Brian decided the only part he was going to enjoy was "private study" when, as far as he could tell, he would be left with a few other pupils in the school library or in a sixth form room to study independently. The one good point, which filled him with relief beyond measure, was there would be no more PE; no more ritual weekly humiliation and embarrassment in the gym and on the sports fields.

Despite his worries, Brian settled into sixth form life quickly and reasonably comfortably. The difficulties and hurdles he had anticipated either did not materialise at all or he found he could easily surmount them. He liked the separateness of the sixth form from the lower five years. Sixth-formers were expected to attend morning assembly, sitting on seats at the back of the hall, not on the floor. They were also expected to set an example to younger boys around school and take part in supervision duties. Brian did his bit at lunch times. Pupils sat at specified octagonal tables in the dining hall in mixed age groups, from first to upper sixth years. Brian was used to serving food to his younger family members and was comfortable in the role of table supervisor over seven younger boys, aware of the irony that he was probably the only one of the eight boys who had free dinners. He enjoyed no longer having to wear the uniform he had once been so proud of wearing. The sixth-form "uniform" consisted of a special tie, a "smart sports jacket," dark trousers and a plain-coloured shirt. His sixth-form clothes consisted of John's hand-me-downs and clothes he had bought with his own earnings. He liked the exclusivity of the three small sixth-form rooms, cut off on their own landing from the rest of the school on the top floor of the main teaching block, with panoramic views from the windows across Batley and high Pennines beyond. To his relief and pleasure, the atmosphere was different in the sixth-form. Teachers were more relaxed and informal. Mr. Parkinson did not perform the dreaded beginning-of-term register ceremony and never took a formal register. Instead, he glanced around the room to see who was missing before completing his class register.

The ethos among the pupils was better too. A few boys, those who had been in bully-gangs, or hangers-on, tried to perpetuate the power hierarchies which had pertained lower down the school but they found themselves adrift in the sixth form. Many of the sixth formers were new to the school. They came from schools in nearby towns in order to gain good science, technical and geography A levels and they neither knew nor cared about the existing power patterns among established Batley High boys. Most boys responded well to the grown-up spirit of the sixth-form suite, abandoning the petty rivalries, macho posturing and physical bullying of the lower years and adopting instead a cheerful clubby attitude, where they could happily network new friends on a more adult basis than before. One day early in the first term of the sixth form Brian was startled and pleased when the Head Boy pulled up halfway down Field Hill on his motor scooter and offered him a lift home. He did not enjoy the experience of riding pillion on the wobbly scooter and was not sure where to put his feet but it thrilled and pleased him that the Head Boy was treating him as a mate. He knew nothing about rugby, cricket and other sports, or about girls, and so he never felt himself a full member of the sixth-form club but he was a good listener, a good mimic, and he possessed a sharp-edged, sometimes cutting, sense of humour. It all helped in finding a niche in the club, giving him a measure of comfort and security.

The A level English literature course was disappointing. None of the set texts entirely grabbed his attention, particularly the poetry, which he mostly forgot immediately after taking the exam although lines from Lawrence's *Snake*, Yeats's *An Irish Airman Forsees His Death* and *When You Are Old* seeped deeply into his memory cells, as nursery rhymes learnt at infant school do. Mr. Parkinson bravely began with Chaucer's *Prologue to The Canterbury Tales* in Middle English, with Coghill's modern translation beside.

It was almost a disaster, trying to teach this to a group of boys who had not studied Latin or a modern language for more than a year and who rarely heard English spoken in anything other than standard form on the radio, or industrial Yorkshire in everyday life. Drama consisted of a compendium of three plays: *The Knight Of The Burning Pestle*, *The Rivals* and *The Importance Of Being Earnest* which Mr. Parkinson taught conscientiously, giving Brian a sense of the history and development of English drama prior to the modern age. Brian had enjoyed *Macbeth* at O level. The language, sound and poetry of Shakespeare stirred him and although the A level Shakespeare text, *The Winter's Tale*, was more complex and ambivalent than *Macbeth*, it roused his interest and curiosity. *Wuthering Heights* grew on him gradually. He read novels enactively and uncritically. He was interested in the characters as real people, not as literary devices, and settings and themes were real places and real issues to him, not authorial constructs. He became deeply interested in Heathcliffe and Cathy as a real man and woman. Wuthering Heights and Thrushcross Grange were real places to him and he treated the questions the story raises as real-life issues.

The modern prose text was C.P. Snow's *The New Men*, a 1950s novel set in a Cambridge University college whose principal characters are dons and their wives. He re-read the novel much later in life and found the authorial voice pompous and sententious, the setting cloistered and incestuous and the characters too small-minded, rigid and weak to sustain and carry the big themes the author overstrives to explore. But the world and lives portrayed in the book fascinated the seventeen-year-old Brian. This special place with its special people – a Cambridge College and its dons – was the successor in his fantasies to the glasses boy at Infants, to Jennifer and David at Juniors, to the posh fowk in Millburns and Shepleys, to wanting to be a teacher. It became the object of his desire: the life, the place, of his dreams, even though he knew a place at Cambridge was as unattainable to him as a life on Mars.

It was clear the sixth-form English group was never going to gell or become in any way interesting or exciting. Mr. Parkinson struggled to teach the subject in an interesting way to a group of boys who, apart from Brian, were not readers and whose interests and ambitions were far removed from English literature. Brian cut himself off from the group and generally maintained his interest in the course but there were times when even the ever-calm, ever-patient Mr. Parkinson visibly despaired over the indolent indifference toward literature among the group and Brian despaired with him, wishing there was a Philip in the class with whom he could share the parts of the course he enjoyed.

In the new clubby atmosphere of the sixth form, Brian was surprised to find himself befriended by two other boys, Jim and Don, who were both initially placed in the A Level English group but soon dropped out, preferring to concentrate on their chosen science and technical A Levels instead. He knew them both by sight in the lower school years but their paths had never crossed. The two were already firm friends. Both lived in Birstall and came from established working class families, which was (and probably still is) considered a better background than coming from Staincliffe Council Estate. The two boys played sports but sport was not their main interest. Neither of them had ever associated themselves closely with the swaggering element at the school but both were physically strong, mentally assertive, capable of aggression and neither could be pushed around. They had more kudos and respect in the mainstream life of the school than Brian. Jim lived a few doors down from Shirley and Jimmy at Howden Clough and went out of his way to make a friend of Brian. Don went along with Jim but to the ever-sensitive, watchful, nervous Brian, Don often seemed to be standing-back, observing him quizzically, a slightly amused knowing smile on his face, as if he could see underneath Brian's carapace. Both boys liked Brian's mimicry skills and his sly sense of humour. Jim was an excellent mimic in his own right and though they were amused at his shyness and nervous reserve, Jim and Don both, to different degrees, opened up to him, letting him in on their lives, which he enjoyed sharing, in a semi-detached way.

Brian's only experience of sharing intimacies with a friend was with Philip who, even more than himself, was complex and multi-layered emotionally and sexually. Jim and Don were straight heterosexuals. They did not push or probe Brian about his sexual nature but assumed he was the same as them. He spent hours with them, listening to accounts of their sexual adventures with older girls at the not too distant Bretton Hall Training College, knowing it was fantasy, mind-sex, but intrigued, amused and fascinated by this very different inner world from his own. The three of them stayed good friends throughout sixth form and Brian would occasionally meet up with Jim at Howden Clough for a year or two after leaving school. Brian was never quite sure what he gave to Jim and Don apart from being a passive listener but they gave him solid uninhibited friendship and warmth and, just by often being seen with them, they also gave him security and a place in the mainstream heterosexual world of Batley High sixth form.

The new boy, Charles, who studied history with Brian down at the Grammar School, was different altogether from Jim and Don. He had been educated until then at a private school in the south of England but his mother, who was recently widowed and lived in nearby Tingley, had fallen on hard times financially and thus Charles found himself a sixth-former at Batley High. On the surface he had the smooth confidence (and accent) of a public schoolboy. He was much more open and transparent than

Brian, telling him quite unashamedly it was his mother's lack of money and straightened times that brought him to Batley High. His unembarrassed honesty about his family circumstances impressed Brian although he bridled when Charles made it clear he thought he had come down in the educational world and was only at Batley High due to a lack of money at home. Underneath the confident surface, Charles was lost in the rough-and- ready world of Batley High and he tended to cling to Brian, who was more tolerant of his namby-pamby southern private schoolboy ways than other lads. From the beginning Charles and Brian competed with each other verbally, each trying to prove to the other the superiority of himself, his family, values, culture – *everything.*

Charles was already a firm supporter of "Tha Cownsahvartive Pahrteh" and his political opinions raised Brian's hackles and made him think seriously about politics, for the first time in his life. It was perhaps because of meeting Charles and being thrown together with him into an adversarial friendship that Brian realised he could never fundamentally be anything other than a socialist, if not always a supporter of the Labour Party – especially when its slippery leaders of the 1990s appended that slippery prefix "New" to its name. Brian was aspirational by now and knew what his ambitions were. He wanted to be a teacher. He wanted to move out of his working class community and Batley and become a member of the middle class. He eventually wanted to own a car, a television, a house, a telephone – and go abroad for holidays. But he loathed the unfairness of the private education system and the first-past-the-post privileges which inherited wealth and class bring to some people, while others have to work hard to move up in the world, if they move up at all. He wanted all forms of inherited privilege to end and fair distribution of wealth and opportunity for all to take its place in England. It was a true-blue Tory – Charles –

who unknowingly taught him to think about and believe in such ideals in a clearer way. Until then, his support for Labour had been instinctive; unquestioningly imitating Bob's, Mary's and towder-ends' political leanings during his growing-up years.

Both Charles and Brian, for quite different reasons, found studying history A level at Batley Grammar a difficult and ultimately unrewarding experience. Charles was intelligent and he was a desperately anxious hard worker but he was not academic.

"Honest, Harstie. Ai tell yew. Mai aideah of 'heaven' is cricket on ah sammers day dewn et thah ewld scewl in Sarreh. Ew, end tea end cream bans. In tha refreshment tent, aarftah."

"History" for Charles meant The Queen, and all the monarchs of England before her, and visits with his mother to the palaces and stately houses royalty still lived in, or places they used to live in. It was most definitely not the complicated dense stuff of the A level course at Batley Grammar, which Charles struggled valiantly and tenaciously with for two years but never really mastered.

By the time he reached sixth form, Brian was becoming more and more driven to achieve his aspirations and ambitions and when new knowledge and ideas captured his interest and imagination, he worked hard on mastering them and became fascinated with ideas for their own sake. Reading C.P. Snow's novel on Cambridge life fascinated him and as a result of that fascination he went on to read more twentieth century novels, especially those situated in worlds beyond his own social background. Evelyn Waugh was a particular favourite. He liked the humour (and did not entirely grasp the satire) but above all else, it was Waugh's chronicling of "upper classes lives" that fascinated him and he voraciously read every Waugh novel he could lay his hands on. The cultural concepts and notions Mr. Palmer introduced in the art room – and left him to work out for himself – also fascinated him, and set the foundation for a lifetime's interest in art and culture. But throughout sixth form he was still fundamentally insecure and full of demons – about his sexuality, his family and his social class. He was now much more self-aware and he found mixing in all-male heterosexual groups increasingly stressful, except when in the company of Philip and to a lesser extent Jim, Don and Charles.

It was the difficulty of fitting into the Batley Grammar group and working out its culture and ethos, rather than the course itself, that put him off A level history from the start. At first he felt even more of an outsider at Batley Grammar than he did in the Batley High metalwork shop. He felt he was a triple outsider now: the new boy joining a group of twenty-odd boys who had all known each other for five years, and on top of that he was queer, and a lower working class queer at that. He felt he was a bent lower working class outcast trying to fit into a straight, uniformly middle and aspirational working class group of Grammar School boys, all of them strangers. The Grammar School history group, as it turned out, were cheerful and friendly toward Brian and never showed any hostility or sense of their own superiority, actual or supposed. He knew how to blend in and was a good listener and although the history course left him cold, and he never felt anything but an outsider at Batley Grammar, he was fascinated with the gossip of the insiders he sat among and working out the culture of the school, what made it tick, rather as he used to absorb the world of Millburns Grocery Stores, took up a good deal of his time and attention. It was not the same for Charles, who had to face a simmering background competitiveness from Grammar School boys confronted with this very visible minor public schoolboy in their midst. Charles had the classic public schoolboy looks, manners and accent that, for example, David Cameron has, and he made some of the clever Grammar School boys bridle.

The Grammar School was housed in cramped Victorian buildings and when Brian first went there and struggled down crowded corridors to find the sixth form history room, the cheerful physical chaotic atmosphere reminded him of Healey Secondary Modern when he was eleven. There was neither the space nor the corridor discipline he was used to at Batley High. It all looked quaint to him, with teachers swirling around in black academic gowns among the boys, cheerfully joshing with them or angrily cuffing them out of the way. The whole institution seemed steeped in swaggering competitiveness, among teachers as well as boys. It made Batley High look calm and amenable in comparison. It was the same in the history classroom, a tiny room in the oldest part of the school, next to the Headmaster's House. The room was crammed with twenty or so growing adolescent boys, and their A level history teacher. To Brian, the history room exuded the very history of Batley Grammar, a school full of history, unlike Batley High which was just going into its fifth year of existence. Batley Grammar School was founded in 1603 and its most famous old boy was Joseph Priestley, a radical thinker and discoverer of oxygen. (The radical postmodern novelist, David Peace, was also educated there, a few years later than Brian.) The school was regarded as one of the best smaller grammar schools in the West Riding and was ranked just behind the surrounding bigger grammar schools in Bradford, Wakefield and Leeds in the verbal league tables of the time. Most of the staff were Oxbridge graduates and from the first day of stepping into the school it seemed to Brian that the pinnacle of success at Batley Grammar was to gain an Oxbridge place. Other universities were regarded as second best and teacher training colleges were considered distinctly third class.

Competitiveness and rivalries simmered between boys. Swats were teased unmercifully by wits and wags and swats retaliated by sneering at wags when they misunderstood a subtle point of history. To Brian's amazement and intrigue, the same situation pertained between the boys and their history teacher. The wags and the wits spent much of their energies subtly, in a coded way, needling the poor man – about his private life, his unmarried state, his sexuality, while the swats watched every word he said and were quick to dive on the slightest historical error he might make. Brian was in awe of the teacher but pitied and empathised with him too. He was in early middle age, balding and a little stout and always suntanned, which was unusual in the West Riding of 1963. Brian soon learned from class gossips that his tan was the result of long travels abroad to ancient historic sites during every school holiday. The gossips told Brian about the teacher's history degree from Trinity College Cambridge which gave him kudos among the academically ambitious boys and challenged them too, making them constantly want to bring him down from his high academic pedestal. Brian impassively watched the constant simmering battle between the teacher and the boys with just a faint smile on his face, as protection in case of a possible attack upon himself for not joining in the goading. The teacher was more than capable of putting boys down when they goaded him too far, keeping them in place with a sharp erudite word but often he seemed hurt and genuinely wounded, like an outsider animal being attacked and excluded from the main pack.

Brian and Charles lacked the benefit the other boys had of familiarity with the teacher's method. He gave the class the basic outline of the component parts of the course, mainly through dictated notes, but he also talked wide-rangingly around the core, often referring in detail to wider-reading, historical texts which he expected the class to have read carefully in their own time. He was deeply involved in the academic history world and was excited by the great up-and-coming radical historians of the time, such as Christopher Hill. At the end of every week the class had to produce a well argued, referenced and constructed A level essay, fully covering the topic of the week. It took Brian a long time to comprehend the methodology and by the time he understood it, it was too late. He struggled to understand the methodology throughout most of the course but was afraid of approaching the distant academic historian at Batley Grammar for help. The only other channel of help he could go to was his O Level history teacher, Harry Schofield, but pure arrogance, stubbornness and pride stopped him from seeking help from that quarter.

Brian thoroughly absorbed the clever-grammar-schoolboy-makes-Oxbridge ethos at Batley Grammar but he did not absorb the course or the teacher's method. Toward the end of the course, when he at last understood what was expected, he worked hard on preparing a good answer to the weekly essay title and was rewarded with one or two marks of sixteen out of twenty – equal to a higher A level grade. But it was too late to catch up by then. He had spent nearly two years fascinated by the culure of Batley Grammar but bored by the course itself, unsure of the method, and lacking the confidence to admit his uncertainty and seek help. The discourse and culture of Batley Grammar was initially alien and intimidating to him and this, combined with his deep sense of his own outsider-ness, put him off A Level history at the Grammar School from the start. He decided early in the sixth form he could cope with English but "gave up" on A Level history, until right at the end of the course. In doing so, he gave up the idea of gaining a university place, regretfully deciding the "third class" option, a teacher training college, was the future place for him.

The general studies course at Batley High was both enjoyable and interesting, including science sessions with Mr Calvert. Brian was placed in a group full of boys keen on science but Mr Calvert's stance in the general studies class was to put the social, economic and political importance of science first. It was a time when the Prime Minister, Harold Wilson, and radical ministers like Anthony Wedgewood-Benn, (now Tony Benn) were talking about exciting things such as "the white heat of technology" changing the face of Britain and bringing about a great and glorious future. Mr. Calvert was as excited with the wider ramifications as he was with the science itself and he explored science by discussing inventions such as the bi-metallic strip which brought about huge improvements in people's lives, such as its use in thermostats in central heating systems. Brian became caught up in these ideas and to his pleasure found himself understanding the "simple" scientific discoveries introduced by Mr. Calvert; ideas he had previously found alien.

Mr. Parkinson took a pragmatic approach to current affairs. Rather than formally drilling the group in current issues he instead urged them to listen to serious programmes on the radio and watch current affairs on TV, but above all else, he insisted they should read what he called a "quality" newspaper, bringing in copies of *The Observer* and reading and discussing detailed and lengthy articles to show the group what he meant by "quality." At home, Bob and Mary read *The Daily Herald*, a popular broadsheet (before popular newspapers became "tabloids") with strong links to the Labour Party and Trade Unions. Bob and Mary thought it was a newspaper for their sort of fowk, as indeed it was, and they would not dream of reading any other national newspaper. (*The Herald* became *The Sun* in 1964, when Brian was beginning his upper sixth year, but its socialist-unionist roots did not become lost forever until 1969 when it was taken over by Rupert Murdoch and profits entirely superseded editorial principles and ideals.)

Brian took Mr. Parkinson's advice and bought *The Observer* every Sunday, paying for it with his own earnings.

As far as he was concerned, reading *The Observer* was another way in: a means of becoming posh, although by now he had stopped using that term, being more interested in becoming "an intellectual," and "middle class," positions which he knew were not necessarily synonymous with being posh. When he could, he watched TV programmes such as "Monitor" and "Panorama," the latter hosted by the clever adversarial Robin Day, the former by the intellectual Hugh Wheldon. (Bob and Mary finally got round to renting a TV just before Brian's seventeenth birthday toward the end of 1963. Before that, they made do with the wireless.) And when "The Michael Parkinson Show" and "That Was The Week That Was" came on the TV screen he lapped them up, excited to be a spectator of the "stars" of the time (this was before "celebrities" became common usage) and to be "in" on what the clever, mainly Oxbridge educated, new young satirists such as David Frost were saying about the world out there beyond Chapel Fold and Batley. Sometimes his fascination with these "intellectual" programmes irritated Bob, who would switch channel to an old Hollywood film on ITV, purely, it seemed, to thwart Brian. The "posh" newspapers and television programmes became the latest in a long line of escapes from his own world – from the glasses boy, to Jennifer, to Millburns, to Philip and Charles, to Batley Grammar and idle dreams of a place at a Cambridge College.

True to form, Mr. Palmer pursued his own line in "the arts" lessons of the general studies course. He dutifully discussed dance, music and theatre reviews in the quality papers but made it clear his real interest was in visual art, taking the group through an express history of Western art from the 15th to 20th centuries. Brian found himself fascinated and captured by the art to which he was introduced, from Breughel to Miro. More than anything, Mr. Palmer wanted to *stretch* the general studies group. He decided to do this by introducing the general studies class to the idea of an extended study, challenging them to choose an artist they particularly admired and to base the "long essay" on the chosen artist's work. Breughel's scenes of mass humanity, enclosed in a regulated landscape full of individual people and lives, deeply stirred Brian. At the other end of art history, he was fascinated with the surrealists and especially Miro's vivid colours and odd shapes suspended in air, yet solid on canvas. But he chose to write his long essay on Van Gogh, whose later post-impressionist works astonished, moved and intrigued him when Mr. Palmer first introduced them in the O level art course. He borrowed a biography of Van Gogh and a book of his paintings from the school library and spent hours poring over his life, seeing the life and the person in the paintings. He became deeply engaged, empathetic, with Vincent's fragile personality and his tortuous progress to creative genius. He was fascinated by Vincent's emotional and financial dependence on his mainstream brother and family, even when he was in the deepest grip of creative outpouring. The essay Brian produced was rushed and chaotic, like Van Gogh's brushstrokes, but bereft of their magnetic impact. Mr. Palmer did not seem to mind, smiling to himself when he saw the emotional and intellectual effect discovering a little of the life and work of Van Gogh had made on Brian.

Mr. Parkinson took it upon himself to develop a decent sixth form literature section in the school library. His selection consisted of Penguin paperbacks, around the time when the Penguin cover colour became reddish-orange, succeeding the green of earlier times. Brian was attracted to the bright new paperbacks, thinking them chic and "intellectual." They contrasted greatly with the battered old hardbacks at Staincliffe Library and the gaudy cowboy and love story paperbacks his family read, buying them cheaply from second-hand stalls on Dewsbury Market then passing them on. Much of his "private study" in the library consisted of listening to the chatter of those around him, sometimes joining in, doodling on notepaper, or poring over atlases, maps and art books. He made an effort to read the new paperbacks but his first choice, Aldous Huxley's *Point Counter Point,* was unpropitious. His desire to be "an intellectual" did not stretch to unravelling the complexities of the upper-crust, post-First World War metropolitan sophisticate world of Huxley's novel. Nowadays GCSE and A Level English literature courses force students to read something of their "literary heritage" by including compulsory pre-twentieth century texts. Brian, on the other hand, should have been forced to read *post* nineteenth century works in the sixth-form. He found Chaucer, Dickens and Beaumont and Fletcher more accessible and gave up on Huxley after fifty or so pages and apart from gobbling-up all of Evelyn Waugh's early satires, he did not begin to read serious post-nineteenth century writers, dramatists and poets again until he began his teacher-training English course.

Brian re-sat the 'O' Level English language at the end of his first term of sixth form. The teachers at Batley High were unhappy with the English language results of the summer before. They were suspicious over the accuracy of the Examination Board's marking and chose an alternative board for the re-sit in English. Brian gained a grade 6 (a low grade C in current terms). It meant he had the basic five 'O' Levels he needed for a career in teaching.

*

It was some time during the first term of 1964 that Brian first came across a word which shocked him to the core: a word which as soon as he saw it, he knew defined him sexually. The word was "homosexual." He had never seen or heard the word before. He knew words like puff, pansy, nancy-boy, queer, fairy and other nod-and-wink phrases and innuendoes:

"He's a bit – yer knaw …Ont feminine side."

"He's – yer knaw – wun er them soo-ert…"

He first came across the word three years before homosexual acts between consenting adults over the age of 21 became legal in England. The legalisation of homosexuality was already being discussed in quality newspapers such as *The Observer,* which Brian was by now in the habit of reading, and it was in that newspaper that he first came across the word. His mouth dried up when he read it and then looked up its meaning. His tongue felt like some thick slug inside his mouth, preventing him from breathing normally and making his heart beat faster. His hands trembled as he stared and stared at the printed word in front of his eyes – in *The Observer,* which was right about everything! Sweat built up in his armpits and trickled down his arms. He stared and stared and stared at the word. And he thought:

"That's me. That's what I am. I'm a homosexual."

It was the first time he had seen a word describing his own sexuality that he could accept. Until then he had known he was different sexually from the majority but words like "puff" and "queer" and "fairy" did not equate with him and so his sexual nature hung in limbo. When he first saw the word in *The Observer* it was a Revelation: it described *him*. He accepted what the word said about him totally, ineluctably, right there and then and that acceptance would remain inside him always. It described him: the sexual part of him and there was no point denying it – to himself at any rate. The fact that homosexual acts among consenting adults were "illegal" seemed to him nonsensical. How could you make an intrinsic part of a person's make-up illegal? A true criminal *chooses* to break the law. A true homosexual does not choose his or her sexual nature. In one way, discovering this new word gave him a real sense of his true place in the sexual world, his true nature: it was a rock he could rest upon, in place of the insecure uncertainty he had felt about his sexual nature until then. Discovering the word solved the problem of his "difference." He had a "proper" word now; a word which articulated his difference precisely.

Discovering he was homosexual was a relief but he believed it would be a problem for everyone else he knew, and others he might come to know in the future, if they found out – except Philip. Although neither of them knew the word, Brian and Philip had talked about being attracted to their own sex, before Philip changed and began courting Claire. Surely Philip at least would accept Brian's new-found sexual status? Apart from Philip, he resolved there and then that no one else would ever share his new-found identity. He would keep it a secret from everyone: from his family; from the people he mixed with at school and at work; from the community he lived in every day of his life. He did not know the term "closet sexuality" at that time, but that is what he resolved to become: a closet homosexual. He knew absolutely, or he thought he knew absolutely, that everyone hated homosexuals: all those scathing sneering words: all that innuendo. Homosexuals were a loathed, despised, hated minority and not even legal, but marginalized in a murky corner of society, a corner where Brian did not want to be. He wanted to be a teacher. He wanted to be "legal" and he reasoned that meant he had to stay in the majority, which meant keeping his homosexuality a secret from the world, no matter how much he accepted it inside himself, unequivocally and without caveat.

He may have accepted his homosexuality when he first saw the word at seventeen but it did not follow that he liked or welcomed his new-found sense of himself. Yes, he knew he was homosexual but he hated being in the closet just as the whole heterosexual world (he thought) hated homosexuals who were "out" – another term he did not know in 1963. So there was a sense of liberation, a sense of moving from the darkness inside him into a place full of light, in being able to articulate, to himself, his sexuality. But there was a great sense of burden too. A sense that for the rest of his life he would have to carry the weight of his new knowledge about himself inside and a conviction he would never be able to share his true identity with others.

While he was struggling with the Middle English of Chaucer, with the new-found syntax and vocabulary of *The Observer* and with the methodology and culture of studying history at Batley Grammar, deeper inside, Brian was struggling with his new secret awareness of his sexual nature. Until he came across the new word he had kept a big distance between his mind and his sexual body and, by extension, between his body and the bodies of the boys and men he found sexually attractive. He was "in denial" about his sexual body and, by extension, about the fact that those he found attractive had sexual bodies too. Masturbation for Brian was quick and secret and involved touching himself as little as possible. The fantasies he conjured up which led to ejaculation were similar: quick, vague and inexplicit in sexual detail.

Discovering the word "homosexual" led Brian into thinking more explicitly about the physical details of sex. Until he reached seventeen, he had not moved-on sexually from his thirteen-year-old self; the Brian who banished the boy he played with when he wanted to explore sex further than the fully-clothed wrestling matches. Until he knew the word "homosexual" he had never thought in any depth about what "cock-sucking" actually involved. It was just an ugly idiom scrawled on the stinking public urinal walls at Batley Market Place, and had nothing to do with *him*. Similarly he had not thought in a graphic physical sense about anal sex between two males. Now he knew this word he began to think about these physical acts of sex and although, on a sensual level, he found the thought of some of these acts arousing, he rejected the thought of ever himself performing these acts with another person. He did not think of *why* he rejected the idea of having sex with another male. He just knew, or thought he knew, it was impossible. Much later in life he thought his decision to abstain from sex with another male was caused by a deep primordial fear of rejection, inside himself. In order to perform these acts with another he would have to show, not hide, his Mary-Ann-ness. And when he thought about coming-out, or having sex with another, the imprint of rejection by Bob in those early years of his childhood took over, preventing him from acting, fearing he might re-experience the feelings that rejection brings, remembering his infant years, when he curled himself into a ball of empty abnegation.

*

After Brian discovered the word "homosexual" in *The Observer*, he changed. The change was largely internal although there was some change too in his external behaviour. Inside, the predominant feelings of confusion and puzzlement about who he was, and why he was different, diminished. He felt he knew who he was now and although he was aware of the difficulties being different sexually bring to a person he felt calmer, more in control, inside. At least he could now articulate to *himself* what he was. On the outside he became marginally more confident in his interactions with others, less nervous and sensitive to criticism, less fearful of being rejected or derided. The new-found confidence took the form of working more systematically on carving out an external personality and life history for himself and, coincidentally, of being more thorough at hiding much of his true sexual self, his true background, his true feelings.

Although the new-found knowledge about himself brought him relief, it also made him more conscious of how alien the culture and values of his contemporaries at Batley High and Batley Grammar were to him and it made him feel how alien *he* was, inside those predominantly heterosexual cultures. He coped with the situation in two ways. He put on a front to the rest of the world behind which he hid his true self. It enabled him to at least *exist,* if not to belong, in the alien culture around him. But there were times when school, the outside world, acting and hiding, were too much of a strain and as the sixth form progressed, he took more and more time off school, preferring to be at home: cleaning, tidying, cooking, reading and dreaming in the solitude of the daytime house at Chapel Fold, when everyone else was at work or school.

Lack of money became more of a problem as he grew older and wanted more things, in order to keep up with his contemporaries. Toward the end of the lower sixth, an enterprising garage near Batley High opened a new car wash service; the first in the town. More and more people, including members of the aspirational working class such as Mr. Danes, Mr. Dewhurst and Mr. Fitzpatrick at Chapel Fold, were buying cars. It became all the rage among the car-owners to have their cars washed at the new place Down Batley on a Saturday, especially in the winter months. The garage and car wash manager contacted Batley High and Batley Grammar to ask for reliable sixth-formers to help with the Saturday car wash rush and Brian, Jim and John (the latter was in the Batley Grammar history group) found themselves with Saturday jobs, thanks to teachers who knew they needed the money and recommended them as reliable sensible workers.

The work was physically hard and monotonous. The car wash was primitive compared with today's high-tech places. The sprayer doused the car in pre-wash water and then in pre-drying water. Everything else was done by hand by the three Saturday lads. The work involved waving the car drivers into the car wash and pressing the water sprayer buttons to douse the cars. In winter, cars were caked in mud and the car-washer lads had to sponge-off stubborn dirt as well as sponging the cars down, using soapy buckets of warm water which had to be constantly emptied and re-filled as the lines of cars came in, before dousing the cars again, then drying them down by hand with wash leathers. There were quiet days when the three car-washers hovered, with not much to do, but usually it was non-stop hard work from eight till one, with an hour off for lunch, followed by a long afternoon session from two till six. In wintertime, the car wash was freezing and wet, with nowhere to get warm.

Jim was an easy amiable workmate who made Brian laugh with his mimicry of broad Yorkshire and his tall stories of sexual exploits with the Bretton Hall girls. John was serious, intellectual and political – more like a stern teacher than a pupil. Brian, like any young person his age, was beginning to question authority figures. He had experienced that minor clash with the two teachers at school and was contemptuous of the dictatorial ways of Cyril Burns. The boss at the garage was a small bald hyper-active man who sometimes went into sulks and moody glares directed at the three Saturday boys. But Jim, Brian and John found they could easily deflate his efforts to intimidate them by adopting an icy politeness. Sometimes he embarrassed them, trying to be their mate, rather than their boss. One Saturday he conspiratorially showed them pornographic snapshots, taking the grubby photos out of a dirty white envelope he kept in the garage pay booth, which doubled as his "office." Brian was repelled and disgusted by the snapshots showing a naked fat old woman in humiliating poses and a man's errect penis approaching her mouth or vagina. He was glad to see Jim and John were both as repelled as him. The three of them looked politely at the pictures, making no comment and all were relieved when a regular client sounded his car horn for service in the washing shed. It gave them a reason to leave the boss – alone in his booth with his pictures and dirty white envelope, looking crestfallen and dismayed by their apparent indifference. Brian distanced himself from the pictures. They confirmed his disinterest in the female body and their nastiness reinforced his conviction it was best not to involve himself in sexual activity with others. The Saturday car wash wage, with additional tips, gave him a measure of financial independence to buy his own clothes, cigarettes and other "luxuries" during the school term; luxuries which would otherwise have been unattainable, unless he left school to work full time.

During Brian's lower sixth year his brother David worked for a local bookie, a Mr. Frayn, who wanted a "chalker-upper" for just a few hours on horse racing days. Brian found himself doing this job during the Easter holidays in his two sixth-form years. He knew nothing about gambling and had no interest in horse racing, unlike his older brother John, and Bob, who both loved "osses an bettin." Frayn's premises consisted of a little wooden hut perched on the side of the road just beyond Howley Moor. Inside was a small area with benches where punters studied the form before placing bets at the counter, behind which David or Mr. Frayn sat and took the bets. There was a small blackboard on the wall in the punters' area and "chalking-up" involved writing the odds on the races that day and rubbing them out and changing them as the odds fluctuated. The changes to the odds were called out by whoever was behind the counter. Frayn's was a complete mystery to Brian and he spent much of his time there studying the punters, while the punters studied the form. Most of them seemed miserable and dour, absorbed in the betting and nothing else. But there were some gains in working at Frayn's. He was forced to make himself write legibly on the blackboard – something that came in useful in his later career. And there was the wonderful bonus at the end of the day when he was driven from the little wooden hut all the way down to Batley in Mr. Frayn's brand-new purring Jaguar saloon. The last time he had been on this route was when he had "driven" his youngest sibling Michael up to Howley in the battered old maroon Tansad, just a few years earlier.

Baby-sitting, paper rounds, car washing, chalking up and packing mattresses provided Brian with a small income and some financial independence during sixth form. Using some of the money he earned, he had his first independent holiday, taking time off from Rest Assured to spend a week with Philip on the Isle of Man, in the summer between the lower and upper sixth, when both boys were nearing eighteen. Their holiday bore no resemblance to the sort of holidays that many eighteen year old young men (and women) take together today: clubbing, binge drinking and having casual sex in worldwide locations. On the surface at least, Brian and Philip were two "nice" middle class boys and they stayed in a "nice" B+B in Douglas, chosen by Philip's fastidious Mum, where they behaved themselves impeccably. In those days on the Isle of Man, the birch was used as punishment for under-age drinking (it finally ended twenty years later, in the early 1980s) and the most risqué thing they did during the whole week was buy two halves of beer in a pub one evening, downing them quickly, terrified a police man was going to walk in at any moment demanding to know their ages. It was a hot summer and the beaches were packed with bathers. Philip could not swim and he resisted Brian's efforts to get him to strip off into swimming trunks, for fear of exposing his thin frame and body acne to the world. The two boys spent most of the week wandering along the beach front, picking out people they fancied, comparing notes, although by now Philip was much keener on girls than boys.

No matter how hard Brian tried to distance himself from sex and keep his own sexuality firmly stopped-up inside, inevitably it often surged, inside and around him. When Philip persuaded him that Saturday night to make-up a foursome at the new bowling alley in Wakefield, Brian enjoyed playing bowls but being paired-off with Claire's friend embarrassed him. Surely Philip *knew* he was more interested in some of the boys, dressed in fashionably tight jeans, playing in nearby games? Three years after it was first released in 1961, the film version of West Side Story was still running and on another Saturday night Brian and Philip watched the film in a Leeds cinema. Brian was enchanted by the dance, the music and the drama, but most of all he was infatuated with the sexuality of the young male actors in the film. They filled him with a swooning, yearning longing.

None of the boys at school infected Brian with the same longing intensity as the actors in West Side Story but behind his cool distant mask he was attracted to some and in secret ways some seemed attracted to him. During free periods, one boy started contriving situations where he stood or sat close to Brian, "accidentally" brushing into him or leaning across him and touching him in a furtive way but showing nothing of his feelings on his face. Brian was attracted to this boy but reacted to his approaches in his usual way: tumult inside; frozen indifference outside. During one free period, Brian was sitting in the library desultorily reading a Penguin paperback with a few other sixth-formers lounging around, including the boy, who casually came over and stood behind his chair. He leant over, saying nothing, and pulled the chair onto its back legs, with Brian still seated on it. Brian feigned indifference to what the boy was doing, unsure about his motives, but inside he was stirred by the boy leaning over him and by the sensation of the back of his head touching the boy's crotch. Suddenly Jim, who was sitting nearby, leapt to his feet, furious with the boy. He grabbed him by the shirt front and pulled him away from Brian, threatening to beat him up if he did not leave him alone. The boy made a quick exit. Brian felt deflated and puzzled. He wondered why Jim was so angry but did not ask, as he was clearly in no mood to talk. Many years later, thinking back on the incident, Brian realised that for all his tall stories Jim was more sexually savvy than him. The boy was signalling his wanting oral sex but Brian did not recognise the signal. Jim saw the signal, did not like it, and stopped it developing.

One of the privileges of being in the sixth form was being allowed, if you had a free period at the end of the day, to leave school a few minutes before the mass exodus of the younger boys. In his final year, Brian had free periods at the end of most afternoons. He took advantage of the early-leaving privilege, rushing downstairs to the cloakroom to collect his overcoat before the big exodus started, during cold winter months. (This was before it became fashionable among teenagers to walk the streets skimpily dressed, no matter what the temperature or weather conditions.) Don was allocated to cloakroom supervision duty at the end of afternoon school and was usually already in position, waiting, when Brian reached the cloak room. Brian would run into the cloakroom and Don, smiling sardonically, would follow him into the narrow aisle. He would then deliberately block the exit, silently challenging Brian to escape, watching his reactions closely, as if he were a laboratory animal he was experimenting with. Brian tried half-heartedly to push past and escape but Don pushed him slowly and determinedly into a corner, forcing him to sit down with him on the bench, beneath winter coats hung on the pegs above. Don held him down when he struggled to get up, still smiling, seeming to enjoy observing Brian's confused reactions to the "game." When the end-of-the-day bell rang, Don would let Brian go, readying himself for the rush of younger pupils invading the cloakroom. Brian was aroused by Don's power games, played only when no one else was around. But he was unsure whether

Don was goading him, experimenting with his reactions, or whether he was genuinely sexually interested. The old terror of rejection and derision prevented Brian from ever finding out. It was safer to passively put up with, and secretly enjoy, the entrapment game and wait, agitated and tremulous, for the arrival of the the younger lads, to gain his half-reluctant, half-relieved, escape from Don.

As the final year dragged on, it was clear Brian was not going to gain good enough A level grades for university entry and so he applied for teacher training college courses instead. He was disappointed inside, politely listening to some of the Batley Grammar boys talking of the universities they were bound for – Oxford, Cambridge, Edinburgh, Leeds – making him feel distinctly "third class." He was observant enough by the age of eighteen to see that some of the "first class" boys at Batley Grammar – sons of solicitors, vicars and teachers – were going to their destinations as much due to the advantages their class, family backgrounds and values bestowed on them, as on innate intelligence. He resented it and resentment negatively distorts a person's psyche, although he would not realise that until many years later. He kept his disappointment and sense of inferiority secret, smiling on the surface when his family and his teachers expressed their pleasure at how well he was doing in going to college at all.

He spent hours scrutinising training college prospectuses, wondering about his future life in one of these places. Some colleges demanded O level maths and so were discounted. Others had compulsory PE components, others specialised in infant and primary school education. These were eliminated from Brian's final selection, leaving just a few remaining colleges from which to choose. The system demanded students applied to six colleges, placed in rank order. The application was then circulated by a clearing organisation to the six chosen colleges and students were left waiting several weeks until invited for interviews, or not.

Brian would have been happy studying English literature for three years. He told himself he was not interested in anything else. In truth he lacked confidence in his ability to study anything at college level other than English. The training colleges existed until the 1960s to train primary and secondary modern school teachers, while the universities supplied grammar and technical schools with graduate teachers. It was another cause of resentment that if he went into secondary teaching it would almost certainly not be in a grammar school. But things were slowly changing by 1965. The introduction of comprehensive schools in some areas of England was beginning to blur the old training boundaries and the change of title in the early 1960s from "training college" to "college of education" reflected this change. There were only two colleges, his first and second choices, to which Brian really hoped to go. Both were in pleasant locations in the Midlands: as far away from Batley as the moon, to Brian. The favoured colleges put a strong emphasis on the main subject course and rather less emphasis on compulsory education and subsidiary subject course, which appealed to him.

Probably because he lacked maths O level, and also due to the narrow scope of the five O Levels he already had, Brian was invited to just one interview, at Bingley College of Education, his sixth choice. Until 1963, Bingley had been a women's training college with a good reputation for turning out competent infant and junior school teachers, many of whom would go on to become headmistresses, mainly in schools in the Yorkshire Dales and West Riding. When Brian applied for a student place, early in 1965, Bingley was struggling to attract male students, a situation which no doubt helped in his selection for interview. He had gained an interview for entry into the lower ranks of higher education by the thinnest whisker and he knew it. He resented the situation and was disappointed not to be going to university but he desperately wanted a college place anywhere and so he duly attended an interview at Bingley.

The town of Bingley is less than twenty miles distant from Batley but in 1965 travelling there involved a slow bus to Bradford, followed by a long wait for another slow bus to Bingley, followed by a hard twenty minute walk up a long steep hill to the college campus, making Bingley seem much further from Batley than it was. Brian set off for the interview on a clear-blue-sky-cold-sharp-air-day; the sort of weather that always uplifted him. He set off despondent and disappointed he was not going to a university interview or to one of his first and second choice colleges in the Midlands. But he fell in love with Bingley before he even saw it. More precisely, he fell in love with the journey and the landscape, seen under the clear cold blue sky, as the second bus started to climb from the centre of Bradford to the Manningham Road and on to Shipley, Saltaire and Bingley.

The Manningham Lane area of Bradford now is largely inhabited by British Asians and in 2001 the area saw some of the worst race riots ever known in Britain. Thirty six years earlier it was a different place. For Brian, travelling on the bus through Manningham in 1965 was a repeat of that day in the middle 1950s when his big brother Bob took him and David to Battyford, and he saw his first real Pennine country, and fell in love with the Calder Valley and its green hills, black drystone walls, mill cottages in clusters and glistening river in the valley under a pure cold blue sky. He gazed at the spacious grand terraced stone houses lining the Manningham Road and at the side streets climbing from the main road to hills and drystone walls above. He gazed as the town houses of Manningham gave way to the countryside. Hills, fields and grazing sheep took over from terraced steep streets as the bus approached Shipley and Bingley. He gazed at Bingley as the bus pulled in to his stop. He saw a huddle of Yorkshire stone houses, shops and offices, in a narrow valley, with glimpses behind the High Street of the Five Rise canal locks. Grand stone terraced houses, like those in Manningham, climbed a steep hill to the college campus and behind the hill were higher distant glimpses of Ilkley Moor. He loved the landscape and the feeling of enfoldment it gave him. He loved the small college campus set in lush green wooded grounds at the top of the high hill with its wonderful expansive Pennine views. He knew he wanted to *be* there, from leaving Bradford to arriving in Bingley town, to walking up the steep hill and finally seeing the college for the first time.

On the journey back to Batley he thought of the two middle-aged male lecturers (both of them ex-primary school headmasters) smiling at him, encouraging him, as he shyly blundered his way through the interview, before offering him a place, content with his five O Levels and interview performance. He could hardly wait for September to come and knowing his student place at Bingley was secure, he became more and more disillusioned with school. He forgot how Batley High had excited and stimulated him when he started in the second year. Now all he wanted was to leave. He was sick of the burden of secrets he carried around with him in his Batley life and dreamt of becoming another person from September in his new life as "a student" at Bingley. He took more and more time off school and his smoking habit increased. He did not stop to think of the course his life had taken, of his family, his community, his country, over the thirteen years he had spent at school since September 1951. His last few weeks as a school pupil were just a flat boring time of waiting: waiting for the day of the final exam, and when the final exam ended, he walked out of Batley High, smiling. He was happy to put everything behind and he did not look back. He looked only forward.

By 1965 his older sister Moira was married and had already given birth to her first child Tim but she still kept in touch with friends she made when she worked in London and Filey. A few days after leaving school, Brian called in on Moira for a long morning's gossip. He told her how much he was looking forward to college and how he was not looking forward to a fourth summer holiday job at Rest Assured with abominable Cyril and demanding Joe. But he needed the money and Mary needed his keep to tide them through the long twelve weeks before starting college. Moira offered to contact a friend in Filey who worked at Butlins Holiday Camp to see if she could find a summer holiday job for Brian. He jumped at the chance of escaping for the summer; not just escaping Rest Assured, Cyril and Joe but escaping Batley and Chapel Fold, escaping his life there; a life which had become stifling during those last few months of school. One week later, he began a holiday job at Filey Butlins as a Kitchen Service Hand; ready and eager to experience his first long spell of living away from the family, Chapel Fold and Batley.

Butlins Holiday Camp and the Rest Assured bedding factory were similar. At Rest Assured, the factory floor was designed down to the last detail to manufacture bed mattresses and workers were there to facilitate the process of manufacture. Workers were just another facet of the process, from the men who hauled in the raw materials at the beginning, to the men who wrapped the finished products and hauled them out to the delivery lorries. It was an endless process of raw materials "in" at one end, and finished products "out" at the other. It was the same at Butlins: raw new-campers "in" on their first Saturday; followed by six days of processing the campers through everything Butlins had to offer, followed by campers "out" on the second Saturday, before the whole process started again with the next cohort of holiday-makers. As at Rest Assured, the Butlins staff existed to facilitate this vast process of manufacture. Bedding was manufactured at Rest Assured. Butlins manufactured holidays for thousands of people during every week of the summer holiday season.

The site and personnel infrastructures at Butlins were clearly delineated. The first site you came to was the Reception area, whether you were staff, or holidaymaker. From Reception you were processed-on to the next appropriate site. There was a site housing the holiday campers, all laid out in a neat grid. There were the holiday-makers' communal areas: dining hall; drinking bars; entertainment halls; children's play areas; indoor and outdoor swimming pools. In a dingy corner of the camp was the staff chalet area and its dining hall, toilets and wash block. Staff facilities were dingier and shabbier than those used for the holiday-makers. At Rest Assured, office and management staff had separate quarters from factory floor workers and on-floor managers each had an office on the factory floor. There were similar divisions at Butlins. Managers and administrators (such as Moira's friend) did not reside on camp but lived locally and travelled in each day. The workers, from Redcoats and entertainers at the top of the ladder, to toilet cleaners and kitchen service hands at the bottom, were students or seasonal workers and most were housed in staff chalets. There were unspoken demarcations and tensions simmering under the "we're-all-happy-campers-and-staff-together" surface. The tensions were between local and incomer seasonal workers; between students and regular seasonal workers; between Redcoats and other workers, between chefs and service hands; between holiday guests and staff.

On his arrival at Butlins, Brian was rapidly processed from reception to his sleeping chalet. His bedroom at Chapel Fold with its two single beds, set of drawers and a wardrobe was hardly luxurious but the chalet screamed "Spartan" at him, with its rough plaster walls, small window, concrete floor, one hand washbasin, one wardrobe, two sets of bunk beds and minimal bedding. Only sub-mariners and Russian cosmonauts could possibly live in more cramped conditions, he thought. He shared the chalet with two other young men. One was a tough streetwise seasonal security worker from Manchester who, apart from his numerous tattoos, made no impact at all on Brian. Sometimes in bed at night Brian heard the security worker and his latest girl sneaking into the chalet, followed rapidly by the breathy sounds of furtive greedy sex. The third occupant of the chalet was Tony, a small squat handsome boy of Brian's age from Essex who was starting art college in London in September. Apart from exchanging names and a brief "hello" when they first met, Brian rarely saw the tough lad from Manchester again and to his relief his and Tony's paths rarely crossed. Tony was what Brian's Mam would have called a "morngy bugger." He had a whiny nasal broad Essex accent and an inferiority complex about his small height and light weight:

"Aw gawd. Look at me. Oi'm bewlt loike a fackin' beyntum 'en, en oi ownli woigh eit fackin' stown. Wot fackin' chick's gonnah look twoice at me? I ain't got no charnce: ge'in a bird."

Brian agreed inside. He wanted to tell him *he* certainly could never fancy him, with his awful whining voice and huge inferiority complex. When Tony's whining really grated, he just wanted to tell him to fuck off. But he smiled politely and kindly.

"Don't worry, Tony mate. Bein' five foot three an' eight stone isn't the end of the world. You'll soon find a 'chick' that fancies yer, I'm certain."

Tony did find a chick eventually and spent most of his free time in his chick's chalet and Brian was relieved not to see him too often, after those first few meetings.

All those National Curriculum makers and enforcers who believe the world is just an objective, solid place – as a machine or a tool is a solid objective thing – would love the Butlin's kitchens. They ran like a machine and people working in them were component parts, keeping the machine going in the process of feeding a thousand holiday makers three meals a day. At one end of the process, bulk food came "in" from delivery lorries. At the other end, meals were taken "out" to the dining room to be consumed by happy-campers. It was undoubtedly a smooth machine, between "in" and "out." It had to be: hundreds of people not being fed at the time they expected could have led to nasty scenes. At the "in" end of the process, porters lifted the bulk food from lorries and brought it into the kitchens. Chefs then cooked the food in vast quantities: enough for two sittings with hundreds of campers per sitting, for breakfast, lunch and dinner.

The kitchen service hands stood in a line of four behind a stainless steel topped serving table. It felt familiar, to Brian, but it was a long narrow table, unlike the double mattress size table in the packing section at Rest Assured. Porters then placed containers and trays loaded with food onto the table in front of the service hands who were unenthusiastically waiting, with serving spoons and spatulas in hands. Porters delivered stacks of hot plates to the "in" end of the serving table and "hands" then ladled food onto plates. Gary, Alice, Brian and Hugh might be the day's "hands," on breakfast duty, say. Gary began with an empty plate upon which he served a fried egg from the hot tray. He then passed the plate to Alice who added two rashers of bacon before passing the plate to Brian, who added two pieces of grilled tomato and passed the plate to Hugh, who finished with a spoonful of steamed mushrooms. Porters then loaded the breakfast plates onto heated trolleys waiting at the "out" end of the serving table, where waiters were ready to wheel the trolleys to the final "out" – through big swing doors into the dining hall where the campers waited. And: V*oila!* Breakfast for the five hundred!

Kitchen Service Hand work was tedious and monotonous in the extreme. Day after day, Brian rose at six thirty, stumbled across the camp to the kitchens while donning regulation clothes over jeans and tee-shirt before serving hundreds of eggs onto plates, from seven till nine. Then back to the chalet to sleep before the next duty, from eleven thirty till two, serving four slices of cucumber hundreds of times onto hundreds of plates. Then a brief period off-duty till five before the final shift of the day, serving two scoops of mash onto hundreds of plates. Then at last, he was freed, at seven, until six thirty the following morning. It was a routine that never varied, day after day. The worst part of the job involved having to stand in one spot up to eight hours a day at the end of the hot steaming kitchens. The "hands" wore sandals with no socks and perspiration dripped down legs and onto feet until the sandals were soaked in stinking sweat. The chef-in-charge, a sour foul-mouthed Geordie with a long mean face, was known as the nastiest bastard on camp.

"Why-ay man, gerra fookin moo-ev on wi them tay-it-ers. Thems'll be frozzun bah the tayme tha coos-tum-ers gerr-em."

"Why lass, luke at tha way-ee tha's slapped them pee-ers onter thee-ah. It lukes lyke a py-el er shite. Doo it er-gen. Prop-er, lyke."

The good thing was that insurrections among his junior chefs were rife and most of the time he was quelling them, damning them to perdition and worse, which meant he could only give the "hands" intermittent doses of his malevolent attention.

After a few days working at Butlins, Brian felt as if he had turned into an atom caught up in an overwhelming, meaningless, ever-active greater force, or a tiny pebble on a tidal beach constantly being swept, back and forth, back and forth, by a giant overpowering sea. He felt a sort of "none-ness." It was not like the sense of abnegation he felt when he was threatened or overburdened by who he was; it was just nothingness. He felt as if he were just some *object*, being swept around constantly by this huge relentless force – Butlins. It was not only during working hours he felt like this. It was the same during off-duty hours. He sometimes roamed the site watching happy-campers and Redcoats at play. But he could not detach himself from the force. He could not be a detached observer. He was swept-up into the relentless force of "entertainment" everyone was trapped in, like desperate squirming fish in a net. He could not wander quietly into a bar and sit and reflect in a corner with a beer. He was *swept* into the bar among a crowd coming from nowhere, but always *there*. When he ordered a drink he was *sucked* into the manufactured jollity of the barmen, waiters and campers. And when he sat down there was always a crowd, willing him to join in the fun, or the compere for the night was calling out to him to "sing-along." It was the same in the urinals. Waves of men leapt up to "The Lads" room the same time as him. They unbuttoned, the same time as him, and pissed the same time as him, shook drops off – the same time as him. The pressure was relentless. *The Animals* pop group had a smash hit at the time which was emblematic for Brian of how he felt, being at Butlins:

"We Godda Ged Ouda This Place,
If it's the LAST thing we E-VER do!"

There were quieter moments on duty in the kitchens when it was possible to get to know the other service hands. The regular team Brian worked with, which included himself, Gary, Alice and Hugh, and sometimes a Scots lad, were quite fragile gentle people, except the Scot. The main team of four were bemused by the frenzy of Butlins and it was a sense of their shared "outsiderness" that brought them into a situation where they could almost be described as friends, in that they did sometimes talk to each other on a personal, quiet, unfrenzied level. The casual seasonal workers at Butlins did not, generally speaking, make friends. No one did really. It was casual temporary seasonal work and true friendship needs time to grow, develop and mature. Quite a few workers had sex together and these conjoinings rarely went further than just the sex. The Scots lad once made a sexual advance on Brian. They were swimming in the indoor pool and suddenly he grabbed Brian and wrapped his body round him, gripping him in a tight vice, pinning him inside his legs and arms so that Brian could feel the lad's erect penis pressed against his stomach. Brian reacted as he had done with the boy on the outhouse roof. He struggled and shouted, forcing him to release his grip, as other swimmers started to notice. It was the publicness of his advance that Brian hated: he was no better than the two dogs, copulating on the green at Chapel Fold. When they were not indulging in always furtive-seeming sex, casual workers would occasionally create their own force and break out *en masse* on a trip to Filey together on their day off, or to one of the village pubs nearby for a night's drinking binge. Brian was good at listening but was deeply wary, shy and unsure in the company of people he did not know well. Working at Butlins was the first time in his life he had spent more than a few days away from family and familiar surroundings. Initially he spent most of his time listening, watching, observing, soaking-in the mores, characters, culture, accents.

Gary was a mature College of Education student in his late-twenties from a small Northumberland town. He told Brian he left grammar school at sixteen with good O Levels, for the lure of earning a wage in a local factory. He learned his mistake and in his early twenties realised his "vocation" was to teach. He was genuinely, evangelically passionate about becoming a teacher. Brian was shocked, listening to Gary, and kept quiet about his own impending teacher-training course. In truth he had never really thought about *teaching*. When he was nearly thirteen and

Mr. Locke had talked to his class that day he had just blurted out "teacher" because it was the only posh job he could think of.

Alice was a shy girl, around Brian's age, from Sierra Leone. She was taller than him by several inches and when they were next to each other, standing at the serving table talking, he had to look up to her. She was very slender and very black and when she smiled, which was often, she showed the loveliest white teeth he had ever seen. She had only been in England a few weeks and would be staying with her aunt in Leeds while she trained to be a nurse at St. James's Hospital. Brian loved to hear her African accented English, her perfect grammar and wide lexicon:

"When ah hev fenished ma medical traynin' an curriculum at Leeds, ma vocation is tu go back home to Sierra Leone an' implement tha skills ah hev learned to aid tha sick an needy."

It was a novel situation for him to be thrown together with someone even quieter and shyer than himself. As the days passed he became determined to bring Alice out of her shell, by gentle teasing and coaxing. At first she giggled and blushed when he spoke to her. He teased her over seeing her blush – under her deep black skin. Brian had no idea of the effect his teasing was having upon Alice, because sexual attraction simply did not come into the equation for him, and so it was Gary who told him he should cease the teasing, unless he meant to take the friendship further. According to Gary, Alice had "fallen" for Brian. After learning this, he kept his distance and Alice became even quieter, sinking deep into herself, leaving Brian feeling guilty, inept and foolish.

Hugh had just finished his first year at the London Royal Academy of Music. His parents were consultant doctors in a big Birmingham hospital and, he told Brian, they had "kicked up a stink" over his profligate spending and the mountain of debt he had accumulated during his first year at the Academy and forced him to take the holiday job, banishing him from spending the summer at the family holiday home near somewhere in France with the peculiar name of "Gra-arse," as Hugh pronounced it. Hugh was sometimes persuaded to play the battered upright piano shoved in a corner of the staff dining room and the flowing, sweeping, beautiful sounds he produced, astonished and amazed everyone. Hugh did not really talk *to* anyone. He just talked. And people listened, or ignored him. Hugh did not seem to care either way. He was repelled by the food he had to serve every day. He called it "tasteless pap" and conducted a running monologue on the food he would *like* to serve. Brian had never heard of most of the dishes he named:

Hugh: "Ah, lovely. Beef Wellington."
Brian: *"What?"*
Hugh: "Pommes Lyonaise."
Brian: "*Eh?*"
Hugh: "Canard a l'orange."
Brian: "Mmm, yer. I like that, too."
Hugh: "Do you *really?*" ...

Inevitably the temporary semi-friends began to question him about *his* life. He had spent most of his life hiding behind masks and avoiding the limelight and, when he was forced to talk about himself, his reaction almost automatically by now was to deny his real self. It was due to the profound fear inside of rejection and his deep sense of his wrongness and he would pretend to be someone he was not. He did the same thing now when the others questioned him, and this time he did it with a vengeance, knowing his questioners were temporary, present-time people with no knowledge of his past life and unlikely to know him in the future. So he started to tell outright lies: the sort of lies he had last told to the hair-pulling junior school teacher at the bus stop after school and to Mr.

Margetts, when he gave Brian the lift in his Hillman van that stormy day. But this time he lied as a young adult, not as a child. He told deliberate lies to credulous people who believed he was telling the truth.

He was Brian Hirst and had just left Batley Grammar with ten high grade O Levels under his belt. For good measure he named all ten subjects, including maths, a science, French and Latin. He had just taken three A Levels and if he gained three A grades there was a place waiting for him to read English at Churchill, then Cambridge University's newest college. He said it all matter-of-factly and, he hoped, convincingly, just adding a tone of reluctance, a sense that he did not like to be probed about himself (which was true), in the hope it would put them off asking more questions. And it did. It worked. They seemed to believe the thumbnail fictional sketch he had given and did not probe him again. He had told pure lies about himself to these credulous people who, when they thought about him at all, seemed to like and respect him. He imagined their shock, maybe outrage, or worse ridicule, if they ever found out the truth. But this knowledge was outweighed by the feeling of sheer relief he felt when telling these lies: lies that gave him the balm of not being the Brian he was, just for those few weeks of working at Butlins. And he lived with his lies quite contentedly, relieved temporarily from the resentment he was more and more feeling about who he was, or rather, the shame-haunted person he saw himself as being.

Brian's A level results came out near the end of August 1965. Bob and Mary had "graduated" from being solely radio-renters, to becoming radio *and* television-renters. It would, however, be another ten years before they owned a telephone and so Sheila collected Brian's results sheet from the post at Chapel Fold and he arranged to telephone her during the afternoon on "results day." All the Butlins student-workers were due to receive their A Level results that day and a booze-up at a nearby pub in the village of Hunmanby, to which everyone seemed to be going, was arranged for that evening, where everyone could celebrate, or drown their sorrows. The real Brian had already decided the other Brian had gained his three A grades and he would be celebrating his place at Cambridge that night.

On exam results day Brian was working breakfast shift only, which meant he had a free day from 10.00am. It was a beautiful hot summer sunny August day. After completing the shift he ran to the staff canteen to devour a lukewarm breakfast which had probably been standing on its plate on the trolley for at least two hours. He was starving. He was always starving during all those weeks he worked at Butlins and there was never enough food. The two slices of margarined toast that came with the congealed egg, bacon, tomato and mushroom, had gone hard, stiff and curly at the edges and he grumbled to himself about the stingy bastards at Butlins, not even allowing more than two pieces of toast, just a measly slice, cut in half. But it was a great day. He was happy and he told himself he didn't give a toss about exam results. He would be "getting out of this place" soon and going to Bingley, whatever A Level results he achieved. Wolfing down breakfast, he planned his day. The staff wash rooms would be empty. He would begin with a long bath and hair wash. Then he would telephone Sheila from the phone booths near the main entrance. Then maybe walk into Filey via the shore and buy fish and chips, and then walk back before finishing the day in the pub at Hunmanby.

He bathed, washed his hair, shaved, put on clean clothes, washed his sandals and then strolled through the relentless omnipresent activity-force that was Butlins, smiling at the insanity of it, to the telephone booth. Sheila did not sound herself when she answered the phone. She sounded dull, flat, pensive.

"Gu on, tell me the worst. What did ah get?"

"Yer what, love? Oh! Your *exams*. Hang on. It says here "C" for A level English; "O level pass" for A level History; "Grade 2" for O level General Studies. Is that good?"

"Mmm. Not bad, really."

There was a long silent pause. He wondered what was wrong. Sheila was rarely so silent.

"Brian love. I've got something awful to tell you. Your Glynne was knocked off his bike. By a lorry. At those cross roads near the Butchers Arms up Staincliffe. Yesterday morning. Don't ask, love. He was killed."

His hands started to shake. His heart thumped. His legs felt like jelly. The phone in his hand felt like it was sending lightning flashes through him. The phlegm at the back of his throat began to rattle. Water spurted from his nose and eyes. He wanted to scream.

"No. No. No. It hasn't happened. He can't be dead. NOT Ower Glynne."

"Are you there, Brian, luv? Are you all right?"

Some words came out. They sounded like when you try to talk under water, in the bath.

"Yeah. 'll ring temorreh."

He threw the phone from his hand and yanked open the stifling booth door and ran back to the chalet, everyone and everything passing in a blur. He flung the chalet door open. Thank God. Tony and the other lad were not there, as usual. He sunk himself face down on the bed and beat his fists and feet on the mattress and repeated: "NO, NO, NO!" It could not have happened. He could not be dead. Granmas die, Grandads die, dogs get run over, budgies get crushed under cages. But NOT this. Not Glynne. Not his cousin, who he suddenly realised he loved as much as when they were little. "NOT OWER GLYNNE!" The tears turned to howls of rage and anger. It was the grief and rage of a child, screaming at the death of another child; a child unable to accept death. He could not believe he was making this noise. What if someone passing outside heard his racket and came in? "FUCK THEM! FUCK THEM!" He howled and cried and sobbed. And eventually he fell into a coma-like sleep.

He slept several hours until Hugh banged on the chalet door at nine and came in, telling him he was late. Everyone had set off for the pub. He was still dazed and stunned but he remembered the instant Hugh woke him what Sheila had told him earlier that day. And just as instantly he decided he would say nothing about Glynne, to Hugh or anyone. He was terrified he would cry and blubber, sob and scream, make a pathetic whimpering fool of himself. He would find a mask to put on and hide behind it, until tomorrow, when he would telephone Sheila again. Hugh, who never really noticed anyone, did not see his red face, his sore eyes, his crumpled damp clothes. He pulled Brian outside, urging him to hurry so they could catch up with the others at the pub, unknowingly handing him a mask to hide behind:

"How were the grades then? Get what you needed?"

Gratefully Brian grabbed the mask and put it on. He shrugged modestly, self-deprecating.

"Great, yeah. I got three As."

"Well that's good then. Come on. Let's run."

Until that night, Brian had only once been drunk before, when he was nearly fifteen and drank those three pints of Tetleys Bitter at his brother John's Australia leaving party at Batley Carr Club. Since then he had drunk an occasional half a pint with Philip in pubs in Wakefield, Leeds and Isle of Man. Sometimes on babysitting nights his brother-in-law Jimmy would supply him with a gill bottle of Guinness and tonic water (which he believed was a good mixture to gradually "wean" Brian onto drinking beer) and he would drink the Guinness-and-tonic, munch his way through a bag of crisps and smoke a cigarette or two while watching a film on TV. The little beer he had tried gave him a headache and he did not enjoy the taste. He had never tried wine or spirits.

It was madness in the pub when they arrived. Everyone was shouting about exam results and drinking heavily. Brian shrank from the shouting and heavy drinking but someone goaded him into trying vodka. He drank it in one go, amazed it seemed to have no taste and no effect once it was swallowed. Before too long he was standing with the hard drinking set who were greatly amused by his amazement over the easiness of drinking vodka. Gary was nowhere to be seen. Alice did not go to pubs and Hugh had disappeared. The drinkers plied him with vodka after vodka, until the modest, quiet mask slipped off completely and a noisy raucous carnival mask came on. The last thing he remembered was swallowing another vodka, swaying in the middle of a crowd of mysteriously swaying onlookers, all of them laughing at this extrovert clown who had suddenly burst out from shy Brian. He was shouting at the top of his voice.

"Ph-waw, ph-waw. S'fuckin eashy, drinkin' vodka. Ah go' three As. Ah g – thr – s …"

And then blackness. Complete blackness. Until he woke ten hours later with head and body throbbing and thudding and found himself still fully clothed, just intact, on his bed in the chalet. He had no recollection of what happened between collapsing in the pub and waking the following morning. Some of the others must have carried him back. He lay on the bed for a while, coming round slowly, wondering what happened. Who brought him back? What would the others say when they saw him? God. It was awful. Then Glynne's face came into his head and he cried for hours, quietly. After, he phoned Sheila and told her he could not get time off for the funeral. He was terrified of making a fool of himself, imagining blubbing in front of everyone if he went, and was deeply ashamed of his cowardice. He worked the evening shift and no one said a word about the night before.

He stayed another week at Butlins but could not stop thinking about Glynne. He withdrew inside himself, avoiding contact and talk with everyone. He decided to go home, to Chapel Fold. He had saved just enough money to keep him going until college began at the end of September when he would get his first term's grant cheque. When he returned to Chapel Fold no one commented on his absence from the funeral. Mam told him Auntie Louie was in pieces. He dared not go to see her. David told him how terrible the funeral was. All his brothers had broken down and wept. Talking to Mam and David just made him feel more of an outsider than usual: the homosexual in the middle: the queer one: the one full of shames: the one not sharing in the family grief.

He took to staying in bed until late. And going every afternoon to a pub further down the Halifax Road not far from the Butchers Arms crossroads where Glynne was killed – a pub where he was unlikely to bump into anyone he knew. And downing two pints of beer. And getting a headache and sleeping it off until after tea. And going to the pub again in the evening and drinking two more pints. And going straight to bed on his return to Chapel Fold, with another headache pounding. And sleeping. He wanted only the anonymity of the pub and the drowsy oblivion the beer induced for those few weeks between returning from Filey and leaving for Bingley.

But underneath the sadness and grief, he was young and full of hope and eager anticipation for his future. And the day soon came to leave for college. And Mam walked all the way with him to the bus stop at the end of Chapel Fold, gossiping about this and that. She stood with him at the bus stop, nattering, until the Dewsbury bus pulled up. He boarded the bus and stowed away the big blue cardboard suitcase with the Qantas Airline sticker, which his brother

John had given him, and found a seat. He looked out and saw his Mam waving from the bus stop. He waved back, till the bus dipped down the hill toward the Track Road crossroads. And Mam disappeared.

Moira at Butlins: Late 1950s

Brian aged eighteen. Summer 1965

The Halifax Road Bus Stop